WHEN BRITAIN

AND REFUGEES DIED

THE TRAGEDY OF DEPORTATION

AND THE *ARANDORA STAR*

IN 1940

by

BRIAN LETT

Della Cresa Publishing 2023

This book is dedicated to my granddaughters Cassie and Phoebe, with love and all good wishes for the future.

www.brianlettauthor.com
www.gordonlettfoundation.co.uk

Other books by the same author:

SAS in Tuscany 1943-5 – Pen and Sword 2011
Ian Fleming and SOE's Operation Postmaster – Pen and Sword - 2012
The Small Scale Raiding Force – Pen and Sword - 2013
An Extraordinary Italian Imprisonment – Pen and Sword - 2014
SOE's Mastermind – Pen and Sword - 2016
Gordon Lett, Amico dell'Italia – ISRA, Pontremoli [in Italian] - 2018
Italy's Outstanding Courage – Della Cresa Publishing – 2018, Italian edition 2020
Hitler's Hangmen – Greenhill Books - 2019

Printed by Amazon KDP

INDEX

INTRODUCTION

This is a sad and tragic story. It details how a government of a democratic nation, fighting desperately to survive against forces of the extreme right in Europe, temporarily lost sight of fairness, justice and democracy, and took actions that led to the tragic death of hundreds of innocent people, and the acute suffering of thousands more. It was, as British Foreign Secretary Lord Halifax said at the time, a very bad business. The government was that of Great Britain and Northern Ireland, its leader was Winston Churchill. The moment was when Adolf Hitler unleashed the German *blitzkrieg* in northern Europe in Spring of 1940, forcing the British Expeditionary Force to retreat and cower on the beaches of Dunkirk, praying for evacuation and survival. Miraculously, by 4 June 1940, nearly 340,000 men had been evacuated back to Britain, and Churchill's government waited for the previously unthinkable – a German invasion of the British islands. A period of near panic ensued which lasted until late July, when parliamentary democracy began to re-assert itself, and normal British standards began to return.

By the time that war against Germany was declared on 3 September 1939, Great Britain and Northern Ireland was playing host to two very different communities that had arrived from mainland Europe. One was the German/Austrian community, made up in the main of Jewish and political refugees from Nazi terror and oppression; the other was the Italian community, which included some Jewish and political refugees from Fascist oppression, but which was in the main made up of Italians whose families, over the preceding eighty or ninety years, had come to Britain to work – in modern terms most had arrived as economic refugees. The two communities became joined in their suffering.

The German/Austrian refugees had been granted refuge by the British Government in their time of greatest need – that was a tradition of which most British citizens were rightly proud. They had, of course, been individually vetted, and then permitted to enter the country, and to take shelter under the protection of the British state. Many only intended to stay in Britain in the short term, and hoped to move on to other countries such as the United States to secure their future. All were grateful to Britain for their refuge, and hated Nazi Germany.

The Italian community, by contrast, had put down roots in England, Scotland, Wales and Northern Ireland over many years. Although they usually married within the Italian community, many Italian residents had children born in Britain who were therefore British citizens, and some had themselves become naturalised British. Their British born children, if old enough, were called up into the British armed forces once war with Germany had broken out. The majority worked in the catering trade, and by 1940, many of the best chefs in London and other major cities were Italian. For most of them, Mussolini's Fascist government in Italy was almost totally irrelevant to their lives.

It has always been the case that if, when a war starts, one of the combatant countries has within its borders a number of citizens of an opposing country - "enemy aliens" as they were called - a decision has to be taken as to how to treat them. The essential test will usually be where the sympathies of those citizens lie – are they with the host country or with its enemy. If the latter, they are a potential danger, and whatever precautions are necessary must be taken to prevent them helping the enemy.

In the United Kingdom, after war broke out, first against Germany in September 1939 and later against Italy in June 1940, many thousands of Germans, Austrians and Italians were arrested and imprisoned, and thousands were deported in dreadful conditions to far flung corners of the British Dominions. Churchill's order on 10 June 1940 was to "Collar the Lot"- to arrest all enemy aliens - and to deport as many of them as possible as quickly as possible. That policy led to untold suffering by thousands of "enemy aliens", and to the deaths of nearly six hundred of them. For a few weeks, the British Government, fighting a lone battle to preserve democracy in Europe, behaved in an abusive and totally undemocratic way towards a section of those under its care and protection.

This book seeks to discover why Churchill and his government behaved in the way they did, and whose fault it was that so many anti-Nazis and anti-Fascists were crammed onto a number of requisitioned ocean liners and deported far from Europe. Whose fault was it that so many of them died? Whose fault was it that for a time so many Jewish refugees were treated as badly by the British as their co-religionists still in Germany were treated by the Nazis?

The concept that Churchill and his wartime Coalition Government simply panicked in their approach to "enemy aliens" was first propounded in the House of Commons on 10 July 1940. The whole question of the Government's internment and deportation policy was raised in an adjournment debate on that date. The debate was initiated by Major Cazalet [Conservative] and Miss Eleanor Rathbone [Independent, Combined English Universities]. Because the British Government was a war time coalition, normal party divisions did not apply. Colonel Josiah Wedgwood [Labour] described the Government as: "an administration which is too easily swayed by the Daily Mail and by the agitation of uneducated, panicky people...I see in this wave of internment cum Daily Mail panic, from which we have been suffering lately, a wholly incorrect view of what [the situation] is..." Viscount Wolmer, later Lord Selbourne, [Conservative] adopted a similar line, referring to the "panic view" and concluding with the words: "We should treat this matter in a common sense way and not in the spirit of panic." Samuel Sydney Silverman [Labour] said that it was not unfair to describe the Government's policy as a policy of panic, adding: "People do unjust and cruel things when they are afraid." Reginald Sorenson [Labour] said: "It is true that at a time of difficulty and apprehension moods of panic are generated, but it does not follow one should give way to such moods. Some people, when the mood of panic is on them, assume that the only thing is to splutter out hatred, to become insensitive and more inhumane...I am glad that now an attempt is being made to counter-balance that mood of panic."

The author will endeavour to tell the story faithfully and fairly, according to the information that is now available in the National Archives, the Imperial War Museum and elsewhere. It will be for the reader to reach a verdict upon the conduct of the British government in the months of May to July 1940.

CHAPTER ONE

THE GERMAN/AUSTRIAN COMMUNITY IN BRITAIN, AND THE APPROACH TO INTERNMENT

Following Hitler's rise to power in Germany in 1933, it became increasingly clear to the British Government that another war with Germany was a real possibility. By the late 1930s it became a probability, and Government thoughts turned to what action might be necessary against German and Austrian nationals within its borders - enemy aliens - if war did break out. Britain had had the experience of a similar problem in the First World War. It was then that the classification "enemy aliens" had been given to citizens of enemy countries who were living temporarily or permanently within the United Kingdom. In 1914, at the beginning of the First World War, Britain had the benefit of a new home intelligence department, known then as the Special Intelligence Department [later renamed Military Intelligence Five: M.I.5], led by army Captain, Vernon Kell. It had been set up in 1909, and was under the control of the War Office. M.I.5 had the task of identifying possible enemy spies, and of advising on the internment of enemy aliens. Throughout that war, the British Government struggled with the problems of internment. The Isle of Man was eventually chosen as the principal internment centre. The basic approach was that the Home Office [assisted by the intelligence from M.I.5] should decide who should be interned, the police would arrest them, and then the War Office would have the responsibility of running the internment camps to which they were sent. Throughout that war, the British authorities experienced numerous difficulties, and there were various changes of policy. Perhaps the most pertinent comment is that in World War One the British gained considerable experience of the difficulties of mass internment, and the problems that it could cause.

After the First World War had finished, careful consideration was given to what had been learned from it. This included the question of what to do with enemy aliens if a new war broke out. In 1923, the Committee of Imperial Defence decided that there was in fact little point in interning a large number of enemy aliens if it took a large number of your own men to guard them. It was thought that a better course would be to expel them all from Britain – to send them back to their home countries, providing that they would not be of value to the enemy's war effort. The latter proviso meant that there would be some exceptions, and therefore some provision for internment had to be made. The Home Office and the War Office both agreed on that policy.

However, the historical British attitude towards refugees from oppressive foreign regimes was one of sympathy. Once Hitler and the Nazis came to power in Germany in 1933, the flow to Britain of refugees began, and as the Nazi regime became more oppressive and expanded its boundaries, it increased very significantly. Between 1933 and the outbreak of war, Hitler took over Austria, the Sudetenland, and then the rest of Czechoslovakia. Great Britain showed a mercy and understanding towards refugees from Nazi oppression, particularly the Jews, that was lacking in many other European countries. Whilst alert to its duties to its own citizens, the pre-war British Government had allowed refugees to come to Britain provided that they had a sponsor who could speak to their good character, and guarantee that they would not prove to be a financial burden on the state, for instance by providing the refugee with a job. Many of the refugees who arrived were professional men and women, and many were highly skilled. There were many well-established Jewish families in Britain, some in positions of power and influence. However, as we will see, Britain also had a significant number of anti-semitic, home-grown fascists – led by men like Sir Oswald Mosley, Bt, of the British Union of Fascists.

In November 1938, came *Kristallnacht.* This was the name by which the worst yet Nazi pogrom against the Jews became known. On the night of 9/10 November, numerous Jewish owned shops and synagogues were smashed or burned. The violence was incited and orchestrated by the Nazi party. The name *Kristallnacht* translates as Crystal Night – so named because the streets were littered with the broken glass which came from the shattered windows of the Jewish shop fronts. Jews were murdered, and some committed suicide in despair. The following day, wholescale arrests began, and the German concentration camps began to fill with Jews. It was the final signal to the Jewish community that it was no longer safe to stay within the borders of the Nazi Reich, and, in the following months,

Jews streamed out of Germany to seek refuge elsewhere. Many of the refugees from *Kristallnacht* arrived in Britain. There were already a number of Jewish charities working to help the refugees, and their work increased significantly.

In particular a scheme was devised by private citizens to bring into the safety of Great Britain thousands of unaccompanied children from Germany and Austria who were being threatened by the Nazis – nearly all of them Jews. Provided that a sponsor was available in the sum of £50 [worth a lot more then than now], and that a home had been found for each child, the Home Office gave permission for them to come. Beginning in December 1938, ten thousand children arrived in Britain under the scheme, known as *Kindertransport.* Naturally, the refugee children's families were thankful that their children had reached a place of safety. There is a memorial tablet in the Houses of Parliament which records the thanks of those children, and those of their parents who survived the war, to the British Government for allowing the *Kindertransport* scheme, which undoubtedly saved the lives of those ten thousand children. They would otherwise have perished along with their families in one of the Nazi concentration camps. Both the children and the adult refugees who fled to Britain needed an immediate safe haven from Nazi oppression. Prior to September 1939, Britain provided that. For many of the adult refugees, however, Britain was only to be a temporary home, whilst the refugees made the necessary applications for visas to a final destination, the most popular choice being the United States. For the children, the safe haven of Britain would be necessary only until their parents joined them, it was a cradle to protect them from the Nazi excesses after *Kristellnacht.*

However, by this time, war was obviously looming. Various scenarios were being considered by the Government's planners, one of them obviously being internment. Although Germany appeared the most likely opponent in any future war, the possibility of the involvement of Mussolini's Italy was also considered. Captain Kell, who had in effect founded M.I.5 back in 1909, was still in charge of it – now Colonel Sir Vernon Kell, KBE, CB. Several reviews of the likelihood of the need for internment took place, and the initial view was that the total number of internees would "not exceed 600-700".

The principles decided in the 1920s were still being adhered to – intern those whom it might be dangerous or counter-productive to return to their country of origin, but simply expel the rest.

M.I.5 was required to work with the Home Office to define the categories of enemy aliens to be interned on the outbreak of war, to complete lists of those enemy aliens who should not be allowed to leave for defence reasons, and to work with the Home Office to make arrangements for the control of aliens, including the policy regarding deportation. It was also M.I.5's job to ensure that the War Office made arrangements for the provision of internment camps. On 30 January 1939, Kell gave the Home Office Prison Department a "very rough guide" to the numbers who would need to be interned [although it was the War Office who would be responsible for the camps]. He now estimated that there would be 3,000 internees in the whole country, of whom 1,300 would be in the Metropolitan area. Thus the number of prospective internees had already increased more than four-fold. It is interesting to note that at this stage the M.I.5 figures included Germans, Austrians and Italians – Mussolini was expected to join Germany if war was declared.

By 7 February 1939, eight days later, the figure for prospective internments had increased to an initial intake of 3,250, rising to 5,500 after a month. A memorandum of 10 February 1939 comments that: "while most of these refugees would be technically alien enemies, most of them will be more favourably disposed to this country than to those they have been forced to leave", but continues by suggesting that, in the case of heavy enemy bombing, it might be necessary to intern enemy aliens for their own protection from an enraged British public – referred to as the "inflamed eye of the man in the street."

In a memorandum dated 5 May 1939, and passed on to M.I.5, Mr Lionel de Rothschild, a leading member of the British Jewish community and an ex-Conservative MP, suggested that: "in the interests of the refugee himself it will be better to remove him into a place of safety, rather than expose him to the risk of physical damage inherent in contact with a community suffering from the psychological reaction of its first experience of intensified bombing raids [which everybody expected]. An infuriated population is not likely to stop to enquire if the male of foreign appearance, or whose speech shows traces of enemy origin, is an alien enemy or a refugee" However, the memorandum goes on to stress it was important to separate refugees from other enemy aliens [i.e. potential pro-Nazis]: "It is essential to consider the state of mind of the refugee who, in many cases, after suffering from several years of every form of inhuman treatment…is compelled in his place of temporary sanctuary to submit to separation from his wife and family…". In short, Mr de Rothschild was accepting that internment might be necessary, but emphasizing that refugees should be dealt with as a separate category and not mixed up with everybody else. His point about the effect of separating refugees from their families appears subsequently to have been ignored or forgotten.

Whilst the planning as to what to do about enemy aliens in the event of war continued, so too did the arrival of thousands of new refugees. A "stocktake" of German and Austrian refugees in the 10 February 1939 memorandum recorded that 7,000 males had already been admitted to the United Kingdom, visas had been granted for a further 2,000, and a further 7,000 were expected to arrive before the end of March. Many of them would be in transit to other countries such as the United States, but could not be expected to move on for several months. Thus, the British Government knew that increasing numbers of refugees arriving in the United Kingdom would lead to a greater number of so-called enemy aliens being present in Britain in the event of war with Germany, and potentially a greater internment problem, but the government of Neville Chamberlain still allowed the refugees to come. Britain's doors remained open.

Importantly, refugees were not admitted to Britain without careful checks as to their identity and background. There were a number of organisations set up in Britain to help refugees from Nazi oppression, particularly Jews. Most of the organisations were based in London at Bloomsbury House. One of those who worked to arrange for the refugees' entry into the United Kingdom was a man called Julian Layton. Layton [who finished the war with the rank of Lieutenant Colonel, attached to the Home Office] was Jewish, and his parents had come to the UK from Frankfurt, Germany in 1890. Layton was born in 1904. He built a career for himself in the United

Kingdom as a stockbroker, but retained family ties to Germany. His sister had married a German and lived in Frankfurt. When the Nazis came to power, Layton became involved in helping Jewish refugees to flee from oppression. He got all of his family out of Germany in 1934, and continued to work to help other would-be refugees to escape to Britain. Together with other prominent British Jews, Layton helped to find sponsors for those who wanted to come. As Nazi oppression worsened, and the flood of would-be refugees increased, Layton was involved in the setting up of a camp at Richborough, Sandwich, Kent, which, with significant financial support from the British government, provided for 3,000 refugees who did not have sponsors. The idea was that these refugees should include youngsters, who in the camp would be taught English, before being moved on to suitable countries where they could start a new life. Many wanted to go to the United States, and Richborough could provide them with the necessary language skills and education to do well there.

After *Kristellnacht* in November 1938, the Nazis arrested thousands of Jewish men. However, at this stage, they would be set free by the Nazis if they could show that they had another country to go to, and then went there. Layton worked in Vienna, helping by arranging approval for as many of those who applied to go to Britain as he could. He was obliged to liase with the Nazi Adolf Eichmann, who was later executed as a war criminal, and to submit to him a list of those selected to go to Britain.

Significantly, Layton was alert to a danger of the Nazis substituting their own secret agents for the selected candidates, and to avoid the identities of genuine candidates being assumed by Nazi stooges, all of the selected candidates were photographed, and the photographs checked when they arrived in Britain. Layton in fact never discovered any Nazi substitute amongst the refugees, but clearly he knew that there was a danger that the Nazis would try to infiltrate their agents into Britain masquerading as refugees, understood the damage that they could do, and put measures in place to ensure that no "cuckoos" arrived with his genuine refugees. Layton remained very much involved with Richborough Camp once it was set up, and would visit every weekend.

In August 1939, shortly before war was declared, the British Government of Neville Chamberlain made the decision to set up a series of tribunals in the event of war to judge whether individual German, Austrian or Czechoslovakian "enemy aliens" were or might be a danger to national security and therefore should be interned, or whether they might be allowed to stay at liberty. The Lord Chancellor's Office [the predecessor to the modern-day Ministry of Justice] assisted in the setting up of tribunals, and was told that: "the Home Secretary is hoping to avoid any general measure of internment of aliens. Of the Germans and Austrians in this country, most of whom are refugees, the great majority are entirely friendly to this country." Ninety-six suitable barristers were sought to sit on the tribunals. Although apparently no exact figures were available, it appears that by the time war broke out [3 September 1939] there were about fifty thousand Germans and Austrians in the United Kingdom, of whom thirty-five thousand were refugees.

On the outbreak of war, the tribunals were set up, and, in the event, both County Court Judges and senior barristers were used to make up the numbers. The proceedings of the Tribunals were not open to the public, and the enemy alien was not allowed to have a lawyer, although he [or she] could bring a friend with him, and witnesses. The Tribunal would act upon such information as was available on the enemy alien from the police or M.I.5, with their evidence taken in private, and upon representations from any refugee organisation. The enemy alien was allowed to give evidence, and to call witnesses. However, the Tribunals were not a court of law. They were appointed by the Home Secretary to help him in the discharge of an administrative function - internment. Proof of guilt of any offence was not necessary. The Tribunal's task was to assess whether, if allowed his or her unrestricted freedom, the enemy alien might pose a risk to the security of the nation. The Tribunals were instructed that such a risk might be found either because of pro-Nazi sympathies, or extreme left, pro-communist ones. Germany and the Soviet Union had signed a non-aggression pact, and it was only considerably later that the Nazis turned on the Soviet Union.

Upon the basis of suspected Nazi sympathies or extreme left wing views which might cause a threat to the security of the nation, the enemy aliens were placed by the Tribunals into one of three categories: A, B or C. Category A were supposedly the most dangerous and they were interned. Category B were those about whom there was some element of doubt, and therefore they were made subject to certain restrictions but allowed to remain at liberty. Category C were friendly aliens in need of no restrictions. The Tribunals were undoubtedly variable in their performance and standards, but in the result, a significant majority of the enemy aliens who came before them remained at liberty at this stage of the war.

Facing a difficult situation at the beginning of the war, the Chamberlain government was no doubt trying to be fair, and to honour Britain's reputation for justice. It had been accepted before the war began that the great majority of German, Austrian and Czecholslovak refugees were friendly to Britain. By way of example, Julian Layton, who was responsible for arranging for the Internment Tribunals that took place in Richborough Camp, later said that of the 3,000 young inmates in the camp, 2,300 proved their loyalty to Britain by joining the Pioneer Corps – initially, the only military unit that accepted "friendly enemy aliens."

Where it was felt that the Tribunal had made a mistake, it was possible to present fresh evidence to the Home Office and to appeal. A number of internees were released from detention after this process had been used.

In the early days, various prison camps throughout the country were set up and used for those detained. Two of the better known were at Seaton and Paignton in Devon. They contained both internees [Category A only at this stage], and German or Austrian seamen captured on various German civilian vessels which had been attacked and captured or sunk, who ranked as prisoners of war. Both the camps at Seaton and Paignton had been in use as holiday camps before the war – ideal in the summer, uncomfortable in the cold and damp of a seaside winter. Paignton was a camp for those who had enough money to pay for rather better food and accommodation, Seaton was for those who could not, or chose not, to pay. In winter, the poorly built cabins were very cold, and on occasions the pipes froze. Unfortunately, the War Office, who administered the camps, decided to lump all the German, Austrian and Czech prisoners together, and did not distinguish between Nazis and Jewish refugees. In the result, despite the fact that the government's thinking behind its internment of Germans, Austrians and a few Czechs had been considerate and perhaps as fair as possible in time of war, the application and administration of the policy was faulty from the start.

CHAPTER TWO

THE ITALIAN COMMUNITY

The other community in Britain which was to be substantially affected by internment was very different. The Italian community had been fully embedded in the British Isles for many years. Since the second half of the nineteenth century, Italians had come to Britain to work, and had established a network of small businesses throughout the four countries of the United Kingdom. Most worked in catering – running restaurants, cafes, fish and chip shops and ice cream parlours. By 1939, many of the best chefs in the top class restaurants of London were Italian. Although most arrived in Britain as economic refugees from the poverty of their villages in Italy, many established a successful business, or rose to the top of their trade.

Italy was and is a very diverse country, with most of its wealth in the cities of the industrial north. In poor areas when there were too many mouths to feed in a family, emigration was the obvious solution. The emigrants would travel to find work abroad, and when they were settled with small established businesses, they would often be able to provide work for others from their extended family, or from their village. They would preserve their links with the "old country", and would return home when they could. In 1931, there were 29,000 Italians resident in Britain, of whom 20,000 had been born in Italy. London alone held about 15,000 Italians, but there were Italian communities all over England, Scotland, Wales and Ireland.

By June of 1940, Italy had been under the rule of the dictator "Il Duce" Benito Mussolini and his Fascist regime for nearly eighteen years. It was on the 29 October 1922 that Mussolini was invited by the weak King of Italy, Victor Emmanuel III, to become Prime Minister, and that his Fascist party first effectively took control of the country's affairs. Over the next two years, he and his Fascist party worked to increase their hold on the country, until, in June 1925, Mussolini felt strong enough to announce to the Chamber of Deputies: "We are not a ministry; we are not even a government, we are a regime." Mussolini's fascist regime dominated the whole of the country. Violence was a significant feature of Fascist politics, but

Mussolini was also sufficiently astute to appreciate the value of appeasement and accommodation. He did not seek to depose the constitutional monarch, Victor Emmanuel III, who remained weakly on the throne throughout the Fascist period, and Mussolini reached an accommodation with the Roman Catholic Church in February 1929 which avoided any open conflict between church and state.

Mussolini's Fascists took control of the press and the radio, and enforced a strict censorship of all news items. They also took control of local administration. The mayors of the Italian comunes were re-named *podesta*, and were no longer elected, but were appointed. Thus all town halls came under Fascist control. However Mussolini allowed each region to retain its local identity and customs, always of great importance to the local people. Youth was important to the future of the Fascist regime, and so Mussolini took over control of the Boy Scouts and other youth organisations. If you wanted to play youth football, you had to join a Fascist Youth team. Fascists also controlled the arts, the theatre and music. For many younger Italians, by 1940 Mussolini's Fascism was all that they had known, or could remember. They were used to Fascism, and they had learned to live with it, even if they did not agree with many things that Mussolini did. Patronage and corruption were rife.

Although Fascism had thrived in the towns and industrial centres, it at first had little effect on most of the peasant farmers of rural Italy [the *contadini*]. It never made much difference to the *contadini* who was running the country. Their life was always a very hard one. Their main battle was with nature. Changes of government did not substantially affect their daily lives. Fascism was generally unpopular in the countryside, but most forms of government were. As stated, most of the Italians who emigrated to Great Britain did so because they came from poor areas of Italy where there was little work. Many of the economic migrants to Britain came from *contadini* stock. As Fascism in Italy grew in strength and became more extreme, political refugees and Jews joined the economic migrants, but in very much smaller numbers than the Germans and Austrian refugees fleeing from Hitler.

Having consolidated his hold over Italy, in 1930 Mussolini turned his attention to Italians living abroad. In the United Kingdom,

Italians, whilst assimilating the British way of life very happily, tended where possible to live in their own communities. In London, those from Emilia Romagna, Tuscany and Compania lived in Clerkenwell, those from Piedmont and Lombardy in Soho, and so on. Mussolini decided to create a series of "Little Fascist Italies" throughout those parts of the world to which Italians had emigrated. The Italian communities in Britain mixed very happily and successfully with local people, but retained strong family and emotional ties with Italy. They regularly sent money home to help their families in the impoverished villages there, and almost always recruited new staff to help them in their burgeoning businesses from their home villages in Italy.

In the early years of Italian Fascism, it was not unpopular in Britain. Many politicians believed that Mussolini was doing a good job – that he was bringing order to Italy after chaos, and pushing back against the rising tide of communism. In World War One, Italy had, of course, been Britain's ally. Since the Russian Revolution of 1917, and the rise of Bolshevism and Leninism, there was a genuine and widespread fear in Britain and other European countries that communism was the significant threat, and Mussolini was initially praised for resisting communist ideology, and reversing a drift towards communism. In 1927, five years after Mussolini had come to power, Winston Churchill visited Italy and met Mussolini, and upon his return to England, he gave a press conference in which he praised both Mussolini personally and his regime, saying [as reported in the Times, 27 January 1927]:

"I could not help being charmed, like so many other people have been, by Signor Mussolini's gentle and simple bearing, and by his calm, detached poise in spite of so many burdens and dangers…If I had been an Italian I am sure that I should have been wholeheartedly with you [Mussolini] from start to finish in your triumphant struggle against the bestial appetites and passions of Leninism…Externally your [Mussolini's] movement has rendered service to the whole world…Italy has shown that there is a way of fighting the subversive forces which can rally the mass of the people, properly led, to value and wish to defend the honour and stability of civilised society. Italy has provided the necessary antidote to the Russian poison."

An organisation had been set up in Britain in 1922 called the British Fascisti. It was a right-wing organisation that adopted Mussolini's politics, and was the fore-runner of the various British Fascist groups that emerged in the 1930s – the largest and most notorious of them being Mosley's British Union of Fascists.

In 1932, Mussolini appointed Dino Grandi as Ambassador to London. Grandi was a committed and active Fascist and a former Foreign Secretary of Italy. Grandi's job was to spread the Fascist gospel amongst Italians in the United Kingdom, and to increase the party's grip on Italian nationals abroad. This was done through the clubs and societies that the Fascists took over or founded, each referred to as a *fascio*. In a guide to Italians in London printed in 1933, the following assertion was made: "The ten million Italians dispersed around the world are no longer a detached appendix of the fatherland, but the fatherland itself, which through them expands in the world in the elements of its power and glory." Taking those words at their face value, it is possible to understand why later M.I.5 might worry about members of the *Fascio* in Britain, but the situation was complicated.

The Fascists published a weekly newspaper in Britain called *L'Italia Nostra* between 1928 and 1940, and news from the various "Little Italies" appeared every week in it. *L'Italia Nostra* had two objectives: to build a sense of Italian identity [of a Fascist kind] amongst the emmigrants – called *"Italianita"* or Italian-ness – and to promote Fascist propaganda. As with Fascism at home in Italy, Fascism became increasingly difficult to avoid in the United Kingdom for Italians, as Grandi and his Fascist team did their work.

Grandi was particularly active amongst the Italian community in London. As at home in Mussolini's Italy, the idea was to catch the children young, and embed in them the Fascist way of life. Italian schools were encouraged in London and elsewhere. The directors and teachers in the schools had to be Fascist, and the children would parade in the playground, giving the Fascist salute. In the same way as schools in Italy indoctrinated the children in Fascism from an early age, so now the Italian schools tried to do the same in Great Britain and Northern Ireland. The Roman Catholic church in Britain supported the sending of children to the Italian schools – a preferable education to that in a Protestant school. Many Italian children were offered free summer holidays in Italy each year – these were at Fascist summer camps, funded by the Fascist state.

Long established Italian cultural and working men's clubs in Britain were taken over by the Italian state, and became *fascio* clubs. Thereby, nominally all their members became members of a Fascist organisation in Britain. Mussolini, through Grandi, was trying to exert the same control over ex-patriate Italians in Britain as he did over his fellow countrymen at home. Regular tasks such as sending money home to Italy through the Italian consulates were far easier if the sender was a member of the Fascist party – you gave your Fascist party number, and matters proceeded smoothly thereafter. In reality, if you wanted the Italian State [through the consulates] to help you, you had to be a member of the Fascist party. However, in order to judge how much or how little membership of a *fascio* club in Britain actually meant in any individual case, it was necessary to judge both the individual and the community in which he or she lived - something which it later became clear M.I.5 never bothered to do.

By way of example, there is, in the very north of Tuscany, near where that province meets the borders of the Liguria and Emilia Romagna, a village called Bratto, perched high in the Apuanian Alps above the city of Pontremoli, Massa Carrara. In the first half of the twentieth century, and for centuries before that, Bratto was a small, poor, farming village. Its inhabitants worked hard to support their families. They fought an eternal struggle against nature, working long hours to gain a living from the earth, or working in the forests making charcoal. The patron saint of the village was St George, the same as for England, and the church was named after him. Because there were often too many mouths to feed, some of the sons of the village had to travel far to look for work. In the second half of the nineteenth century, some travelled as far as England, and set up small businesses there – making ice cream, selling fish and chips, setting up cafes and later restaurants, and working with mosaics. For the Brattese, the focus of their emigration was usually London. Once they had made their modest fortunes, many would return home to enjoy in Italy a comfortable retirement.

During the post First World War depression and the rise of Mussolini, national domestic politics remained of little interest to the Brattese – they were too busy fighting to make a living from the soil and forests. Generally, however, they disliked central government of any kind, and the taxes that the governments inevitably imposed. They continued to send their children to London to work, and some of those who had run businesses in London passed their businesses on to their sons and returned to Bratto to enjoy a comfortable retirement. Others preferred to remain in London. When war was declared between Britain and Germany, in September 1939, rather more Italians returned home from Britain than had previously been the case – not because they were pro-Fascist, but because of the danger of bombing, particularly in London. Long before the London Blitz in the autumn of 1940, there were dire predictions as to how extensive the civilian casualties from German bombs might be. There had been some bombing during World War One, its horrors had been extensively witnessed during the much more recent Spanish Civil war, and it was thought now to be inevitable that hundreds of thousands would die from German bombs – hence the evacuation of British children from its cities and major towns when the war began. Also, many Italians remembered the internment that had been imposed on enemy aliens in the First World War [although not on Italians since Italy had been one of Britain's allies], and had no wish to be interned as an enemy alien in Britain in the new war, should Mussolini join in on Hitler's side. In the event, Italy did not join the war until June 1940, and therefore for Italians in Britain in the autumn of 1939 and early 1940, there was the option to go home to their villages in Italy if they wished, and thereby avoid being bombed by the Germans in London or interned in Britain should Mussolini bring Italy into the war. The village of Bratto was made up of a small number of large families – in the village graveyard, the same surnames appear time and time again – Bardini, Beschizza, Cattini, Cocchi, Corsini, Necchi-Ghiri, Schia and others. A time came when most of the families had relatives working in London. Thus, when war between Britain and the Germans broke out in September 1939, the village of Bratto, like many others in Italy, was quite closely connected to what was happening a thousand miles away in London.

A good example of a Brattese who was born in Bratto but brought up in England is Luigi Rafaele Stefano Beschizza. This book will follow his story. Luigi was born in Bratto in 1918. Luigi's father had first gone to England to work in 1907, working in the catering business and running a cafe. He returned to Italy to serve in Italian army in 1915, married Luigi's mother in 1916, and went back to England at the end of the First World War. Luigi's mother joined her husband in England in 1920, initially leaving Luigi with the family in Bratto. This was not uncommon in rural Italy in those days. The breadwinners would go to Britain to work and the smaller children would be left with their extended family in Italy. Four years later, in 1924, Luigi travelled to London to join his parents. The family lived in a flat above their café in Goldhawk Road. From the age of six until he was fourteen, Luigi went to school in London, and learned to speak fluent English with a London accent. At the age of 14, he went to work in the family café, and later his father opened a second café not very far away in Hammersmith Broadway. Luigi was not very tall, but was an athletic young man and a good footballer. He was a happy go lucky individual. By the outbreak of the Second World War he was twenty-one, and thoroughly enjoying his life in London.

Luigi Beschizza was in no way involved in Italian politics. Many years later, when asked to describe his attitude to Mussolini, Luigi replied: "All I knew was that we had a government in Italy headed by Mussolini. I wasn't anti-Fascist, I just didn't know about them." Being a good footballer, he was at one stage asked to join the young Fascists football team in London, but said no. He did belong to the *fascio* run Italian Club in the Charing Cross Road, but that was only so that he could go dancing there with his friends on Saturday evenings. Luigi was proud of being Italian, as most Italians are. Italy is a country with a fine history. The civilisation and achievements of the Roman Empire are not forgotten, nor is Italy's fine heritage of art and music. However, despite his national pride, Luigi was totally apolitical.

In addition to the economic refugees who came from Italy in search of work, there were also a number of Italian refugees from Mussolini's regime. A number of organisations in Britain helped refugees, and Julian Layton's work with the Germans and Austrians has already been mentioned. The International Department of the Labour Party involved itself with them. Mr William Gillies was the Secretary of the International Department, and was one of the Party's experts on refugees. He worked to help them over a number of years leading up to the outbreak of war, both German/Austrian and Italian, and came to know many of them personally. He was therefore extremely well placed to know who amongst the refugees were genuinely pro-British, and of value to Britain. The Labour Party ran a significant propaganda campaign against Hitler and Mussolini, and in the wartime coalition government, they were the acknowledged champions of the many refugees in the United Kingdom. Mr Gillies was concerned that the necessary government departments should know who the leading anti-Fascist Italians, and genuine friends of Britain, were, and therefore made a point of informing the Home Office of their names in writing. As early as 1937, he took the trouble to send to a Mr Cooper, the chief of the Home Office Aliens Department, a list of Italian nationals who were Britain's friends, giving the reasons why the Home Office could accept his assurances i.e. proof of their genuineness. The list included Decio Anzani, who was the Secretary of the Italian Section of the League of the Rights of Man, a fiercely anti-Fascist and anti-Nazi organisation, and had lived in England since Mussolini's rise to power. Anzani was said to have been one of the best-known anti-Fascists in the Britain. Mr Gillies went so far as to say that in the case of danger, the men on his list should be protected because they were valuable to Britain.

In August 1938, Mr Gillies again sent a list of anti-Fascist Italians to the Home Office, this time to a Mr Clayton. On this occasion he especially emphasised the value of Mr Anzani and a Dr A.F.Magri. He supplied the list in duplicate. Dr Magri and Mr. Anzani's names appeared at the top of the list. Gillies recommended that one copy of his list should be given to the Security Services. Then, in May 1940, before Italy entered the war, Gillies was asked, by what he described as a member of the Special Services, to again supply a list, and he did so. Thus Mr Gillies had made the sympathy towards Britain of these men and others absolutely clear on three occasions before Mussolini declared war on 10 June 1940.

CHAPTER THREE

WAR WITH GERMANY

TRIBUNALS AND INTERNMENT

The declaration of war with Germany [and therefore Austria] on 3 September 1939 was the trigger for the long-planned programme of internment. The Internment Tribunals went into action, placing "enemy aliens" into one of the three categories previously described: A, B or C. Obviously, refugees from Nazi persecution would be expected to be anti-Nazi. Whether they were pro-British, was a secondary question, but since Britain had given them refuge, it was to be expected that they were. However, there was nonetheless a concern that some of these might be "cuckoos" - Nazi agents masquerading as refugees - something that Julian Layton had taken measures to prevent. The British Government was also very wary of those refugees who might have extreme left-wing politics, particularly if they were declared communists. The Nazis had made a non-aggression pact with the Soviet Union. Although Britain was not at war with the Soviets in 1939, they were regarded as an obvious danger. The Tribunals were instructed to consider this, despite the fact that, since Britain was a democracy, communism was not illegal, and there was a British Communist Party. In a number of cases, the Tribunals decided that Communist enemy aliens were a security risk, and therefore locked them up as Category A.

Of course, such a system of categorisation could only be as good as those who were chosen to apply it. Eventually, a total of 120 tribunals were put in place, and every enemy alien was entitled to a hearing before one. The Home Office issued a series of memoranda to provide guidance to the Tribunals. However, the tribunals were one man affairs, and the decision would therefore depend on what that one man thought. Usually, the decision maker was an experienced and distinguished lawyer, but not necessarily one with any experience of German or Austrian culture, which would usually affect the enemy alien's evidence to some degree. The enemy alien would have the opportunity to give evidence, and would be questioned by the tribunal. He would have no lawyer, and would not know the content of any confidential information supplied to the tribunal about him or her by M.I.5 or others. Evidence from refugee organisations was regularly taken where the subject of the tribunal was a refugee. They would make representations as to his known character and background. Category B provided the tribunals with some discretion – providing for the imposition of restrictions on an individual that fell short of internment. Although only about 1% of those who came before the tribunals were interned as Category A, many were placed in Category B for no particularly good reason, and geographically the tendency to place enemy aliens in Category B or C fluctuated enormously. However, the principles of British justice survived the beginning of the war as best they could – every enemy alien had a hearing and a chance to put the case against his or her internment. There was also the   appeal tribunal for those who wished to challenge their categorisation.

One of those who came before a tribunal was Leo Kahn, who can be taken to have been a fair judge of how tribunals should work, since he was a lawyer. Kahn described himself as middle class, he was from Cologne, he was Jewish, and he was a liberal. In Germany, he had had little involvement in politics, although he had flirted with Marxism for a very short time. From 1933 onwards, with the rise of Adolf Hitler, Kahn believed that there was no future for him in Germany, and began to prepare to get out. In 1934, he spent nine months in England, studying the English language, and establishing contacts. He returned to Germany to do his doctorate in law. He kept in touch with Britain in the meantime, making two short visits to a friend in 1935 and 1936. Then in 1937, Leo Kahn came to Britain with the intention of staying. He was still a single man when he arrived for what he had declared would be only a temporary visit. Having no intention of returning to Germany, Khan managed to arrange for his fiancée and her sister to follow him to Britain a little later on. Kahn's parents died in 1938, and his own sister emigrated from Germany to Uruguay.

When he arrived in 1937, Leo Kahn went to Bristol, where there was a circle of Jewish refugees. Once there, he managed to borrow £50 from a friend, a large enough sum to get him started in Britain. As a German Jewish lawyer who spoke English, he soon found himself working for the Jewish Refugees Committee in London – helping his fellow countrymen to escape to Britain. When war was declared, Leo Kahn, like everybody else, had to go before an Internment Tribunal. He went before a Magistrate in Wealdstone, London. He understood that Category A was for those found by the tribunal to be a potential risk to British security, but like many others [undoubtedly including a number of tribunal members] Leo Khan found it difficult to understand the difference between Categories B and C – neither led to internment, and the lines of discrimination between the two seemed blurred.

Kahn was supported at his hearing by a representative of the Jewish Refugees Committee who gave references. He was still working for them. Kahn was asked whether he had ever been in prison or in a concentration camp, and said no. To his surprise, Kahn was then pressed as to whether he had been in a prison in Berlin in 1924 – at which time he had in fact been a schoolboy. He denied it, and was asked to supply his fingerprints, which he did. He was asked to return for a second hearing once his fingerprints had been checked, which he also did. It was duly established that he was not the Leo Kahn who had apparently been in prison in Berlin in 1924. He was asked whether he needed to travel around the country for his work, and he said he was not sure. The tribunal then came to the decision that there was no evidence that Leo Kahn was "unreliable", and therefore that he was not Category A. He would retain his liberty. The Magistrate who chaired the Tribunal told Kahn that they had found nothing against him, and that Category B would be "enough." Category B entailed a restriction on Kahn's movements. Perhaps if he had said that he needed to travel, he would have been placed in Category C. A Category B finding was unfair on the evidence, Kahn was clearly anti-Nazi, and nobody suggested that he was a dangerous communist.

Kahn's fiancée had by now become his wife, and was a teacher, teaching English to foreigners. When she appeared before a Tribunal, she was placed into Category C. Her sister, however, was placed into Category B, almost certainly because she had not yet found an occupation. Kahn, the lawyer, thought that it was all a bit silly. It was clear that the Tribunals did not really know which criteria to apply. However, in the early part of the war, it did not matter. Kahn, his wife and his sister-in-law all remained at liberty.

Another example was Raimund Pretzel, one who was obviously anti-Nazi because, under the pen name of Sebastian Haffner, he had written two of the most anti-Nazi and pro-British books available at that time. Despite this, he was for some reason interned as a Category A enemy alien. It was only the energetic intervention of his publishers which prevented him from later being deported, and he was eventually released. His Jewish wife had also been interned.

Ulrich Alexander Boschwitz was born into an affluent German-Jewish family in Berlin in 1915, during the First World War. His father was a factory owner, but died before he was born. It is not clear whether he gave his life for Germany in the war, or died for some other reason. Boschwitz was undoubtedly of Jewish blood, but his father had converted to the Roman Catholic church, and his mother Martha was a committed Protestant, with no Jewish connections until she met his father. Ulrich was never a practising Jew, and was brought up by his mother in the Protestant faith. Ulrich's mother took over the running of the family business after her husband's death, and when Ulrich left school he undertook a business apprenticeship in preparation for taking over the business himself. Adolf Hitler's rise to power completely changed his life. When on 1 April 1933, the Nazi regime declared a national boycott of Jewish businesses, the Boschwitzs found themselves categorised as Jewish, Ulrich by blood and Martha by marriage. By 1935, Ulrich and his mother found it necessary to leave Germany, but they were not allowed to take their family's fortune with them. They went to Sweden, and in Sweden, Ulrich wrote his first novel, which was published in Swedish in 1937. He used the non-German pen name of John Grane. The novel was a success, and Ulrich continued to write, completing his second novel *The Traveller* in 1938 after watching the horrors of *Kristallnacht* on 9 November from Brussels. *The Traveller* was published in English in 1939 under the title *The Man who took Trains*, and Ulrich and his mother moved to England the same year. The book was totally anti-Nazi, and told of the horrors and general awfulness of Nazi persecution of the Jews. It was in some ways autobiographical – Ulrich's own family had suffered much of what his character in the book, Otto Silbermann, suffered. Ulrich Boswitch was in the same category therefore as Raimund Pretzel – he was demonstrably anti-Nazi. He and his mother were not initially interned, but that was to change later.

Ludwig Baruch was born on 2 March 1917 in Hamburg. His parents were non-practising Jews, whom he described as middle class intelligenzia and left wing, which was the family tradition. As Ludwig grew up in Hamburg, he experienced only subdued anti-semitism. His father initially worked for a German company in Hamburg, but then moved with Ludwig's mother to work in Liverpool. Ludwig followed them there in September 1930, at the age of 13. Although he found Liverpool shabby after Hamburg, Ludwig settled in well, and made plenty of friends. He experienced no animosity because he was German, or because he was Jewish. When the Nazis came to power in Germany in early 1933, it came as a great shock to Ludwig's parents. His mother broke down for weeks. Young Ludwig had already joined the Young Communist League, and believed that only the Communists could deal with the Nazis – it was, he thought, the only way to survive. By the time that Britain declared war on Germany on 3 September 1939, Ludwig had gained a reputation as an active Young Communist within the British Communist Party. He was twenty-two.

Despite being an obviously anti-Nazi Jew, Ludwig Baruch was interned following a Tribunal hearing which found him to be in Category A, presumably because of his communist sympathies. He was sent to Seaton Internment Camp in Devon. There he found himself imprisoned with some Nazis, some German merchant seamen, but also many other Jews, including Rabbis. Ludwig appealed his internment, and appeared before the Appeal Tribunal. There, because of his communist beliefs, he was asked the question: "If there was a conflict between them, would you back the Soviet Union against the United Kingdom?" A simple "no" might have got Ludwig Baruch released, but he replied that it was a theoretical question, and that therefore he could not answer it. His answer condemned him, his appeal was refused, and his detention at Seaton continued.

A report received by M.I.5 dated 23 February 1940 concerning the Jews held at Seaton Internment Camp was apparently ignored. It came originally from a non-Jewish anti-Nazi who had recently been released from that camp. It read: "The Nazis are organised and there is at least one Gestapo man amongst them. They are bitter and arrogant and display their hate on every possible occasion. They constantly sing bloodthirsty anti-Semetic songs. They have beaten up Jews on several occasions...surely it would be possible to separate the sheep from the goats...in round figures, the Nazis are 3% out of the 600 internees." However, nothing changed, and still the Nazis were not separated from the Jews.

Seven weeks later, on 10 April, a Mr D.McLeod of the War Office wrote a memorandum about the camp at Seaton which was passed on to M.I.5. It asked for the release into useful employment of a group of German seamen who were held there. Mr McLeod explained that they were all trade unionists who had belonged to United States and Scandinavian Unions. Trade Unions were outlawed in Nazi Germany. They had initially refused a grant of 30 marks that the German government was making to all captured seamen, but later accepted it and invested it in British War Bonds – a contribution to the British war effort. They were obviously anti-Nazi. Mr McLeod's suggestion was dismissed out of hand by M.I.5, and one comment on the file speculated that Mr McLeod should be placed in a mental hospital.

Returning to the Internment Tribunals, of course it was not only Jews who appeared before the tribunals. Franz Stampfl was born on 18 November 1913 in Vienna, Austria. He was the fourth of seven children, and the family was Catholic. His father was a surgical instrument maker. Franz studied art and was a good athlete, excelling at javelin throwing and skiing. At the age of 23, he went with the Austrian Olympic team to Berlin for the 1936 games. There he saw Hitler's Germany at first hand, and was shocked by its militarism. In 1937, he moved to England, and for a while studied art at the Chelsea School of Art. When Hitler took over Austria in 1938, Franz Stampfl, as an Austrian student in the United Kingdom, was served with notice by the British Government that he must leave the country unless he showed that he had a unique and necessary skill.

Franz managed to do this with the support of the Olympic Gold Medal winner Harold Abrahams. He got a job as an athletics coach in Northern Ireland. From there, returning to England he took up a job at Queen Elizabeth's School, Barnet, Hertfordshire, as athletics coach, enjoying very considerable success. It is said that one of Stampfl's great abilities was to put equal emphasis on the training and development of the body, and the training and development of the mind – making sure that his athletes were both physically and mentally fit. He initially avoided internment, but that was not to last.

It was not only enemy aliens who were interned. As a part of Britain's pre-war democracy, many home-grown British Fascists had declared themselves, and had joined right-wing parties such as Mosley's British Union of Fascists. After the outbreak of war, a system of internment was also imposed for British nationals who were believed to be a danger to national security. Regulation 18B of the Defence [General] Regulations 1939, made subject to the Emergency Powers [Defence] Act 1939, empowered the Home Secretary to arrest and detain British subjects whom he "had reasonable cause to believe to be of hostile origin or association or to have been recently concerned in acts prejudicial to the public safety or defence of the realm", provided that such person was given the opportunity to make representations to an advisory committee appointed by the Secretary of State. An Advisory Committee had been set up in September 1939 under the chairmanship of Sir Walter Monckton KC, later succeeded by Norman Birkett KC. The Regulation 18B powers were used against British citizens. Many British Fascists were detained in due course – only a trickle at first, but after Churchill became Prime Minister in May 1940, many of the leading figures in the British Union of Fascists and other British fascist organisations found themselves in custody. However, as a matter of law, British subjects who were interned could not be deported. They were British citizens and were entitled to live in Britain. Therefore, if a German, Austrian, Czech or Italian had become a British citizen, although they were still liable to internment [as all British citizens were] under Regulation 18B of the Defence Regulations, they could not be deported.

Frank Sigmund Hildesheim was 63 years of age. He had been born in Glasgow on 20 March 1876. A number of his siblings were also born in Glasgow. His parents were Germans who came from Hamburg, and his father worked for a number of years in the jute trade in Glasgow. They were Jewish, although Frank was never a practising Jew. Frank lived in Scotland for about ten years after his birth, and attended a local school until the age of ten. The family then returned to Hamburg. Because they were born in Britain, Frank and his siblings were entitled to British citizenship. Frank became a marine engineer, and between 1905 and 1910, he returned to work in Britain for the Vickers company. He married a British national from Australia, Helga Petersen, and had a son and daughter, both born in Hamburg. Throughout World War One, Frank worked in Germany as a marine engineer, for some of the time on U-Boats. After that war, Frank continued to work in Germany, and became an expert translator in the field of technical nautical engineering. Since he was not a practising Jew, he survived longer than many of Jewish origin, but in 1938, he decided to seek a future in Britain. He applied for and received the British passport that he was entitled to. By so doing, he was allowed to renounce his German citizenship – however the law was that if he did not leave Germany within a year of taking British citizenship, he would revert to German nationality. He arrived back in Britain in March 1939. His adult daughter wished to remain in her job in Germany, and his wife initially was reluctant to leave their daughter alone. Their son was already living and working in the United States. Frank therefore came to Britain alone, and penniless.

At the outbreak of war, things looked bad for Frank – he was a highly qualified marine engineer who had worked for Germany throughout World War One, and he had only months before claimed British citizenship and come to Britain. Frank was duly detained, under Regulation 18B [since he was British], on 5 December 1939. He was not detained as an enemy alien, although the decision to detain him under Regulation 18B effectively put him into Category A. Initially, his detention under Regulation 18B meant that he was held in Wandsworth Prison. He appealed his detention, and on Wednesday 24 January 1940 he appeared before the Appeal Committee, chaired by Norman Birkett, K.C. By this time, his wife was in detention in Germany as an enemy alien – i.e. a British citizen in Nazi Germany. His daughter apparently remained free.

It is clear from the transcript of the appeal hearing that Frank Hildesheim was open and honest with the Committee. However, he could not get away from the facts that, although born in Scotland, he had chosen to live in Germany for most of his life, he had expert knowledge as a marine engineer, he had worked on U Boats in Germany during World War One, he had only recently come to Britain, and his wife and daughter were still in Germany. The Committee appears to have liked him, but felt that he must constitute a risk to national security because of his particular expertise, and his background. It refused his appeal, but recommended that he be held in an internment camp with other Germans and Austrians, rather than in a prison. This was no doubt intended to be a kindness. However, when Frank's wife, Helga, finally arrived in Britain shortly after the appeal hearing, also penniless, she stayed with cousins of Frank's just north of London. It was a significant blow to the couple when they found out that Frank was going to be moved to the internment camp at Seaton in Devon, many miles away. Mrs Hildesheim was allowed to visit her husband in Wandsworth Prison on 24 February 1940, and the record kept of the visit includes that they were: "both very depressed owing to the fact that they had both been informed of Mr Hildesheim going to a concentration camp…" Frank was duly transported to Seaton. The intended kindness of the Appeal Committee had mis-fired. A little later, things would get even worse for Frank Hildesheim

Thus, although the tribunal system did not work very well during the early months of the war, there was at least an initial hearing and a right to appeal – both for British subjects and enemy aliens. That changed after the arrival of Winston Churchill as Prime Minister on 10 May 1940, and the disaster of Dunkirk. Very quickly and quite unexpectedly, Britain found herself overwhelmed by the Nazi forces in Europe, and facing an imminent invasion. When Mussolini joined the war on 10 June, no doubt expecting easy pickings from the British Empire once Britain had been defeated, thousands of Italians living in Britain were arrested without any hearing at all.

With Churchill as the driving force, the British Government decided on 31 May 1940 that all Category B enemy aliens should be interned. All of a sudden therefore, the difference between Category B and C became vitally important. The knock came on Leo Khan's door, and he was arrested. He was taken to a police station, and then on to the internment camp at Kempton Park Race Course. Kempton Park, empty of race horses, was now filling up with internees. The horses' accommodation became that of the human prisoners. Khan was held at Kempton Park for about three weeks, and then moved to Warth Mills, Bury, Lancashire. The Austrian Franz Stampfl, the athletics coach, also now found himself arrested and interned, as did Ulrich Boschwitz and his mother. Ulrich had only to say: "If you think I am pro-Nazi, read my book." *The Man Who Took Trains* was powerful anti-Nazi literature, and had been published in English, albeit under the pen name John Grane. Ulrich was clearly anti-Nazi, and had been a refugee from Hitler's Germany since 1935. Despite this, both he and his mother were initially sent to internment camps on the Isle of Man. After a few weeks there, Ulrich was nominated as a "dangerous enemy alien" and was sent for deportation. Frank Hildesheim, the British citizen who had been sent to an aliens internment camp in what had been intended by the Appeal Tribunal as an act of kindness now also found himself marked for deportation, despite the fact that deportation in his case would be unlawful. Germans, Austrians and Czechs who were recent arrivals, and had not yet had the benefit of a tribunal, and those youngsters who had, for instance, arrived under the *Kindertransport* scheme but had now passed the age of sixteen, and were therefore eligible for internment, forfeited any right to a tribunal.

When, on 10 June 1940, Italy entered the war on Germany's side, Churchill's order became "Collar the Lot" – which in the slang of the time meant "arrest them all." Churchill wanted all enemy aliens between the age of 16 and 70 to be arrested, interned and the most dangerous ones to be deported from Britain with all possible speed. Britain was in clear and obvious danger of invasion by Germany, and Churchill's aim was to eliminate any risk from within Britain's shores. There was simply not time, in his view, for any more tribunals to be held. There was a great fear, whipped up by the British Press, that Germany might have secretly put a Fifth Column in place in Britain, to rise up and assist any future German invasion. Churchill's reasoning was: "arrest all enemy aliens, get rid of as many as possible from these shores to distant parts of the Dominions, and we can sort out who is good and who is bad later on". As it turned out, the sole judge of which Italians were to be arrested and then deported was M.I.5, who often had little or no sound information to go on.

In addition to enemy aliens/potential Fifth Columnists, there were a number of German/Austrian prisoners of war being held in England, together with members of the German Merchant Marine who had been captured with their ships, or when their ships were sunk. These too Churchill wanted to get rid of, regarding them as a danger should the German invasion come. There was already some intelligence and some rumours suggesting that German paratroopers might land in the prisoner of war camps and set the prisoners free to help the invasion. However, the problem with the mass deportations that Churchill and his Government envisaged was that the only way to accomplish them was to transport the prisoners by sea for many miles across U-Boat infested waters.

CHAPTER FOUR

THE FEAR OF A FIFTH COLUMN

The term "Fifth Column" dates from events in the Spanish civil war in 1936 – a General Emilio Mola Vidal had four columns of troops attacking Madrid, and claimed that he had a sympathetic fifth column concealed inside the city. This claim attracted much publicity at the time, and the term Fifth Column moved into regular use in the English language. Ernest Hemingway, the well-known American author, wrote a play in 1937, which he entitled: "The Fifth Column". The term came to be used for any persons "hidden in plain sight" amongst the citizens of any country, who supported that country's enemies. The Nazis employed Fifth Columnists in a variety of countries which it invaded, including Holland, and in due course the fear of a Fifth Column became, for a few months, a British phobia. The phobia fuelled the mood of panic after the evacuation of Dunkirk. It was aimed initially at the German and Austrians, and then, after 10 June 1940, at the Italians.

In September 1939, at the beginning of the war against Germany, there were approximately 72,000 adult Germans and Austrians in the United Kingdom. Prior to the Spring of 1940, only 572 of them had been interned by the Internment Tribunals that were set up, in addition to 350 who were "suspicious characters" and had been interned immediately upon the outbreak of war. 6,691 Germans and Austrians had been placed in Category B and subjected to some restrictions, and 64,290 were in Category C, of which 51,324 were refugees. However, there were also some refugees in Categories A and B.

One valuable source of information as to what was going on in Britain in 1939 and 1940 was an anthropological organisation called Mass-Observation. Founded in 1937, it studied all aspects of life in Britain. It still exists today, and its archives are based at the University of Sussex. It reported regularly on the results of its researches. In the second half of April 1940, weeks before the German *blitzkrieg* started, it reported: "April has been marked by a campaign against "the enemy in our midst", the sinister invisible enemy; the Fifth Column. A campaign against the Fifth Column, led with restraint by M.P.s has been whipped up into something different in the Press; a campaign to intern all refugees. The Sunday Press has been particularly active on this subject; several papers have ignored the point made by M.P.s, and the serious weeklies, namely that the Fifth Column may be mainly composed of persons in high positions, British born and bred."

One of the leaders of Mass-Observation, Mr Tom Harrison, was to comment in the New Statesman on 13 July 1940 that public opinion had, in April and May, been influenced by what he described as several weeks of intensive campaigning from "responsible" quarters and from the British Upper class. He complained: "…we never had a word from any responsible person explaining over the radio or in the mass papers the distinctions that could be made between different sorts of aliens. Little was done to prevent the phrase: "Fifth Column" becoming a stunt…" Mr Harrison was complaining that British public opinion was deliberately whipped up to create a fear of all aliens and refugees, and that the Government did nothing to stop it. It was certainly true that there were a number of members of the British upper class who were actively pro-Nazi and pro-Fascist. Some were members of the Right Club, which the author will describe later. At this stage of the war, most of them were still free men and women. The fall of Luxembourg, Holland and Belgium to Nazi forces in May simply served to increase their optimism. It was obviously to the advantage of the British Nazis that as many anti-Nazi Germans and anti-Fascist Italians be interned, and/or deported. The reality was that all refugees were either anti-Nazi or anti-Fascist.

The Daily Mail, owned by Lord Rothermere, was one of the papers that started the anti-alien phobia. In April, it was demanding that "the police must round up every doubtful alien in this country". However, by 24 May, Mr Ward Price of that paper [previously known for his books in support of Hitler and Mussolini, and for advocating appeasement] was crying out: "Act, Act, Act - Do it now: The rounding up of enemy agents must be taken out of the fumbling hands of local tribunals. All refugees from Austria, Germany and Czechoslovakia, men and women alike, should be drafted without delay to a remote part of the country and kept under strict supervision…As the head of a Balkan State told me last month:

"In Britain, you fail to realise that *every* German is an agent. All of them have both the duty and the means to communicate information to Berlin..."

Fuel was added to the fire by a rather more distinguished source in the same month. On 14 May 1940, Sir Neville Bland, who had been British Ambassador to Holland before it fell to the Nazis, presented a memorandum which began with the words: "I venture to submit, with all the emphasis in my power, as a result of our recent experiences in Holland, that immediate steps should be taken to intern all persons in this country [i.e.Britain] with German or Austrian connections." What exactly Bland meant by "connections" is not clear, but he was advocating the most sweeping of arrests and detentions. He justified this by citing his experience of the German invasion of Holland, saying: "Holland, although she left it until too late, was far more alive to the danger created by these people than we appear to be even today. It is clear, either by inference or by direct evidence, that the paltriest kitchen maid with such connections, not only can be, but generally is, a menace to the safety of the country...We know that the Germans have worked out a plan for dealing with this country. We do not unfortunately know what that plan may be. I have not the least doubt that, when the signal is given, as it will scarcely fail to be when Hitler so decides, there will be satellites *all over the country* who will at once embark on widespread sabotage attacks on civilians and the military indiscriminately. We cannot afford to take this risk. All Germans and Austrians, at least, ought to be interned at once. There is, I fear, no time to lose...Intern *all* potential enemies..." Bland's letter was shortly afterwards reproduced by the Foreign Office, and circulated to various British Embassies abroad. Sir Neville's prediction of "widespread sabotage attacks all over the country" does not appear to have been based upon any evidence at all against the large refugee community in Britain.

However, the next day, 15 May 1940, the Government's Joint Intelligence Sub-Committee made a number of urgent recommendations including:

[i] All enemy aliens, both male and female, between the ages of 16 and 70 should be interned,

[ii] Special measures should be taken for the control of non-enemy aliens, with particular reference to refugees from Holland, Belgium and Norway. In the case of refugees from enemy occupied territory, such aliens should be held by the Health Authorities until such time as their entry has been approved by the Security Authorities.

[xvii] Appropriate steps should be taken at once to prepare to deal with Italian aliens as soon as necessary.

Whether there was in fact a Fifth Column deliberately hidden amongst the Germans, Austrians and Italians in Britain in the Spring of 1940 is very much open to doubt. It seems extremely unlikely that any of the German or Austrian Jewish refugees who had fled for their lives to Britain were Fifth Columnists, and there is no evidence that they were. However, the British Government were concerned only with risk, and could argue that Jews and other refugees might be coerced to work for the Nazis by threats being made against the well-being of any members of their families who remained in Germany or Austria, and therefore were within the clutches of the Nazis.

The position of Italians was different. M.I.5 approached the question of Italian aliens by condemning all those who were members of a *fascio* as being active and dangerous fascists. They were entirely wrong, as Professor Bruno Foa later explained. Professor Foa was an Italian Jew, who before fleeing Italy had acted for six years as the legal advisor to the British Consulate General in Naples. He had been a Professor of Law at various Italian universities, until being disqualified from such a position in 1938 because he was a Jew. Professor Foa came to London, and in due course joined the BBC. In August 1940, he prepared and submitted a memorandum explaining what membership of a *fascio* or the fascist party meant, saying: "It should be strongly emphasised that, in Italy, it does not follow at all that because a man is a party member he is of Fascist political complexion. Far from it. Possession of a party card is simply a question of bread and butter; a sheer and very often disagreeable necessity for the ordinary breadwinner…It can be safely stated therefore that membership of the party and/or party organisations is held by nine-tenths of the people as a necessary inconvenience. The possession of a membership card is, in everyday life, as much of a necessity as, say, a birth or citizenship certificate in a democratic country. Without it, the Italian man is…denied such fundamental rights as the right to work, and to seek employment. The political significance of such a membership can be assessed as next to nothing."

In general terms, the same was true of Italians living in the United Kingdom who wished to socialise with their fellow Italians there, or to maintain contact with their families and villages in Italy. Foa also stressed that it was not just German and Austrian Jews who had been fleeing as refugees to Britain, but also Italians. These were people who would in no way help the Nazi regime. Many of them were very talented professionals, now denied the right to practise their professions in Italy because of their faith.

However, throughout May 1940, the phobia against enemy aliens in Britain increased, fuelled by a variety of sources. On 21 May 1940, the British Embassy in Madrid, Spain, sent a telegram to the Foreign Office in London. It claimed: "[Another country's] Head of Mission, who is on intimate terms with the German Embassy here, but is well disposed [towards us], told me that the Germans were jubilant over their successes and were now talking quite openly about the methods they had employed. It was evident that the new weapon was the Fifth Column, and the basis of the Fifth Column everywhere, except in the Iberian Peninsula, was Jewish refugees from Germany and Austria. It seemed that they had been approached individually in Scandinavia and the Low Countries, and told that if they would work for Germany they would be allowed to return after the war and their relatives in Germany would be released forthwith. Otherwise, they would be put on the black list…"

Further, the file has attached to it an undated paper from Mr Bruce Lockhart on the countries of South Eastern Europe, which provides an overview of the situation in that part of the world, and states: "…the events of the last six years have made him [the Jew] the implacable enemy of German rule, living in terror…[but] the dire state of misery and degradation to which large masses of the race have been reduced have created a milleu in which the lower form of spy and informer is bred." In other words, Mr Lockhart was suggesting that if Jews were starving and desperate, they might agree to spy or inform for their Nazi masters. However, any objective observer would comment that the Jewish refugees who had arrived in Britain were no longer living in a dire state of misery and degradation. They remained implacable enemies of the Nazis, and they now had hope, and the support of the various refugee organisations in Britain. Furthermore, they had been carefully vetted before their entry to Britain had been allowed, and had also been examined by Internment Tribunals.

A separate memorandum on the Foreign Office file places the lessons to be learned from German Fifth Column activity in mainland Europe into proper perspective. It emphasizes that: "the German "Fifth Columns" have so far been encountered in countries where there was a large German minority [Poland], or where German influence was always powerful, and the people were to a degree German in origin themselves [Denmark, Norway, Holland]…especially in Holland, pro-Nazi political elements not of German origin were valuable allies…there was the vigorous Dutch Nazi Party, openly anti-patriotic until the last minute." Put simply, the Fifth Column danger came from the indigenous German minority and any pro-Nazi elements, not from refugees.

It is worth pausing at this stage to consider who the German and Austrian refugees in Britain were. 73,400 had been examined by the Internment Tribunals. 55,500 were classified by those Tribunals as "refugees from Nazi oppression". Of those refugees, 975 were doctors, 431 were dentists, 1,579 were teachers, and virtually every skill, trade and profession was represented. More than 80% were Jewish.

However, with the worsening situation in mainland Europe as the German *blitzkrieg* rolled onwards, fears of invasion and of a Nazi Fifth Column in Britain continued to grow. The Joint Intelligence Committee included senior representatives of each of the three armed services, and their recommendation on 15 May had been clear – intern ALL enemy aliens. It is probably from that recommendation that the excuse deployed later of "military necessity" came.

Churchill's view, however, went further than that. The first occasion that he expressed the desire to deport all enemy aliens appears to be in a Cabinet Meeting of 24 May 1940, when he said that he was strongly in favour of such action. It was not long after that he set up the Home Defence [Security] Executive, a secret committee with virtually untrammeled powers.

CHAPTER FIVE

CHURCHILL TAKES OVER

Despite the sinking of the *Royal Oak* in Scapa Flow in October 1939, and the many successes of German U-Boats in the North Atlantic, the early months of World War Two were relatively quiet, and are often referred to as the "Phoney War". Internment of a small percentage of enemy aliens took place in Britain, the British Expeditionary Force was sent to mainland Europe, but there was no indication of what was to come in a few months time. On April 4 1940, seven months into the war, Prime Minister Neville Chamberlain said : "Why was it that Hitler, despite all his long preparation for war, did not at the outset try to strike a knock-out blow at Britain and France? Whatever the reason – one thing is clear – Hitler missed the bus" The following day, the Chief of the Imperial General Staff, General Sir Edmund Ironside, said in the Daily Express newspaper: "Time is against Germany. She cannot forever keep her armies in the battle area, poised for action, and then make no move. Her morale is certain to suffer. Frankly, we would welcome an attack. We are sure of ourselves. We have no fears…It's too late now. We are ready for anything they start. As a matter of fact, we would welcome a go at them." Both Chamberlain and Ironside were soon to be proved completely wrong.

Suddenly, on 10 May 1940, came the German *blitzkrieg*. Within three short weeks, the Nazis had rolled through Holland and Belgium, and had forced the evacuation of the British Expeditionary Force [BEF] from Dunkirk. That evacuation, which has become known in British folk lore as the "miracle of the little ships", was necessary because the defences of the BEF and its French allies had been smashed in a few short weeks of violent combat by the overpowering Nazi forces. Hitler had been steadily building up the strength of his armed forces for years. They were extremely well trained and very well equipped. In contrast, the BEF contained many half-trained soldiers and much outdated equipment. In the period before the war, Britain had been re-arming fast, but not fast enough. Britain had relied on her French allies, and on the Maginot Line, a substantial fortification prepared as a defence against invasion from Germany. However, in May 1940, the Germans simply looped around it and powered through the Low Countries, paying no heed to neutrality. They cut off a substantial part of the BEF and many French and other Allied troops at Dunkirk. The British dug in as best they could on the beaches, and prayed for an evacuation. The beaches became a living hell as German planes strafed them constantly. There were many casualties, and all who were successfully evacuated were utterly demoralised. Between 26 May and 4 June 1940, the fugitive soldiers were carried off the beaches by the Royal Navy and hundreds of civilian small craft who had responded to their country's call. In total, 224,000 British troops were rescued, together with 111,000 French and Belgians, but they arrived back in Britain exhausted, disorganised, and with few weapons apart from the ones that they could carry. A huge amount of military equipment was left behind in France, and although 335,000 troops were saved, they had little to fight with upon their return to Britain. Thousands more British and Allied troops remained in North West France, but, as of 5 June, their future was unknown. France fought on for the time being, but her prospects were bleak.

Therefore, suddenly, Britain was facing invasion and total defeat. The stubborn and combative Winston Churchill faced a desperate crisis within little more than two weeks of taking office. He knew that if the Germans invaded, his period in office might be one of the shortest in British history. As soon as the evacuation of Dunkirk began, Britain and Churchill had to prepare for a German invasion. In late May, Britain had expected that she would lose much of the BEF in France, and when it occurred, the "miracle of the little ships" saved the men, but not the equipment. For a while, Britain stood almost naked in the face of imminent invasion.

Obviously, the key figure in Britain after 10 May 1940 was Winston Churchill. He was Prime Minister and Commander in Chief. It had been Churchill's ambition for many years to become the Prime Minister of Great Britain and Northern Ireland, and finally on 10 May, he had achieved that ambition. He did so, however, at a time of enormous difficulty. Even before the *blitzkrieg* began, the British campaign in Norway, aimed at frustrating a German attempt to take over that country, was rapidly turning into a disaster. The previous Prime Minister, Neville Chamberlain, had addressed the House of

Commons on 8 May, and had lost the votes of 93 members of his party in the adjournment debate that followed – 33 Conservatives voted against their own Government and 60 abstained. Chamberlain resigned. On 9 May, the decision as to who would be his successor was between the Foreign Secretary, Lord Halifax, and Winston Churchill. Halifax declared that he could not be an effective Prime Minister since he was in the House of Lords, and therefore Churchill got the job. On 10 May, he visited the King in Buckingham Palace for official confirmation that he would become Prime Minister, but by the time he left the Palace, Hitler's *blitzkrieg* was well under way as Nazi troops streamed across the frontiers of Holland, Belgium and Luxembourg.

Churchill's grasp on power was tenuous. Neville Chamberlain remained the leader of the Conservative and Unionist party. Lord Halifax, a powerful Conservative, favoured appeasement and hoped to broker a peace with Hitler. Churchill set up a Government of National Unity – a coalition of the major parties with a common objective – to try to win the war. In the very early days of his premiership, Churchill hoped to turn things around in France, and even in Norway. Even when the disaster of Dunkirk came and went, Churchill still urged Paul Reynaud, the French Prime Minister, to fight on, and promised further troops to reinforce North West France. However, when on 14 May Reynaud asked for a further ten RAF fighter squadrons to be sent to France, Churchill refused, saying that they were needed to defend Britain. When the Maginot Line was breached two days later on 16 May, Churchill relented to the extent of sending four fighter squadrons to the battlefields of France. France was Britain's big ally, with an army very much larger than the British had available, and Churchill found himself under immense pressure to support them in any way he could. He had to resist much of that pressure, however, in order to preserve defences for the British mainland.

It had been hoped to keep Mussolini and Italy out of the war, and diplomatic attempts had been made to persuade him to make a declaration of neutrality. On 18 May, news came that Mussolini had officially rejected such a declaration. By 20 May, Churchill was considering abandoning Norway and withdrawing British troops to bolster the defence of Britain. On 25 May, Churchill warned the British Dominions that Britain might soon be invaded. So desperate was the situation becoming that consideration began to be given to a mediation with Hitler through Mussolini. Even Churchill, the "war monger" opposed to appeasement, commented that: "If we could get out of this jam by conceding Malta and Gibraltar and a few African colonies, I would jump at it."

Not long after he became Prime Minister, Churchill had ordered a clamping down on the leaders of British Fascism. Remarkably, most British Fascist leaders were still free, such was the strength of British democracy. In a war against Hitler and Nazism, Britain wished to retain a right to free speech as long as it was possible, but there were limits. The arrest of Captain Archibald Maule "Jock" Ramsay MP took place on 23 May 1940. Ramsay was a member of Churchill's own party, the Conservative and Unionists, and had been sitting with him in the House of Commons until his arrest. Yet he was also the leader of a secret Fascist society called the Right Club, which claimed to have another eleven MPs as signed up members. The secret object of the Right Club was to infiltrate the military, all government departments, and the government itself. It was intended to be the ultimate "British made" Fifth Column organisation, waiting to spring into life when a German invasion came. The author will describe the Right Club in greater detail at a later stage. Many other leading Fascists were also detained under Regulation 18B at this time.

A tumultuous period of British history began in late May 1940. Fears about what Italians living in Britain might do if Mussolini declared war were growing. On 27 May 1940, four days after Ramsay's arrest, Brigadier Harker of M.I.5 wrote to Gladwyn Jebb at Foreign Office saying: "We have already informed you that we have reason to believe that the first act of war on the part of Italy might be an attempt to use the Italian Fascist organisation for attacks on key individuals and key points in this country by the employment of gangster methods. We are anxious that arrangements should be made to forestall all such attempts if possible. Details have been worked out for the arrest of all known members of the Italian *Fascio* and certain suspects as soon as instructions are issued to this effect by the

Home Office…the machinery is ready, what remains is the executive decision."

On the same day, 27 May, the evacuation of the BEF from Dunkirk began. On 28 May, Belgium surrendered to the Nazi forces at dawn. Later that day, Count Galeazzo Ciano, the Foreign Minister of Italy informed Sir Percy Loraine, the British Ambassador in Rome, that war between Italy and Great Britain was now a certainty. On the 30 May, Churchill gave the order to withdraw all remaining British forces from Norway. In response to Reynaud's continuing pleas for help in France, Churchill decided to send further troops to North West France, including the 1st Canadian Division. The fear of a German invasion was increasing by the day. On the night of Thursday 30 May, the Health Minister said that the Government felt the risk of bombing was so real that it must plan for the evacuation of children, and that children for evacuation should be registered before the schools closed for the day on Monday 3 June 1940. On 31 May, the Government ordered that all B class Germans and Austrians should be interned, albeit: "Every consideration should be shown by the police to the persons concerned…it must be remembered that the majority are well disposed towards this country and their temporary internment is merely a precautionary measure." Police were also given the power to intern C Class Germans and Austrians if they had reason to doubt their reliability. Whipped up by the tabloid press, a view was developing that: "Britain must now be regarded as a fortress, and every person within the fortress must be harnessed to the national effort, or put under proper control".

Increasingly worried about a German/Austrian Fifth Column, and also the prospect of an Italian one, Churchill set up a secret committee on 27 May 1940, three days after he had declared in Cabinet his desire to deport all enemy aliens. It was the day after the evacuation of troops from Dunkirk began. The Home Defence [Security] Executive [HDSE] was set up to deal with the perceived threat of a Fifth Column. It began its work immediately, under the chairmanship of the Right Honourable Viscount Swinton. Swinton was a senior Conservative politician who had been elevated to the House of Lords in 1935. He had been a member of Neville Chamberlain's cabinet. The HDSE was tasked with beefing up internal security in Britain, and with countering the dangers of a Fifth Column. Its meetings were in secret, and it relied heavily upon information and advice from M.I.5, also a secret organisation. Many members of the House of Commons did not like the idea of such important decisions being taken in secret. The first meeting of the HDSE took place at 11.30 on 28 May 1940, and it was chaired by Lord Swinton. Three further meetings quickly followed at 1830hrs that day, and at 1130hrs and 1600hrs on the next day, 29 May, reflecting the urgency which was felt.

At the series of meetings held on 28 and 29 May, various significant decisions were taken. Vernon Kell's M.I.5 had already drawn up a list of persons believed to be dangerous to national security, and it seems that M.I.5's views were accepted without question. Some names on the list were there because the persons concerned had been reported to M.I.5 by Chief Constables of Police, others were included because of intelligence that M.I.5 said that it had received through its agents. The first question was what the government should do about the existing British Fascist organisations. Their membership remained substantial, despite the fact that many of their leaders were by now in detention. The British Union of Fascists [BUF], Sir Oswald Mosley's fascist organisation, was the most prominent and largest of the British Fascist organisations, and at the evening meeting on 28 May, it was proscribed, and its newspaper "Action" was banned. In addition to the national leaders of the BUF who were already in custody, it was decided that all its district leaders should now also be detained, together with a number of other members who had been reported to Kell by the police.

As previously stated, on 28 May 1940, Count Ciano informed Ambassador Loraine that war between Italy and Great Britain was a certainty. By then the Dunkirk evacuation had started, and Great Britain looked to be in a very weak position. The British Cabinet was notified by the Foreign Secretary, Lord Halifax, on 29 May 1940 that there would be war with Italy, the only uncertainty was the date. It might be within a week, it might be later. The Cabinet then considered what measures needed to be taken against Italian nationals living in Britain. The general view still was that Italian enemy aliens should be deported back to Italy, except for those whose return would help Italy in its war effort. The Cabinet agreed that it was necessary to remove Italian workers from key factories and installations – such as electricians in power stations – and that large numbers of Italians would need to be interned. It was informed by Kell's M.I.5 that there was a proportion of about 1,000 "desperate characters" amongst the Italian nationals in Great Britain who would not hesitate to commit acts of sabotage, that these men had been identified and listed, and action could be taken against them at short notice. It was agreed that there would be a simultaneous round up of the "desperate characters" when the time came. Further, it was decided that the 1,000 Italian "desperate characters" should be put under immediate surveillance, so that action could be taken against them at very short notice.

The Cabinet agreed that Ambassador Loraine in Rome should inform Italian Foreign Minister Ciano that Britain did not wish to intern large numbers of Italians in Britain, and was ready to send them back to Italy, provided that Italy would do the same with Britons in Italy. The Government plan therefore was at this stage that it would intern the dangerous Italian aliens, and send all others back to Italy

The Cabinet met again the following day, 29 May, and discussed the matter further. Home Secretary Anderson, acting on M.I.5 information, now said that he wished to intern not 1,000 but 1,500 Italian "desperate characters", plus 300 British subjects connected with Italian institutions in Britain [who presumably were believed to have been corrupted into supporting Fascism]. There is no explanation that the author has been able to find for the 50% increase overnight in the number of "desperate characters." It became clear later that Sir John Anderson, the Home Secretary, was relying entirely on what he was being told by the internal security service M.I.5 and the HDSE. It was confirmed that the Italian "desperate characters" were to be interned immediately upon the Italian declaration of war. Then they were to be deported far from Britain. The Admiralty was requested to arrange for a suitable ship to be provided to deport the 1,500 "desperate characters" from British shores to Canada or Newfoundland.

At the same meeting, the Foreign Secretary, Lord Halifax raised the question of a "swop" of diplomatic and other British citizens in Italy for similar Italians in Britain. It was suggested that a ship should be found and got ready for the departing Italians. The Cabinet felt that there should be no question of wholesale internment of Italians in this country, although they accepted that many would have to be interned temporarily. The Cabinet decided that, subject to the views of the French, an offer would be made to Count Ciano to deport all Italians back to Italy, save for those whose retention in the UK was necessary on grounds of national security. Those would include persons with a particular knowledge or expertise which might help the enemy.

Sir Percy Loraine, upon instructions, informed Ciano that while exit permits would be granted to Italians up until Italy entered the war, after it had started, the British Government intended to deport a considerable number of "undesirable" Italians back to Italy, probably via Spain, which although Fascist was still a neutral country. Others who wanted to go back to Italy would be permitted to do so, providing that British national security did not demand their retention in Britain. On 4 June, the Italian Government accepted these terms, and said it would reciprocate by sending back to Britain equivalent British subjects in Italy.

The next day, on 30 May, the spectre of a Fifth Column was discussed in Cabinet. It was argued that a Fifth Column must be guarded against, and that [a] the Nazis were likely to select and train neutral aliens to act as their secret agents [therefore hitherto neutral Italians would have been recruited] rather than Germans or Austrians, and [b] that however badly a German might have been treated by his government, he would remain a German at heart, and in time of war was a greater potential danger than a neutral alien – a very simplistic "once a German always a German" approach. It appears that the HDSE was of the view that all aliens, both enemy and neutral, were suspect – including those of the Jewish faith.

Later in the war, it became clear that Nazis did regularly threaten anti-Nazi Germans and Austrians who were in prisoner of war camps outside Germany that if they did not continue serve the Third Reich appropriately, even in captivity, action would be taken against their wives and families still within German borders. The Nazis were utterly ruthless, and although it may seem extremely unlikely that Jews who had fled from Germany or Austria to the safety of Britain would allow themselves to be blackmailed into helping the Third Reich, if they had left members of their family behind in Germany at the mercy of the Nazis it is possible that they might have done so.

The position in relation to all aliens had already been tightened up by new regulations. Any alien, neutral or enemy, was forbidden to possess a car or bicycle without a police permit, and ordered to comply with a curfew to be indoors in their homes between midnight and 0600hrs if they lived in London, and from 2230hrs until 0600hrs if they lived elsewhere. In addition, all householders now had to report the arrival in or departure from their homes of any aliens to the police.

The HDSE decided that a small list of key areas should be drawn up, within which no enemy aliens should be allowed to reside unless they were vouched for. Also, persons of Czech nationality whom M.I.5 suspected of being enemy agents should be treated as enemy aliens. Following the fourth meeting of the HDSE, on the evening of 29 May, it was decided that the age limit for detention [i.e. the age after which enemy aliens should not be regarded as dangerous] should be raised to seventy.

The minutes of the new HDSE, meeting as it did four times in two days, are a reminder of the devastating effect of the German *blitzkreig* on mainland Europe. The aim of the Executive, and of Winston Churchill, was to do everything possible to protect Great Britain – to create and protect an island fortress. In the early days, a series of vital decisions were taken at speed, despite a lack of preparation and adequate information in relation to enemy aliens. With the sudden evacuation of more than 300,000 British and Allied troops from northern Europe, all of whom needed to be housed and fed in the UK, domestic facilities for the housing of internees quickly became hopelessly overstretched,

Unfortunately, M.I.5 having decided that membership of a *fascio* automatically classified an Italian as dangerous, those like Luigi Beschizza who had gone dancing at the Italian Club were now

classified as dangerous Fascists. There was no time for tribunals –
the Germans were about to invade and the internal alien problem had
to be sorted out immediately. The Government's order was that once
Italy joined the war, all Italians resident in Britain who were known
to be members of a *fascio* would be immediately interned and
speedily deported, and all male Italians between the ages of 16 and
70 [other than the invalid and inform] who had less than twenty
years residence in Britain would be interned. The cut off date was 31
December 1939.

One problem was that there was not the available manpower in
Britain to do the job properly. The police were given the task of
carrying out the numerous arrests, and the Army then had the
responsibility of incarcerating the dangerous aliens until they could
be deported. On and after 10 June, when, only hours after
Mussolini's formal declaration of war, the swoop came, the
necessary tasks were carried out with significant incompetence, and,
it may be, with malice in certain cases, or in furtherance of the aims
of the Right Club. The initial arrests were apparently undertaken
upon the basis of the list prepared by M.I.5 of 1500 dangerous
Italians. That list was, however, wildly inaccurate and included a
number of Italians who were well known to be anti-Fascist, as well
as some who were naturalised British and therefore not liable to be
arrested as enemy aliens.

There can be no doubt that the extreme language chosen by M.I.5,
adopted by Swinton's Executive, and accepted by the War Cabinet,
had a very significant effect upon the fate of the Italian detainees. An
enemy alien who was classified as a "desperate character" by M.I.5
was regarded in the same way as society regards those categorised as
terrorists today. However, M.I.5's judgement was accepted by the
HDSE without question, and it secretly passed on the
recommendations to the British Government, with the result that the
"desperate characters" were treated as highly dangerous, and
deserving of little or no sympathy.

The pressure on the British Government to resolve the problem of
enemy aliens mounted inexorably in late May and early June. On 28
May, a memorandum from the Chief Constables of England and
Wales was sent by them to the Home Office dismissing the

proposition that they knew all about the enemy aliens, saying: "In actual fact, the Police know nothing whatever about the great majority of these persons, apart from what they say about themselves, or what the Refugee Committees say about them...The Chief Constables feel that the only safe plan is to intern every enemy alien until he can prove his liberation is in the national interest...In view of what is now known to have occurred in Holland and other countries, it is felt that not the slightest reliance can be placed even on those aliens who have produced most excellent credentials and whose conduct has been initially innocuous, as it seems reasonable to expect any enemy agent introduced to this country will have been effectively covered so far as credentials are concerned, and that his conduct will be extremely circumspect until the time comes for him to take action."

On 3 June 1940, an intelligence report was received from Ankara, Turkey, saying that the Nazis were considering an attempt to drop arms on prisoner and concentration camps in England. A little later, it was claimed that internees were making preparations to assist enemy parachutists landing in their camps.

On the evening of 10 June 1940, after Italy's declaration of war, Winston Churchill issued an order to Sir John Anderson, Home Secretary and the Minister of Home Security, to "collar the lot" – to arrest and intern all Italian males who had been living in Britain for less than 20 years, and who were aged between 16 and 60 [soon amended to 70], together with all Category B and C Germans and Austrians. That order was to be immediately put into effect. In addition, Churchill ordered that "dangerous aliens", both German/Austrian and Italians, should be deported with all possible speed to whichever far-flung parts of the British Dominions were prepared to take them. Hitler could arrive tomorrow.

To make things even worse, the following day, 11 June, Prime Minister Reynaud told Churchill that France had to seek an armistice, in other words to surrender. On 14 June, the Nazi forces entered Paris unopposed. Britain's General Officer Commanding, Alan Brooke, convinced Churchill that he must now withdraw all British forces from the rest of France. Between 14 June and 25 June, a total of 144,171 British, 24,352 Polish and 42,000 other Allied troops were evacuated by sea from France, together with a number of civilians. This evacuation having begun, the British Government sent a message on 16 June to French Prime Minister Reynaud that it would understand if he had to negotiate an armistice with the Germans. On the following day, 17 June, France surrendered. Britain had lost its senior partner in its alliance. Marshal Petain, a First World War veteran, took over in France. Major questions now arose as to what would happen to the French fleet, and to the French colonies, many of which shared borders with the British Dominions.

Churchill continued to beg arms from the United States, and tried to open negotiations with the Republic of Ireland to create a united, anti-Nazi island of Ireland. The Republic of Ireland had a land border with Northern Ireland. The promised reward was a single, united Ireland after the war was won. This tactic was a stark illustration of how desperate Britain was. Churchill's own party, the Conservative and Unionist party, was prepared to trade away its Unionist supporters to save the mainland from the Nazis. The Republic of Ireland refused Churchill's offer, preferring to remain neutral. It is probable that Eamon DeValera, the Irish President, believed, like many others, that Britain was about to lose the war against Germany, and had no wish to end up as one of Germany's defeated enemies, whatever prize the British might offer.

Desperate decisions had to be taken, and taken quickly. After 17 June 1940, France was no longer Britain's ally. It had surrendered to Germany, and the new "Vichy" government under Marshal Petain had reached an accommodation with the Nazis. Two weeks later in early July, the substantial French fleet was anchored at Mers-el-Kebir, Oran. If it fell into German hands, it would pose a huge threat to Britain's navy. Bottled up in harbour by the British fleet, an ultimatum was issued that the French must scuttle their fleet, or join the British. The French refused. On 3 July, the British fleet fired on their erstwhile allies, destroying the French fleet and killing 1,250 men. It was a truly desperate move, but one that the British Government considered necessary in order to save their country.

Returning to the question of internment, in the urgency of the moment, the British Government trampled all over the human rights of the refugees to whom Britain had given shelter, and their rights under the Refugee Convention, and also the human rights of the many Italian small businessmen living in Britain. Churchill ordered their arrests, and having had them arrested, he decided that they should be shipped out of Britain as soon as possible, despite the U-Boat domination of the seas. Britain was to be cleansed of all and any enemy aliens who might just possibly help the enemy. The Italians would be interned and deported without any sort of trial – there was no time for that – and their status would be sorted out when they arrived in the far flung British dominions. No doubt Churchill was concerned with one thing only – the survival of Britain and the British. However, the accusation came only a few weeks later from MPs from all parties that what Churchill ordered was a panic move, and not the product of a fair and just democratic society. It was emphasised that this was not a war between nations [as the First World War had been], but a war between the creeds of Nazi/ Fascism and free democracy. Freedom and democracy were the causes that Britain was fighting for, and, it was said, Churchill's decision to intern and deport went against the fundamentals of both.

Having made the order on the evening of 10 June, the following morning, Churchill informed the War Cabinet of what he had done. The wholescale arrests had already begun. In due course, this policy led to tragic results.

CHAPTER SIX

BRITAIN'S *KRISTALLNACHT*: 10 JUNE 1940

It was at 1600hrs on 10 June 1940 that Mussolini finally announced that, as from midnight that day, Italy would be at war with Britain and France. Then, at 1800hrs, Mussolini addressed a large crowd in front of his residence in Rome. He repeated the declaration of war, saying: "The Western plutocratic democracies have always stopped the march of the Italian people. Italy has done all it can to resist this horrible war. We are resolved to fight on continental and sea frontiers where our people are suffocating…Germany is troubled for her existence and we are obliged to help her." The Beschizza family from Bratto might well have commented that nobody was suffocating them, and that they were doing very well in business in London. Many other Italians all over Britain would have said the same thing. The suggestion that Germany was troubled for her existence after her troops had rolled successfully through the Low Countries and into France was, of course, ridiculous.

Only days had passed since the evacuation of Dunkirk had ended, and Britain was at her lowest ebb. A German invasion was expected within days or weeks. For two months the Press had been stirring up fears amongst Britons that German/Austrians and Italians in Britain were probable Fifth Columnists. There was a widespread sense of anxiety and fear. On the morning of 11 June, the Daily Sketch thought it helpful to publish an article entitled: "Fight Fear" by a Dr Avon. Summarised in modern terms, Dr Avon was simply saying "if fear, stress and anxiety are preventing you from sleeping at night, go and get some pills from your doctor". The article, however, illustrates how widespread fear was.

Fear could in no way excuse what happened in London, Glasgow and a number of other towns and cities throughout the United Kingdom where there were Italian communities. Fuelled by the Press campaign and Mussolini's declaration of war, mob violence broke out, and numerous Italian businesses were attacked and their premises smashed to pieces. The Italian owners could do nothing but look on. Some were naturalised British, and some had sons who were British-born British citizens already serving in the British armed forces. Few if any of the ex-patriate Italians had wanted war, few sympathised with Mussolini's Fascists.

Most of the shops attacked had been serving their local communities for many years, and their Italian owners and staff were known in the community. The targets seemed to be been chosen simply because of an Italian name above a shop, or local knowledge that a shop was run by Italians. The attacks had nothing to do with where the owners political sympathies lay, or what part they had taken in the local community. The mob violence was a simple venting of mass anger and frustration. Mussolini had declared war, and therefore these families were now the enemy.

Tragedy struck at many families. In Hamilton, near Glasgow, Mariano di Marco owned a café. Mariano had been born in Cassino, Frossinone, on 24 November 1897. He came to Scotland to work, and he and his family had built up the business over many years. It had been long and hard work, but worthwhile as the family watched their business grow. All that they wished to do was to carry on trading. On the night of 10 June 1940, a group of men forced their way in, and completely wrecked the shop – smashing everything from the shop counters to bottles of sweets. Within minutes, the shop and the business were reduced to ruin. There was nothing at all that the family could do to resist the mob. When the mob moved on, the di Marco family were left in a state of total distress.

However, things got worse. That same night, Churchill's "Collar the Lot" arrests began, and no consideration was given to those who had had their business premises smashed up. The di Marcos would have looked to the police to help them after the vandalism of their shop. Instead, when the police arrived a few hours later, it was to arrest Mariano di Marco as an enemy alien. He was taken away, leaving his wife and two daughters alone in the ruined shop in a state of very considerable distress. They never saw Mariano again.

Joe Pieri was half Mariano di Marco's age at 21. He lived with his parents in Glasgow – they ran a fish and chip shop. On the evening of 10 June, he was at home alone, his parents were away on holiday. The family lived, as so often, in a flat above the shop, with a view of the street from the upper floor. Joe Pieri later described what happened to his family's shop and many others. Looking out of the window of the flat, he saw a mob of about 200 men coming down the street towards his shop. They had been stalking the streets of Glasgow that night, hunting for Italian shops and businesses, and as they approached the Pieri Fish and Chip shop, Joe could see that they had with them a hand cart loaded with stones and rubble. Joe quickly realised that it was their ammunition carrier for their attacks on Italian shops. Reaching his family's shop, the mob smashed through the shop door, and began the wanton and complete destruction of everything inside. They threw the shop fittings out onto the pavement and wrecked everything that they could. Finally satisfied that the business was ruined, they moved on to their next target. Pieri later learned that every single Italian shop in Glasgow was attacked in a similar way that night. Pieri himself was later arrested, and later deported on a ship called the *Ettrick* to Canada, where he was imprisoned for three years, many miles away from his family.

In London, there was similar violence against Italian premises, apparently starting with the stoning of an Italian café in Compton Street, Soho, smashing its windows. The violence then spread to other Italian premises, and extra police were rushed in to try and restore order. For many, the arrival of the police came too late. There was no judgement as to whether a café owner was pro-British or pro-Fascist, or whether the owners were recent immigrants or were naturalised British with their sons in the British army. Anyone who was Italian, or bore an Italian name, was a target. Although happily the violence of 10 June was far more limited than that of *Kristallnacht* in Germany, and was not organised by the State, it was nonetheless a terrifying beginning to what was to be a period of considerable suffering for the Italian community in Britain.

In the immediate aftermath of the mob violence of 10/11 June, the journalist and broadcaster John Marus, using the pseudonym Candidus, attempted to redress the balance of prejudice. Writing in the *Daily Sketch* on 11 June 1940, he said: "Mussolini is taking a course to which – as he himself well knows – half the Italian people are bitterly opposed…Hitler cracked the whip, and Mussolini obeyed the man who is now his lord and master; for Italy no longer controls her own destiny. She is delivered body and soul to her traditional foe. Whether Germany wins or loses the war, Italy has already lost it. The sentimental ties between Britain and Italy date back at least a hundred years…but Mussolini's madness compels us to hit back hard at them indiscriminately." Candidus was to go on to become one of the leading Italian language journalists on Radio Londra – the BBC radio station that broadcast to Italy throughout the rest of the war, and was banned by Mussolini, but listened to by numerous Italians.

The *Daily Sketch* on 11 June also reported the beginning of the round up of Italians who were to be detained. Under the headline: "700 Italians held in big London swoop", the article suggested: "the Special Branch for a long time has had under observation a large number of Italians who might have proved dangerous to this country", which was the official government line. The article included however the assertion that: "Italy's declaration of war came at a time when many influential Italians in London were discussing the formation of a Garibaldi battalion to fight for the Allies", and that "in the Italian church in the Clerkenwell Road, Italians were praying for an Allied victory". However, the Daily Sketch's suggestion that the 700 London Italians had long been under the observation of Special Branch was quite untrue, as was proved later.

Hundreds and then thousands of Italians were arrested in the hours and days that followed. To the independent observer, there seemed absolutely no logic to the arrests. Known anti-fascists, the old and the ill, and over six hundred Italians with British citizenship [who were therefore not enemy aliens] were all taken into custody. There was confusion as to identity, and if the initial arrests were based upon M.I.5's list of "dangerous Italians", then that list was gravely flawed. In due course, every Italian male between the age of 16 and 70 was arrested. Italian women too were arrested and interned, but happily far fewer than the men. Families were ripped apart. The period of residence of any Italian in Britain was also regularly ignored [according to the guidelines nobody who had been resident for 20 years or more should have been interned], as was the individual's state of health.

Diplomatic immunity was also regularly ignored. The Italian Consul in Liverpool, Sig. A Rotini, was one who suffered temporary imprisonment in a police cell, before being released and allowed to return to Italy on the diplomatic boat. On 15 June 1940, he wrote a letter of protest on his own behalf and on behalf of the many Italians living peacefully in Britain, saying to the Chief Constable of Liverpool: "One is inclined to believe that the wild and futile rush against Italians had its origin in grave anxiety or perhaps even fear. May I add that fear is not always the best counsellor when a country is in danger. Do you really think that such methods will save your country? Does it really serve your purpose to strike blindly at honest hardworking Italians whose loyal attitude towards Great Britain is beyond question?"

The process of selection for internment and deportation was hopelessly flawed. To aggravate the situation, many of the places of detention to which they were taken were totally unsuited. Whatever preparations had been made for housing thousands of internees proved totally inadequate – probably because of the more urgent need to house all those escaping from Dunkirk.

To some Italians internment came as no surprise. Luigi Beschizza, the cheerful young man from Bratto, later commented that none of his circle of friends or family were pleased about the outbreak of war, and that he and his friends had expected to be interned if it happened, since they were of military age, young and fit. In the days before 10 June, as it became more and more obvious that war with Italy was coming, they already had their bags packed. In June, Beschizza was living at the home of a friend and new employer, and not above the family café in Goldhawk Road. On 11 June, the police came to arrest his host and his host's father, both of whom were Italians, but did not arrest him. He was not on their list at that address. Two days later, a policeman returned early in the morning, this time for him. Beschizza remembers that the policeman was perfectly friendly. When he said that he had not yet had breakfast, he was told to have a good breakfast, pack his bag, and that the policeman would be back for him in half an hour, which is what happened. Beschizza was taken to the local police station, and then on to the Brompton Oratory, which was being used as a processing centre for those to be interned. He describes the police as being almost apologetic, adopting a "we have to do it" attitude. From the Brompton Oratory, he was taken to the Detention Camp at Lingfield Race Course.

Nicola Cua was another young man living and working in London. He came from Italian *contadini* stock, his father and his grandfather had worked on the land. Nicola's father came to London at the age of fifteen because his family in Italy was desperately poor. Life was very hard, and there was simply not enough work to go round. Nicola's father had come to London in 1900, forty years before, and worked, like so many immigrant Italians, in catering. After nine years in Britain, his father went back to Italy, found a bride and married. The couple came to England after their marriage, and both worked there. Nicola's father returned to Italy in 1912 to do compulsory military service, returned to Britain, but then went back to Italy in 1915 when Italy joined in World War One on Great Britain's side, and joined the Italian Army. He served for three years in the war in the Italian Bersiglieri. Nicola was born in Italy in 1916, and first came to England when his family returned in 1919. Both Nicola's parents worked – his father remaining in catering, his mother went out to work elsewhere. The family lived in a small flat in Soho, and Nicola was schooled in London, going to local schools, not to any Italian school. He won a place at the Archbishop Tennyson Grammar School in Kennington, and continued his education there. Both Nicola and his father had lived in Britain for more than twenty years, and therefore, according to the rules, should not have been interned at all.

As he grew up, Nicola's parents retained their Italian links. They would go back to Italy every three or four years if they could afford to, stay in their village there and visit members of the family. In London, the family would visit an Italian club in Greek Street to play cards, enjoy the music and socialise. This was in the days before Mussolini started to take control of the Italian clubs in Britain, and there were no politics in the club. The club later moved to the Charing Cross Road [it was the same one that Luigi Beschizza belonged to]– where Nicola commented that although the club was controlled by the Italian Government [through the *Fascio* di Londra],

Nicola only went there with his friends to play snooker and "chase the girls", like many other Italian young men. They had no interest in politics, and took no part in them, although he recalled that the older men did sometimes have political meetings in the Club. Nicola took part in some sports run by the Club, but he and his friends were there for the fun, not for any Fascist activity. They didn't know what the Fascist government was doing in Italy, and weren't interested. The Cua family had nothing at all to do with Fascism.

After leaving Grammar school, Nicola Cua couldn't find a good job, and eventually went into tailoring, because there was an opportunity there. He got on with his life, and should not have been regarded in any way as a dangerous fascist. However, probably because of his membership of the club in the Charing Cross Road, Nicola Cua was on the list of those to be immediately detained. The Club was raided by police, closed down, and the building was seized by the Custodian of Enemy Property. Nicola was arrested at home at 0630hrs on 11 June. Local policemen came to his family home, only seeking at that stage to arrest him, and not his father. Cua recalled that the policemen treated him very well. He asked if they wanted his father as well, and was told that he was not on their list [although he was arrested later]. The police officers told him that he wouldn't be away very long [which was sadly very far from the truth], and took him to the local police station at Vine Street. From there, he was taken to the Brompton Oratory for processing. He found himself being held with a whole mixture of Italian men, old and young. Cua was then sent to the Lingfield Racecourse Camp, and after one night was sent by train to Warth Mills Camp in Bury.

Gino Guarnieri was another young London Italian who was arrested and interned. He grew up until the age of twelve on his parents very small farm in Italy. His father had worked in England for a while before World War One, but then returned to Italy and worked on the land. Gino had six living sisters, and one who had died, and one brother. His family were extremely poor. Members of Gino's extended family were working in England, and when he was twelve and a half, a cousin offered to take Gino off his father's hands, to finish his schooling in London, and then to find him work. He spoke only in his local dialect, and could not speak proper Italian. In those days, illiteracy in the poorest parts of Italy was common.

When Gino arrived in London he was taken into his cousin's home in Orange Street, Leicester Square, and was sent back to school at St Martin in the Fields until he was fourteen. Leaving school, Gino went to work in the Genaro Restaurant, Old Compton Street, and remained there for four years. After that, he worked as a waiter at Malmaison in Berkeley Street, and after that at the Café Royal for about four years. The Café Royal belonged to Trust House Forte, and the Italian Forte family. According to Gino Guarnieri, waiters had to pay for the privilege of working in the Café Royal, and lived off the tips that they received. They had to pay out of their own pockets for any breakages, or items missed off the customer's bill. Nonetheless, Gino clearly made a living, since he stayed at the Café Royal for four years. He then went into the family business – one of his sisters was now in London, and his cousin had a restaurant in Knightsbridge Green. Gino bought into a restaurant run by other cousins, and was doing well. His business partner was an English born Italian, who was called up into the army after war broke out.

After arriving in England aged twelve, Gino had only returned to Italy once for a visit. By June of 1940, he was twenty-six. He had no involvement in politics, and like many other Italian youngsters in Britain, he didn't think about them. He did belong to the club in Charing Cross Road, but had only been there twice. Gino described it as a family club, for socialising, and said he had gone there to dance. He worked from 0800hrs to 2300hrs each day, and claimed that therefore he had had no time to go to political meetings, even if he had wanted to. But in order to join the Club, he had had to sign up with the Fascist Youth, since the Club was now owned by the Italian Government, and that was a condition of membership.

On the morning of 11 June, Gino Guarnieri was woken up because three policemen had come to arrest him. One of them asked Gino if he was a member of the Club in Charing Cross Road, and Gino agreed that he was. That clearly was why he now appeared on the M.I.5 black list. Gino was taken to the local police station, then to Chelsea Barracks, and from there to Lingfield Racecourse camp. The accommodation for Gino Guarnieri was in the horse stables. When

Gino arrived, there were already quite a lot of Italians being held there, and some Austrians. In due course, Gino was transferred from Lingfield to Leeds, where the camp was an old factory, and the internees had to sleep on the floor. Gino Guarnieri hoped that he would soon be released.

The arrests struck at all levels of society. Dr Gaetano Nello Zezzi was a skilled and successful doctor, with rooms at 95, Harley Street, London. He was the company doctor for the cosmetics company Elizabeth Arden, and had a number of other prestigious appointments. As it happened, he was the personal doctor of the chairman of the Blue Star Line, and had cruised with him on a ship called the *Arandora Star*. However, he was an Italian national, and therefore now an enemy alien. Presumably he had had contacts with the *fascio*, and was therefore on M.I.5's dangerous list. Zezzi was arrested, and sent to the Warth Mills detention camp in Bury, of which more later.

Enrico Muzio was a well-known tenor in his late forties, who, throughout the 1920s and 1930s, had played theatres throughout the United Kingdom in concerts and shows. He had also appeared in film. On 16 February 1939, Muzio appeared at the Royal Air Force Depot, Kidbrooke, in a show arranged by the Balloon Barage Group. He was popular not only for his musical talents but also for his comedy. None of this prevented him too being arrested after 10 June 1940.

Uberto Limetani was an Italian Jew, who had arrived in England as a refugee from the Fascist Italian Government. He was the nephew of Claudio Treves, one of the leaders and founders of the Italian Socialist Party. Limentani was an educated young man, and in due course obtained employment at the BBC. He was obviously anti-Fascist, and of value to Britain. Nonetheless, he was arrested on 13 June 1940, and was taken to the camp at Lingfield Racecourse, like Beschizza, Cua and Guanieri. Limentani described the accommodation in a later report as a horse-box which he had to share with nine other men. He remained caged in the horse-box for nine days, until alternative accommodation became available. On the eleventh day of his detention, he was sent to Warth Mills Camp in Bury.

Decio Anzani was a well known anti-Fascist who had been living in Britain for thirty-one years. He worked as a tailor. He was at the top of the list of those whom Mr Gillies of the Labour Party had three times named to the British Government as being of great value to Britain. History recognises Decio Anzani's fight against Italian Fascism, and the London section of the National Association of Italian Partisans is now named after him. Nonetheless, a knock came on Anzani's door, and he was arrested.

Silvestro D'Ambrosio, born on 30 December 1872 in Italy, had lived in Hamilton, Scotland for 42 years. In June 1940, he was approaching 68 years old. He had five sons, all born in Britain – two were serving in the British Army, one in the Canadian army, and two who were registered for service, but not yet called up. His application for British naturalisation had been filed, but not yet granted. His length of residence in the United Kingdom was more than double that of twenty years, which should have excused him from internment. Despite all this, D'Ambrosio was arrested and interned.

Even some Italians who had gained British citizenship were wrongly arrested and sent to internment camps. Roman Catholic priests, young and old, were arrested - even though their loyalties were to God and the Vatican State - the latter being independent of Mussolini's Italy.

However courteously the arrests may, on occasion, have been carried out, as with the German and Austrian arrests it was often very difficult to see what the justification for the arrests was, and how so many mistakes were made. In the cases of both Germans and Italians, naturalised British citizens were arrested along with true enemy aliens – and naturalised British citizens were deported unlawfully. According to a later memorandum by Sir John Anderson, the Home Secretary, six hundred and one Italians were eventually detained as enemy aliens despite having British nationality. Naturalised British Italians were not aliens – they were now British, and therefore the Government had no power to deport them overseas. They could, in an appropriate case, be interned under Regulation 18B, if they were shown to pose a risk to public security, but not shipped out of the country.

On 17 June, at a conference held at the War Office, it was confirmed that British Nationals detained under Regulation 18B were not to be sent overseas – this included, of course, dual nationals. However, the decision was ignored and the law breached. Two cases illustrate the injustice of what happened. Antonio Mancini had been born in Atina, Frosinone, Italy on 3 August 1885, but came to Great Britain at the age of eight, and lived continuously in Scotland thereafter. He married in 1913, and had six British-born children, the youngest of whom was ten years of age in June 1940. He ran a restaurant business in Ayr, Scotland. He applied for naturalisation as a British citizen after forty-five years residency in Scotland, and his application was granted on 28 April 1938. Thereafter, Mancini was a British citizen. Notwithstanding this, in the avalanche of detentions that followed Italy's declaration of war on 10 June 1940, a knock came on Antonio Mancini's door and he was arrested by police as an enemy alien. No doubt he and his family protested, but to no avail. Antonio Mancini, British passport holder, was marched off into detention and deportation. His internment was illegal [although he could have been detained under Regulation 18B as a British citizen] and so was his deportation.

Gaetano Antonio Pacitto had lived in Britain for forty-five years. Born in Italy in 1875, he came to England in 1895, and started what became a very successful ice cream business in Hull. Gaetano was married, and had had ten children. Tragically, one of these, a son named Giovanni, had been killed in a road accident on 19 July 1927. He had been pushing one of the family's ice cream carts, and was struck by a motor car. Gaetano was naturalised British on 19 June 1939. Notwithstanding all this, like Antonio Mancini a knock came on Gaetano Pacitto's door on 10 June, and despite whatever protests he and his family made, Gaetano Antonio Pacitto was arrested and taken away to be interned. His internment was illegal, as was his subsequent deportation.

A sad case which demonstrates the general mismanagement of the internees was that of the Vivante family. The father was Leonello Vivante, who was a fierce anti-Fascist and ardent liberal. He and his wife and four children had been living in England for three years. After 10 June, despite his liberal background, Leonello Vivante was arrested and interned, as were his two elder sons, since both were over sixteen. The eldest boy was a remarkable classical scholar, and had just won a scholarship to Pembroke College, Oxford, where he had been due to take up his place in the autumn. He was not allowed to do so. He was interned together with his father, happily in their case in the same internment camp, and they were not deported. However, the second son, who was only sixteen years of age and at school in Worcester was taken from his school and interned in a separate camp to his father. Before long, he was deported to Canada, leaving the rest of his family in England. He was then held in custody in Canada thousands of miles from the rest of his family.

Thus from the very start, the British Government's "collar the lot" policy was going badly wrong. Problems emerged almost immediately with the way in which the Home Office and M.I.5 had compiled their lists of "desperate characters". The Italian Embassy in London asked why some of the people on their prepared lists of persons who were to be evacuated to Italy on the diplomatic boat had been arrested. It had been agreed in advance of the declaration of war that diplomats and a number of other Italian nationals could return to Italy – a reciprocal arrangement had been agreed for British subjects in Italy. The Italian Embassy therefore objected to the refusal after 10 June of the British Government to allow some of the Italians on their list to go home. This was investigated by the Foreign Office.

A memorandum from Sir Nigel Ronald, CMG, CVO, Head of the General Department of the Foreign Office is of considerable significance. It indicates that at as early as 11 June, the day after Italy declared war, the flawed reasoning of M.I.5 in categorising Italian "desperate characters" was emerging. The memorandum, dated 22 June 1940, states:

"As discussions with M.I.5 proceeded, there grew up a strong suspicion that in actual fact they had little or no information, let alone evidence, in regard to more than a fraction of the persons whom they had led the Home Secretary to describe to the Cabinet as "desperate characters...they arrested as particularly dangerous characters the two brothers Quaglino and Sovrani, the well-known restaurateurs, on the ground that they were members of the *fascio* and had contributed to the party funds. [Giovanni Quaglino was also Vice Consul for San Marino]. A number of active and well-known anti-Fascist writers and propagandists who have been working with or for the Labour Party here, are still in custody [as at 22 June] and representations in their interest are only given the most distant and unsympathetic hearing. This has not unnaturally increased the deep distrust with which the Labour Party regards the Home Office and the Security Services."

Sir Nigel adds the following comment in brackets: "I confess to some misgivings myself; without for one moment suggesting that the Home Office are tainted with Fifth Columnists, I cannot rid myself of the conviction that many of their methods and habits are singularly adapted to forward all forms of disaffection". Although nominally dismissing any positive suggestion of it, the fact that Sir Nigel suggested the possibility of a Fifth Column within the Home Office may show his real concern that it might be true. He goes on:

"From recent conversations [with M.I.5], it appears that M.I.5 cannot claim to have anything like an exhaustive list of members of the Fascio in this country…Indeed they have admitted subsequently that they estimate that their list of Fascists cannot represent more than 40 or 50 per cent of the total number in this country; unfortunately they had, they said, neither the time nor the powers to make a complete and exhaustive study of Fascist activities in this country. No doubt this is true, and accounts for the atmosphere of sullen and superstitious ignorance behind which M.I.5 invariably take refuge in their dealings with other departments. In any event, there would appear to be some room for improvement if M.I.5 is to prove an efficient organ for counter-espionage."

Sir Nigel went on to deal with mistakes that the police had made, saying: "Further elements of confusion have been contributed by the civil police to this magazine of muddle, despite the fact that they were instructed to leave the personnel of the Italian Embassy alone, the Metropolitan Police invaded several of their private residences, and even arrested a servant of one member of the Embassy. In the provinces, although it had been clearly understood that Consuls were to be subject merely to "house arrest" i.e. cut off from contact with the outside world except for taking in household provisions etc., the

Consuls at Liverpool and Cardiff were actually arrested and taken off to police cells. I suspect that the explanation of this is that all these people were "fascists" i.e. on M.I.5's famous list of "desperate characters"…"

The memorandum went on to make various recommendations, including: "the earliest possible release of the anti-Fascist elements, particularly those already collaborating in the propaganda work undertaken by the Labour Party." The final recommendation embodied a full-on attack on the classification imposed on Italians by M.I.5. Sir Nigel said "M.I.5 should be pressed to produce for inspection… the evidence they are using in classifying certain persons as dangerous…They must be further pressed to state clearly their reasons for advocating the indefinite detention in internment, whether here or in Canada, of the more dangerous elements included in their 1,500 "desperate characters"…"

On 24 June, Mr William Gillies, still working hard on behalf of those he felt were valuable anti-Nazis, presented his lists of them to Sir Alexander Maxwell at the Home Office by hand. On 27 June, he sent copies of the lists to Sir Nigel Ronald. He was arguing for the immediate release of those already in internment such as Anzani, Magri, Limentani and the Treves brothers, twelve men in all, and supplied profiles of each. He named many others whom he feared would soon suffer the same fate, but whom he believed to be anti-Fascist. On 28 June, Sir Nigel wrote to Mr F A Newsom at the Home Office emphasising that Secretary of State for the Home Office was most anxious that they should be immediately released. They were, said Sir Nigel, important to the propaganda work that the Labour Party was doing. "We should, therefore, most earnestly beg you to bring all possible pressure to bear on those responsible for these persons' detention to liberate them without further ado. If, of course, the Home Office require our support in any representation they may be making to M.I.5 or anyone else, you have only to let us know, and we will do all we can." A reply came on 24 June 1940, from Mr F.L. Farquhar of the Home Office, to Mr Gillies, saying that the whole question of internees had been handed over to Sir John Moylan, who had been Receiver for the Metropolitan Police since 1918, and who had dealt with all alien questions in the war of 1914-18. Farquhar said:

"I had a long interview with him yesterday, and he told me that as far as he could make out the various authorities concerned had concentrated first of all on deporting to Canada as many as possible of the "desperate characters" i.e. those Italians who should not be sent back to Italy, and whose retention in this country was undesirable. As will be recollected, M.I.5 had led everyone to believe that the number of these desperate characters was about 1,500. On being asked to produce this number, they said they could only find about 750. In an attempt to complete the quota which M.I.5 had failed to make up, the department of the War Office which looks after internees had made an arbitrary selection of a further 400 which they had taken out of the 20/30 age group. This party, numbering approx. 1,100, were to be sent to Canada on a ship leaving on 30 June or 1 July. Sir John Moylan said he was doubtful whether M.I.5, who still clung pathetically to membership of the *Fascio* as their one and only criterion of what constituted an undesirable or a dangerous character would be able to make any rapid or efficient classification. I am afraid that it becomes more and more clear that little reliance can be placed on M.I.5 in helping us to sort the sheep from the goats…all we can do at the moment therefore is to keep in touch with Sir John Moylan and hope that he will be able in reasonable time to produce some sort of order out of the existing chaos."

The most important points are that: [a] by 22 June 1940, the British Government knew that M.I.5's classification of Italian "desperate characters" was unreliable. It is to be noted that by 22 June, no Italians had been deported – the first deportation ship carrying Italians sailed on 1 July 1940; and [b] this was confirmed on 24 June 1940. The Home Office, the Police and the Foreign Office all knew. However, still nothing was done to ensure that those deported on 1 July were in fact properly classified as "desperate characters", and to prevent the gross miscarriages of justice and tragedy that followed.

CHAPTER SEVEN

THE RIGHT CLUB – THE REAL FIFTH COLUMN?

Following his arrest on 23 May 1940, Captain Archibald Maule "Jock" Ramsay MP was detained in Brixton Prison for more than four years under Regulation 18B. His country home was Kellie Castle in Angus, Scotland. His London home was at 24 Onslow Square. Born on 4 May 1894, at the time of his arrest, he was 46 years of age. He was described by the Daily Herald as a "tall, handsome, eagle looking man, scion of one of the oldest families in Scotland." Ramsay had been commissioned into the Coldstream Guards, and had fought in the First World War until 1916, when he was seriously wounded and sent home. He was eventually formally invalided out of the army in 1920. Captain Ramsay was known to his family and friends as "Jock". He was married and had four sons. In 1931, he had been elected as a Member of Parliament for the Conservative and Unionist party in South Midlothian and Peebles, Scotland, had been re-elected, and remained their MP at the time that war broke out. Therefore, he had served under Prime Minister Chamberlain and briefly under Winston Churchill.

Ramsay had for a long time held extreme right-wing views, and in May 1939, with war looming, he formed a secret organisation called the Right Club. The Club announced itself to those who knew of it as anti-Jewish, anti-Freemasonry and anti-Communism. According to what was said against him at his Detention Appeal Hearing, the true objective of the Club was: "to spread subversive and defeatist views amongst the population of Great Britain, and to obstruct the war effort of Great Britain." In reality, the Club was intended to do far more than that. It aimed to overthrow the British Government when the time was right, and replace it with a pro-Nazi Fascist government. At his appeal hearing, Ramsay said that he had been convinced for ten years that international Jewry was a real menace to the peace and happiness of the world. However, he denied that the Right Club was subversive or intended to undermine the war effort. He also denied that he was any sort of Fifth Columnist for the Nazis. However, in truth, Ramsay hoped one day to lead a Fascist Government in Britain, looked to Germany for support, and was prepared to use violent means to bring the British Government down.

The Right Club was a Fascist intelligence organisation, infiltrating the military, government departments, and the government itself. Once war broke out, the Club went underground, and kept its activities totally secret. The membership of the Club was kept entirely confidential by Ramsay, there were no public meetings, and there was no literature explaining the objects of the Right Club, or confirming its existence. It was therefore the very opposite of Mosley's British Union of Fascists or Arnold Leese's Imperial Fascist League [another Fascist network], and was more dangerous than both because of its secrecy. The membership list for the Right Club was kept by Ramsay in a locked leather-bound book. Members were divided into Wardens [the most senior], Stewards, Yeomen, Keepers and Freemen. They paid a fee to join. William Joyce, later known as "Lord Haw Haw" because of his propaganda work from Germany for the Nazis, was a "Warden member". Joyce was executed after the war for treason. Amongst the other members known to M.I.5 were men called Richard Findlay, and Luttman-Johnson, both of whom were known to be strongly pro-German. Ramsay sought secretly to penetrate not only the military and government departments, but also other British Fascist organisations, so that he would have Right Club members strategically placed amongst his potential Fascist allies when the time for the overthrow of the British Government came.

Ramsay's wife was the Honourable Mrs Ismay Lucretia Mary Maule Ramsay, a daughter of Viscount Gormanston and also a dedicated Fascist. She was born on 29 October 1882, and was some twelve years older than her husband. She was extremely well connected in British Society. She had two children by a previous marriage and four by Ramsay. She, like Ramsay himself, was an extreme anti-semite, and may have been partly responsible for indoctrinating Ramsay with Fascist views. She was convinced that the United Kingdom had been deliberately manoeuvred into war by "the hidden hand of Jewry", in the hope that a war between Germany and the British Empire would remove the two main obstacles to a plan for world domination by "International Jewry", German and British power. She favoured the Nazis because Hitler was committed to doing something about the Jews.

When war against Germany broke out in September 1939, Ramsay continued to hold secret meetings of the Right Club at his home, and continued to pursue his scheme of infiltrating government departments. He secretly boasted that he had Right Club agents active in almost every government department. Ramsay used the false name of Freeman when he felt the need for additional secrecy, as did his wife, who became Mrs Freeman. Although Ramsay was the unchallenged leader of the Right Club, his wife was also heavily involved.

When Ramsay was finally arrested and detained in May 1940, a poem was found at his home which it seems he himself had written, and which reflected his view of Britain as war broke out in September. There was a note on the document: "Written the day after war was declared on Germany." The poem was written on House of Commons embossed notepaper, and was a parody of the patriotic song: "Jerusalem". It read:

Land of dope and Jewry,

Land that once was free,

All the Jew boys praise thee,

Whilst they plunder thee,

Poorer still and poorer,

Grow thy true-born sons,

Faster still and faster,

They're sent to feed the guns.

Land of Jewish finance,

Fooled by Jewish lies

In press and books and movies,

While our birth right dies.

Longer still and longer,

Is the rope they get,

But – by the God of Battles

T'will serve to hang them yet.

A pamphlet entitled "War Alphabet" identifies those whom Ramsay and his Right Club selected for particular hatred. Winston Churchill was one of them. The "Alphabet" lists both those that Ramsay supported [H is for Hitler] and those that he would no doubt have liked to have hanged: *"C stands for Churchill, B better describes this blood-thirsty braggart, his boasts and his jibes"*.

Another crude pamphlet gives the words of another song:

Oh! England's heroes show your grit

The LEADER calls to fight the Jew,

The hour has struck: so do your bit

To prove that you are Freemen true.

We're free at last: We're free at last:

We've crushed the snake within our land.

We're marching on: We're marching on:

Saluting with our outstretched hand [the Nazi salute]

Ramsay did not like Sir Oswald Mosley, the leader of the largest Fascist organisation, the British Union of Fascists. However, when Mosley held a meeting of all the extreme right-wing leaders on 9 November 1939, with a view to discussing means of collaboration in their common aim, Ramsay attended. He was quite prepared to use Mosley's Fascists for his own purposes, and indeed needed them, but he was not prepared to accept Mosley's leadership. Ramsay's intention was that in the event of an invasion of England, or a Bolshevik uprising, the Right Club would take over and govern the country. Ramsay clearly hoped for a British civil war, saying on one occasion: "I would welcome civil war, with shots in the streets." As an ex-soldier who had served in World War One, Ramsay knew exactly what war meant, and saw a civil war as his way to power.

On Saturday 20 April 1940, Ramsay chaired a secret meeting of the inner circle of the Right Club. He discussed the policy of the Club, emphasising that penetration in every direction was the key note – he wanted cells of his members everywhere, in all Government departments, and in every right-wing movement, so that whoever eventually took power following an uprising or invasion, the Right Club could take things over from them. Ramsay gave the example of the British Union of Fascists, saying: "If Mosley came to power, we would have someone in his movement who could take over control from them."

Ramsay made one mistake. He stored the locked ledger of Right Club members in the flat of an American, Tyler Kent, who enjoyed diplomatic immunity since he worked at the US embassy in London. However, when it was discovered by M.I.5 that Kent was working as a spy against the interests of both Britain and the United States, the US waived his diplomatic immunity. When police raided his flat, the ledger of members for the Right Club was discovered and seized. It was locked, but was opened, and carefully examined. Presuming that it was accurate [and it carefully recorded the membership fees paid or promised by each member], it demonstrated the power of the Right Club. There were a number of Peers of the Realm listed, and many others in significant positions in British Society and Government, as well as a number of military men. At the back of the book there was an extract, which listed Members of Parliament who had signed up to the Right Club. There were eleven of them.. It is a fair assumption that all the members of the Right Club shared Ramsay's right-wing views. Hopefully not all would have been prepared to use violence against the British Government, but no doubt the MPs who had signed up to the Right Club hoped to take office in a Fascist Government. Ramsay's wife and three of his sons, Robert [Bob], Alexander and George, were listed as members in the ledger, as was William Joyce. Such was the secrecy of the Club that, with the possible exception of its inner circle, an individual member of the Club would never be told who all the other members were, but would only be put in contact with those working close to him or her.

Many women were members. Both sexes could work for the overthrow of the British Government.

One of the obvious dangers to national security was that Ramsay, as an MP, enjoyed parliamentary privilege in relation to anything that he said publicly in the House of Commons. Thus, any sensitive and confidential information stolen by Kent [who stole many sensitive documents] and shown to Ramsay could be disclosed with impunity by him in the House of Commons. The correspondence stolen by Kent included communications between Prime Minister Winston Churchill of Great Britain and President Roosevelt of the United States of America, which were highly confidential. The United States had not at this stage joined the war.

Following Ramsay's arrest on 23 May 1940, the Right Club did not cease its work. The majority of its members stayed free, including Mrs Ramsay and Ramsay's three adult sons. It very soon became clear that Mrs Ramsey was in no way prepared to sit back and accept her husband's imprisonment. She immediately began to plan his escape. Brixton Prison, where Ramsay was being held, was and is an impressively secure facility, which the author has visited many times, but nonetheless Mrs Ramsay expected that before long she would be able to take advantage of one of three things to free her husband: disorganisation as a result of German bombing, a German invasion, or a "revolution" in Britain aimed at overthrowing the elected government, which now had Winston Churchill at its head. Clearly, she expected to be able to utilise members of the Right Club to help her break into the prison, and she also talked of being supported by some of the British Army, a comment which suggests that the Right Club had indeed penetrated the British Armed Forces. She planned that at the right moment she and her supporters would blow open the gates of Brixton prison with bombs – to which she and Ramsay's followers clearly had access, perhaps through their army contacts.

Much of what is known today about the Right Club, and is summarised in the preceding paragraphs, comes from information gathered by agents working for Maxwell Knight, a highly successful M.I.5 spy master. The files containing that information were closed to the public for many years. The reality was this:

[i] There was a home grown Fifth Column operating in Britain which had nothing to do with enemy aliens – it was called the Right Club.

[ii] Its tentacles were apparently widespread through British Government departments and the military. The membership book confirms that many senior members of British Society had signed up to the aims of the Right Club. Penetration by its membership of all the organs of government and the military was the Right Club's main priority, so that it could, in due course, exercise control over what those departments did.

[iii] Although Ramsay was arrested on 23 May, the Right Club did not collapse. It continued its work under the guidance of Mrs Ramsay, other members of the Ramsay family, and various British Fascists who were still at liberty. The Right Club existed during the months of May, June and July 1940, when so many known German, Austrian and Italian anti-Nazis and anti-Fascists were arrested, interned and then deported. There is every reason to believe that the Right Club had agents in the Home Office at this time, in the War Office, and in the Military itself, who may have been able to influence the selection of those to be deported.

Therefore, although there is no direct evidence that tampering by Right Club agents led to the arrests and/or deportation of the wrong people, the suggestion that what happened to so many refugee Jews and pro-British anti-Fascist Italians could not be accidental, and that a British Fascist Fifth Column was at work, is not to be dismissed lightly. The Right Club harboured a deep hatred of the Jews, and must have celebrated the fact that so many of them, and other anti-fascists, were arrested and deported from Britain's shores.

CHAPTER EIGHT

WARTH MILLS INTERNMENT CAMP

None of the Italians internees had enjoyed a tribunal hearing, but they were not alone – the work of the German/Austrian tribunals had ceased some months before, and now there were a number of German/Austrian youngsters who had reached the age of sixteen [the minimum age for internment] but had not yet had the benefit of any tribunal assessment. There were also a number of new German/Austrian refugees who had recently arrived, and so had not been before a tribunal either. Despite this, Churchill's order applied to them all. The order was easily made, but it was very difficult to carry it out effectively, fairly, and in accordance with the human rights of the enemy aliens. As already stated, it proved impossible to find acceptable accommodation for the thousands of prisoners now being seized from the civilian population. As a result of the evacuation of Dunkirk, hundreds of thousands of British and Allied troops had suddenly arrived in the United Kingdom – including Poles, Czechs, Dutch, Belgians and Free French - and more would arrive with the evacuation of the whole of France later in June. The Norwegian Expeditionary Force was also being brought home, together with Norwegian troops as the Norwegian campaign was abandoned. These troops would be vital to the British resistance to invasion, and had to be housed, fed and restored to full fighting fitness. Coming on top of those problems, the mass internment of enemy aliens provided an enormous administrative problem. There was simply not enough room for them. There were many more refugee Germans and Austrians, and now also Italians, living and working in Britain than there were places to detain them. The Isle of Man was designated, as in World War One, as the centre for detention – in normal times it was a holiday island with numerous hotels and guest houses – but during the first few weeks after 10 June, a variety of temporary transit camps were used. As stated, at Lingfield Park and Kempton Park Race Courses prisoners were held in horse boxes. Many of the Italians whom it was intended to deport to far flung corners of the Empire or Commonwealth were passed on from there to a newly set up internment camp called Warth Mills in Bury, Manchester. The plan was that they would then be taken to

Liverpool, put on ships, and deported. The internees who were held at Warth Mills were mainly not young men – they were the restaurant owners, café owners, fish and chip shop owners and ice cream sellers from England, Scotland and Wales, many of them in their fifties and sixties, used to a comfortable, if hard working, life.

Warth Mills was totally unsuited as a detention camp. It was a derelict factory building, dirty and in a bad state of repair. It had been out of use for a number of years, and broken machinery, oil and broken glass covered the floors. The glass had fallen from window lights in the roof, and rain came into the building through the holes that the fallen glass had left. No adequate preparations had been made for its use as a barracks for internees. From the moment of arrival, all detainees, regardless of their age, occupation or state of health were treated like common criminals, despite the fact that they had not been tried or convicted of any crime. This was mainly M.I.5's fault – they had labelled these men as dangerous potential saboteurs and third columnists.

The first batch of internees to arrive included a young Roman Catholic priest, Father [later Canon] Gaetano Rossi. Rossi was twenty-four years of age, and had been ordained the previous summer in Glasgow. He was one of a number of Italian priests who were classified as dangerous enemy aliens and interned. One of those who later joined Rossi at Warth Mills was the Very Reverend Father Gaetano Fricassi, aged 64, parish priest of St Alban's, Ancoats, in the Diocese of Salford. Father Fricassi was in poor health. Born at Pescarolo, near Cremona on 18 April 1876, he had served as a priest in England since 1904 –so for far longer than the twenty years of residence which was meant to bring exemption from internment. Gaetano Rossi, forty years younger, had been born at Palestrina, not far from Rome. He studied for the priesthood in the Seminary in Palestrina, and came to the attention of Archbishop Macintosh, the Roman Catholic Archbishop of Glasgow. Macintosh was seeking an Italian priest who could help him with the substantial Italian community in Glasgow, and he invited Rossi to come to work with him in Glasgow. Young Rossi accepted and went to Scotland in September 1937, with a further two years study necessary before he could enter into the priesthood. He successfully completed the two years, and he was ordained on 29 June 1939 in Glasgow. Father Rossi was to say many years later that he and his father had always been anti-fascist, and that the Roman Catholic church did not like the Fascists because they had taken over the Boy Scouts and all the Catholic clubs. He was happy to be in Glasgow.

Archbishop Mackintosh believed that an Italian priest would help his Italian parishioners to integrate into Scottish society, and to worship more satisfactorily. When they arrived to take up work, many Italians could not speak English, and therefore couldn't express themselves in confession unless it was to an Italian-speaking priest. Their lives were very hard. If running a fish and chip shop, they had to get to the fish market very early in the morning, buy the fish, return to the shop and prepare the fish, and then work in the shop until about midnight. Mackintosh worried that his Italian parishoners, although they did not lose their faith, found it very difficult to practise it. Rossi's role was to integrate with the Glasgow Italian community as much as he could, and to bring them support for their faith. As Rossi himself put it, Italians coming to Scotland found themselves in a very different country to their own, and often felt lost. The young priest put himself about as much as he could in their lives.

Inevitably, the Italian community in Glasgow stuck together, helped each other, and socialised together. There was a long-established Italian club, called the Casa d'Italia, which had been founded by Italians, but had been taken over by the Italian Fascist State compulsorily under Mussolini's rule. Although the Casa d'Italia became a Fascist-run club, it remained the place where local Italians all went to socialise, to play cards and to dance. Father Rossi, as a part of his work for Archbishop Macintosh, regularly went there. Thus it seems he got onto M.I.5's black list.

Father Rossi and the group of prisoners of which he was a part were the first arrivals at the Warth Mills Camp. The guards had clearly been warned to expect a bunch of dangerous men, and treated their prisoners accordingly. Father Rossi himself had been arrested at 0300hrs on 11 June. At the time he was on holiday with two other priests, and staying in a hotel in Lytham St Annes, near Blackpool. He was taken to the local police station, and held there at gunpoint until onward transport was arranged for him and other detainees. The fact that he was in Holy Orders simply prompted a comment that: "Priests are the most dangerous!" Father Rossi was taken to Warth Mills Camp that same night, in a party of sixteen or seventeen detainees.

Rossi later described his time at Warth Mills in an interview for the Imperial War Museum. He said that the party he was with arrived at the Warth Mills camp late at night, and was the first group to arrive. They were taken to a large Nissen hut, which was apparently the prisoner reception centre. It contained five or six tables, at each of which an officer and other soldiers were sitting. All, including Father Rossi, were told to strip naked, and they did so. Once naked, Father Rossi and the others were ordered to present themselves at each of the tables in turn. Standing stark naked in front of each table, Father Rossi was asked different questions about himself, his job and his personal circumstances. The information that he was a priest of the Roman Catholic Diocese of Glasgow made no impression. When he reached a table where an officer had his personal belongings, Father Rossi was asked about his breviary, a prayer book written in Latin. "What is this?" enquired the officer. Father Rossi replied: "A prayer book", but the officer complained that he could not read it because it was in a foreign language. Father Rossi explained that it was in Latin, but that did not satisfy the officer, who confiscated the breviary. Only when the prisoners had been to all of the tables and had answered all the questions that they were asked, were they allowed to collect their clothes from near to the entrance door. All the clothes had been searched, as had any luggage that they had with them. It must be presumed that when Father Fricassi, aged 64, arrived, he too was ordered to strip naked, and was dealt with in the same way. Once the process was completed, Rossi and his fellow prisoners were allowed to get dressed, and then were taken into their prison in the Warth Mills.

All the prisoners had been given individual numbers, and they were known now not by their names, but by their numbers. Happily, unlike the German concentration camps where a prisoner's number was tattooed onto his or her body, no indelible record of his number was placed on any of these prisoners. That meant that the numbers did not stay with them for the rest of their lives, but it also defeated the purpose of de-personalising the unfortunate prisoners into mere numbers. The authorities felt that the numbers would avoid the difficulties and confusion of having to deal with foreign names, and would be simpler to deal with, but in practice the exact opposite happened. When one prisoner's number was called out, another prisoner might step forward for a reason of his own. Brothers might wish to stay together, or sons with their fathers. It was impersonation in its simplest form and it was to lead to much confusion later.

By the time that they were taken into the prison building, it was after dark, and Rossi describes the building as being in complete darkness, no doubt because of a black out in case of enemy bombing. A sergeant led the group of prisoners, who were in line, finding his way with a torch. The prisoners in the line behind the sergeant had no light, and could not see where they were going, or where to place their feet on what was an uneven floor. Pieces of machinery had been taken out of the building, leaving holes where their footings had been. From time to time one of the prisoners would stumble and fall. When they got to the room where they were to sleep, they found rows of canvas beds, with a single blanket on each. The prisoners passed a miserable night. Broken glass littered the floor. It rained in the night, so that some of those trying to sleep became wet. They tried to find dry corners of the room to which they could move their beds. When dawn finally came, the prisoners discovered that they were being held in an old cotton mill which had obviously been abandoned for a number of years.

At breakfast time, the prisoners were told to go into the kitchen to cook their breakfast, but they found that the kitchen was a complete mess, with grease and dirt all over the place. Little if anything appeared to have been done to make Warth Mills habitable for the hundreds of prisoners whom it was intended should be held there. Father Rossi and his companions managed to make tea and porridge in the kitchen, and Rossi sensed a feeling of hopelessness amongst his companions, caused by their dreadful accomodation and their total lack of knowledge as to what their future would hold. Nobody knew what would happen next – whether they were to spend the war in this horrible place, or, if not, where they were going to be taken.

After their breakfast, the prisoners wandered back into their dormitory and sat on their beds in despair. There was nothing else to do – there was no exercise yard or social facility at this early stage. Major Alfred James Braybrook, the Commandant, chose this moment to visit them, ordering them immediately to stand up. No-one was allowed to sit on a bed while he was in the room. Father Rossi described Braybrook as wearing spectacles with one black glass lense, because he was blind in one eye. He was an older man who had seen service in World War 1. After Major Braybrook had introduced himself and run through basic instructions, he left and the prisoners stood or sat around aimlessly until the initial shock of their imprisonment at Warth Mills began to wear off. Then they gradually started to talk amongst themselves. Most of the men were strangers to each other, and a series of introductions began. As the day went on, other prisoners began to arrive, and Father Rossi found himself working as a counsellor for and organiser of all of the inmates of Warth Mills. As a man of the cloth, the other men looked to Rossi as their leader despite his youth, asking him for advice and spiritual comfort. One of the first tasks was to clean up the dining area so that it was fit for use. Father Rossi and the others got on to their hands and knees to clean the floor, which was inches deep in filth. The floors were scrubbed and scraped until they were clean and the stone floor gleamed.

From the beginning of their incarceration at Warth Mills, the sanitary conditions were totally inadequate. Once further groups of prisoners arrived, there were far too few lavatories, and the prisoners had to queue for an hour or an hour and a half to use one. They asked the Camp Administration to provide more lavatories, but were provided only with a number of buckets, placed around the building to serve as extra lavatories. These initially had canvas sheeting around them to provide the necessary privacy, but the canvas did not last very long. It was needed for another purpose - the prisoners cut the canvas up to make pillows – they had been supplied with none, all that they had were bare canvas beds. They made pillows by stuffing the pieces of canvas with grass. Washing facilities were also extremely poor. The prisoners had to queue up to use the taps that there were, there was no hot water, and no showers or baths.

The elderly priest, Father Fricassi, had to endure all of this. He was 64 and not well. His Bishop was to describe him later as always having been violently opposed to Italy entering the war, to such an extent that he would never ever listen to Italian radio broadcasts. He was loyal to Great Britain, and not in any way connected to anybody working to harm her. In 1933, he had been ill for a year following a nervous breakdown, and he was described as being extremely sensitive to physical pain. Father Fricassi lived a life of pious poverty, and it was thought later that his detention was due simply to the fact that he had once let out the parochial hall to a political party – presumably the Fascists. It could only have been this that caused M.I.5 to place poor Father Fricassi on their list of dangerous aliens. On 11 June 1940, Father Fricassi was arrested at his presbytery and detained. When his bishop learned of his detention, he appealed to his Cardinal for help, but to no avail. Father Fricassi remained in custody, and a decision was taken that he was to be deported to Canada.

Rossi commented that the Italian prisoners, all of whom were meant to be dangerous Fascist supporters of Benito Mussolini, in fact held a complete mix of political views. Some were Monarchist, some anti-Monarchist, some left wing, some centrist and some fascists. However, the fascists were substantially out-numbered by the anti-fascists. The prisoners encouraged free speech amongst themselves. A pile of stones was built to act as a form of Speakers Corner, and anyone who had anything that they wanted to say could stand on the pile of stones and address everyone else. All sorts of different political views were expressed, including right wing, left wing and anarchical views, and there were discussions about religion, and, inevitably, sport. Rossi emphasised that there was no danger to anyone, all views were received with good humour. The vast majority of the prisoners were shop-keepers, chefs and café owners - men whose daily lives involved fish and chips and ice cream. There were few professional men amongst them. Rossi commented that anyone genuinely involved in fascism had left Britain before the war actually broke out. All the people he met in the Warth Mills camp, Rossi said, had got nothing against Britain. They were only really interested in their families, and had left Italy to earn money for their families, and to improve their lives. There was no quarrelling amongst the inmates, they all tried to help each other in what were very difficult and unpleasant circumstances. There was not even the usual Italian north/south divide in camp. They acknowledged it, but joked about it. Significantly, the Italian government, whose dangerous fifth columnists these men were said to be, appeared totally disinterested in the prisoners, and made no contact with the camp at Warth Mills. Had they been active fascists, it might have been different.

Once in the camp, and once they had tidied it up as best they could, the prisoners simply had to make the best of their harsh life. Even though they had amongst them almost the complete kitchen staff of both the Piccadilly and Savoy hotels, and the Head Chefs took over the once grimy kitchen and commanded their teams, thanks to a shortage of good ingredients, the food was inadequate and uninspiring. The chefs did their best, and Rossi commented that there was little illness in the camp, apart from pre-existing conditions. The meals were the very modest highlight of their existence.

The prisoners were held incommunicado from the outside world for the first fifteen days – a cause of inevitable distress for men worrying about their families. Many of them knew that, with their arrest, the breadwinner had been snatched from the family, and their families would be in real financial difficulty. After fifteen days, the prisoners were allowed one sheet of paper a week on which to write a letter. They had to leave each letter open, so that it could be read by a censor. Father Rossi wrote letters to Glasgow, but none of them arrived. Rossi's patron, Archbishop Macintosh, wanted to know the whereabouts of his young Italian priest, and wanted to secure his release. Having failed to obtain any information from the British authorities, a message was broadcast on Vatican Radio, asking if anyone knew where Father Rossi was, and telling the world that Rossi was missing. Meanwhile, Rossi received no incoming mail at all.

Uberto Limentani, the Italian Jew working for the BBC, arrived at Warth Mills on about the 24 June. He described it in the following words: "very deplorable accommodation and insufficient hygienic facilities for the 1800 people who were [by now] packed into the restricted space. There was no possibility of having a proper wash, the dirt and grease of the abandoned factory spread all over, the lavatories were practically non-existent. The food, both in Lingfield [where he was sent first of all] and Bury [Warth Mills], was often insufficient, and the evening meal frequently consisted of some bread, a piece of cheese and a cup of tea."

Rossi tried to keep up the spirits of his fellow inmates by organising a variety of activities, including church services and football. There was an empty field next to the mill building, which after a while they were allowed to use for games of football. It was difficult to have an organised game because of the number of people who crowded the field wanting to play. The field was always surrounded by guards with fixed bayonets, which added a bizarre aspect to the encounters. The guards were a mixture of very young conscripts and men who were not fit for frontline duty. They were uneasy to start with, guarding, as they had been informed, dangerous Fifth Columnists – enemy spies and saboteurs. Father Rossi, who stayed at the camp longer than most, commented that once they began to know their prisoners, they relaxed.

Father Rossi soon clashed with Major Braybrook, the camp commandant, over his religious duties. Rossi had managed to contact a local Jesuit priest, and, as he was duty bound to do, wanted to hold mass with the necessary sacred vessels. Rossi contacted Braybrook to request his permission. Major Braybrook refused to give his permission, saying that to hold mass would amount to an assembly of the prisoners which, along with political gatherings and the like, was forbidden. Rossi protested that it was the right of the prisoners to hold religious services, and threatened Braybrook that if he continued to refuse permission, he would make it known publicly that Major Braybrook had personally denied the prisoners their right to worship. Braybrook knew that Rossi had contact with the Jesuit priest, who could make the outrage known throughout British Roman Catholic circles. Realising that he had gone too far, Braybrook then changed his mind, and agreed to let Father Rossi hold services. The services were very well attended. Father Rossi recalled later that everybody came, and that they prayed not for themselves but for the well-being of the families from whom they had been snatched away.

Young Luigi Beschizza was blunt in his comments later. Describing the camp he said: "Warth Mills was a horrible place. It was dirty, the palliases were dirty, the blankets were grubby – I didn't complain, but conditions were horrible." Luckily, Beschizza recalled, the weather was usually fine, and he found a way of getting onto the roof of the mill to sunbathe. A group of youngsters spent most of their time together, and played cards, drafts, and the occasional game of football. Nicola Cua remembered being at Warth Mills for about two weeks. He joined a group of eight or ten youngsters who stuck together, and just tried to have fun. There were quite a lot of men in the camp whom he knew, and he learned at Warth Mills that his father had also been interned, despite his many years in England. Happily, Nicola found his father in the same camp as himself, and they were able to stick together after that.

On 29 June, Uberto Limentani and the group of ex-Lingfield prisoners were summoned by Major Braybrook, who announced to them that a certain number would be leaving on the following day. Braybrook said that a list was being compiled but not yet ready. It would contain the prisoners from Lingfield, whom Limentani presumed were on some sort of War Office black list, together with a balance of single men under thirty. Limentani was immediately concerned that his refugee status was being ignored. He had been keeping company in Warth Mills with a group of Italian refugees, including Max Gentili, Giulio Finzi, G.Janni, Paolo Treves and his brother Giuseppe Treves, all of them confirmed anti-Fascists. The Treves were members of a well-known anti-Fascist family – their father Claudio had been a socialist leader In Italy. The family was of Jewish heritage. Paolo was also working for the BBC, having been directed to them by the Head of Italian at Bedford College, London, a man called Curt Sigmar Gutkind, also of Jewish origin. Gutkind was another refugee to Britain. He had been born German, but also had obtained Italian citizenship before he fled to Britain. Gutkind was interned and sent to Warth Mills Camp.

Limentani was surprised that his name was apparently on Braybrook's list. He therefore spoke to Braybrook, and a number of the other officers at Warth Mills camp, emphasising to them that he had refugee status and worked for the BBC, and was told that if that was so, his presence on the list for deportation would certainly be reconsidered. However, on the following morning, 30 June 1940, when the list of those to go was read out, Limentani's name was still on it. He protested again to Major Braybrook, who answered that there was nothing that he could do, and that the list could not be changed. Limentani spoke to other officers, and one of them, a Captain Croster made a careful note of everything that Limentani told him. Nonetheless, Limentani was marched away with many other Italians from the Warth Mills camp onto the train for Liverpool, and then onto the ship called the *Arandora Star*. He was still classified as a dangerous fascist. Most of his anti-Fascist friends and colleagues went with him. Paolo Treves was one of the very few who avoided that fate – apparently an intervention in his case by Mr Gillies of the Labour Party succeeded. None of the deportees marched out of the Warth Mills camp knew where they were going, but seeing the *Arandora Star*, which was an ocean-going liner, they doubted that it was to the Isle of Man, the internment centre that they had believed was their most likely destination.

In the case of obvious anti-fascists such as Limentani and his friends, the reader may wonder how on earth it came about that they were arrested and sent for deportation – and Limentani's was far from an isolated case.

Father Rossi was not on the list to be sent away in the first batch for deportation, possibly because of the enquiries that Archbishop Macintosh was making. Macintosh had now contacted the Home Office asking about him. Macintosh wanted Rossi back at work in Glasgow. Concerned about his flock at Warth Mills, Rossi had in fact volunteered to go with the first batch of deportees, but was turned down. He wasn't on the list. He was told at this stage that he would be sent with the second batch, which was due to leave in a few days later. However, in the event, he was not included in that batch either. As he was leaving the camp to travel with those selected to go, his number was called out, and he was kept behind. He was not told why, but was put to work in the Camp office, so it may be that Braybrook thought him too useful to deport, or just lost his nerve.

In the Camp office, Rossi's job was to deal with correspondence. There were two official interpreters, whose job it was to translate any documents in German or Italian into English. Father Rossi didn't think that they were very good, and before long, they passed to him all documents in Italian for him to translate. Father Rossi also had to look after all the documents of the prisoners held at Warth Mills, including their passports.

By the end of June, all the Italians except Father Rossi had left Warth Mills. In their place came German prisoners, and Father Rossi found himself the only Italian. Leo Kahn, the German Jewish lawyer, was one of those who arrived with the consignment of Germans at Warth Mills, after some weeks at Kempton Park Race Course. He described Warth Mills as a big, disused factory, containing lots of rusty machinery, which had obviously not been used as an industrial building for a long time. It was still very dirty, and he was worried about the lack of hygiene. Toilets were scarce. The palliases [mattresses] were minimal, and there were not nearly enough blankets. Even though it was summer, the nights were cold, and he foraged for newspapers to keep himself warm. Amongst them there were some very old and some very young prisoners, and the sick, all of whom he and others tried to help. Kahn slept in open, outside the building because the factory was so foul. The only good thing about Warth Mills, Kahn said, was that for the first time they received contact and parcels from their families. He was there for ten days. The Germans, most of them Jewish refugees, seemed to trust Father Rossi completely, and he remained working in the office until he was transferred to a camp at Whitchurch.

The International Red Cross, which inspected all prisoner of war camps, carried out an inspection of Warth Mills on 12 July 1940. Because they were not military prisoners of war, the inmates did not have the benefit of the Geneva Convention, but the Red Cross was determined to check that the conditions of the camp were safe and humane. The visit was nearly two weeks after the *Arandora Star* had sailed, and the Italians had been replaced by Germans and Austrians. The Red Cross found that then there were 1,830 men in the camp. Its capacity was said to be 3,100. At least 180 of the internees were over 60 years of age – the figure would have been considerably higher if those deported had still been there.

The report recorded that the factory was in a bad state of repair. It comprised five big rooms, each containing up to 500 men, sleeping on palliases, with now three blankets apiece. The inmates described the general conditions when they arrived as very dirty, with oil on the floors where they were supposed to sleep. Although it was summertime, when it would not as often be necessary, the Red Cross report records the heating was bad. More importantly, there were inadequate fire precautions – the exits were insufficient for a rapid evacuation and there were no fire extinguishers or water hydrants – and therefore the camp was dangerous. Hygiene was poor – the latrines were in a bad state, there was no hot water, there were no baths, the number of showers was insufficient, there was no sterile or "disinfectant room" for new inmates to pass through. The sick bay had only 30 beds and insufficient equipment. In addition to a significant proportion of older men, there were about 250 men who needed special medical treatment. The inmates reported that they were worried about an epidemic breaking out. Since it was a transit camp, and not intended as a permanent home for the prisoners held there, there was no library, and little for the internees to do. Newspapers were provided, and the internees were allowed to listen to the BBC on the radio. Each inmate was allowed to write two letters per week, plus "official letters" to MPs, refugee charities and so forth.

In short, the conditions in the Warth Mills Camp remained, even in mid-July, a disgrace, despite the attempts by the camp inmates to make them better. They again illustrate the chaos and lack of proper organisation that affected all of the actions that the British Government took against the internees from the beginning of June 1940 onwards. It was panic action that lacked any proper thought or planning. It is perhaps always easy for politicians to issue orders, but far harder for their juniors to carry them out efficiently, particularly if there is a fifth column working within their ministries against British interests, which as we will see, may have been the case. With the sudden horror of an imminent invasion, Churchill and his

Cabinet had abandoned the usual British standards of fairness and justice. Warth Mills should never have been used as a prison camp – it was totally unsuited and in very poor condition. But of course, the "desperate characters" had to be held somewhere.

However bad the physical conditions of a prison camp, a central factor in the quality of life of the inmates will always be the standard of behaviour of its military staff, usually set by the camp commandant. The problem in Britain in June 1940 was that all the better quality troops were urgently required to prepare the defences of the United Kingdom against invasion, so that the guarding of these "desperate characters" was left to lesser quality troops. Their guards would be drawn from the Pioneer Corps, of whom more later, or a hotchpotch of spare soldiers who came from many different regiments, and lacked any esprit de corps. As previously stated, the Commandant of Warth Mills camp was Major Alfred James Braybrook, a Military Policeman who was totally unsuited to his task. His behaviour greatly compounded the suffering and distress of the inmates of the camp. Major Braybrook, was ignorant, corrupt and an anti-semite. Used, no doubt, to dealing with servicemen who misbehaved, and having been told that the prisoners were dangerous fifth columnists, Braybrook showed absolutely no ability to empathise with the unfortunate Italian café owners and German Jewish refugees who actually arrived at the Warth Mills Camp, some of whom had experienced the early days of the German concentration camps. Instead, he stole from them. As internees, they arrived at the camp in their own clothes, and carrying their own possessions, often in suitcases. Upon arrival at Warth Mills, stripped naked, every internee had his valuable possessions taken from him. In return, he got his blankets and some hay to fill his pallias. Any valuables taken from him, the internee rarely got back. Braybrook would "confiscate" items such as gold sovereigns, razorblades, books, jewellery and typewriters and never return them.

When eventually Braybrook's unlawful activities were detected, he was arrested, and he was sent for trial at the Old Bailey. The records show that he was finally convicted in July 1941. His offences were all in relation to prisoners who had been in his charge. He was convicted of stealing £350 [a large sum of money in those days] which had been entrusted to him for the purpose of financing a canteen at an un-named internment camp of which he was the Commandant [almost certainly Warth Mills], and embezzling and stealing other property, including 100 gold sovereigns, two typewriters, some jewellery and 1,040 razor blades, which were a valuable commodity in war-time Britain. He was sentenced to 18 months imprisonment, and so deservedly learned himself what it was like to be a prisoner. However, his sentence was light by modern standards, since he had breached the trust put in him by virtue of his office, and had grossly abused his power. He made an already miserable life for those in his charge a lot more miserable. Documents held at the National Archives at Kew show that he was believed to have stolen a total of £6,000 in cash and goods, although that was never proved in court.

Father Rossi, who stayed on in Warth Mills after the departure of the *Arandora Star* and its successor the *Ettrick*, said that Braybrook was a rascal, describing him as a man who had stolen a lot of gold guineas off the prisoners. Rossi recalled that during his time working in the Camp office, he was asked to put into the stores a typewriter with Norwegian characters. He did so. However, later, it turned out that the internee who owned it had diplomatic immunity, and should not have been interned – yet another mistake. The internee was released, but when he asked for his typewriter back, it was nowhere to be found in the stores, where it should have been. Police officers, who must have already had their suspicions of Major Braybrook, searched his quarters and found the Norwegian typewriter there, together with a large number of other items that Braybrook had stolen from the unfortunate prisoners.

CHAPTER NINE

DEPORTATION

The early shiploads of deported aliens were intended by the Government to be those who were the most dangerous, and who would pose a threat to British security if they remained in Britain when the German invasion came. The governments of the countries to which they were sent were told exactly that – that these men were dangerous Nazis and Fascists. Not surprisingly therefore, they were treated as such both on the sea voyages that they had to make, and by the receiving countries.

The first deportation ship to leave Britain was the *Duchess of York,* which sailed on 21 June 1940, heading for Canada. Officially, she was carrying 2,100 Category A German internees, and 500 German prisoners of war. Comment has already been made on the unreliability of the categorisation by the Tribunals, but the fact that the selection process was, from the outset, hopelessly flawed is most simply illustrated by the fact that amongst the prisoners were four members of the German Consular staff from Iceland. They should, of course, have been awarded diplomatic protection. It is impossible to believe that the four did not make their status clear, but presumably their protests were simply ignored. The fact that they had been deported in error was not realised until 15 July, and an urgent telegram was then sent to the British High Commissioner in Canada asking that they be sent back to Britain.

The *Duchess of York* sailed alone and unescorted. She eventually arrived at Quebec on 3 July. The guard contingent on this voyage was approximately 250, and most had been evacuated from the beaches of Dunkirk. The Evening Chronicle reported the arrival of the *Duchess of York* under a headline reading: "Prisoners of War reach Canada – Loutish Nazis in tense unescorted voyage." Of course, those who were being deported were all meant to be dangerous enemy aliens, and the article no doubt perpetuated that myth.

Italians were to follow, together with more Germans and Austrians. The selection process continued to fail, and, as we have seen, by 22 June, the British Government knew that the M.I.5 list of desperate, dangerous Italians was seriously flawed, but proceeded with their deportation nonetheless. The Government view was: "Get them out, and everything can be sorted out in the country to which we are sending them after their arrival". The inclusion of some of the deportees appears often to be wholly random – just an attempt by the War Office [who were in charge of the camps] to fill the quota of deportations demanded by Churchill and his government. A more sinister explanation may be that agents of the Right Club were involved, and that they used the deportations as a way of getting rid of their enemies from Britain: anti-Nazi Germans and Austrians, and anti-Fascist pro-British Italians.

However, irrespective of the Right Club, the Home Office, the Foreign Office and the Metropolitan Police all knew that M.I.5's intelligence was hopelessly flawed, and that their list of Italian dangerous characters based upon that hopelessly flawed intelligence, by, at the latest, 22 June 1940. Someone should surely have called a stop to the deportations until proper investigation was done. But that did not happen. The panic to deport raged on at full speed. In no circumstances should a British citizen have been deported, that was unlawful. Nor should anybody with diplomatic immunity have been deported. Both these things happened on the next deportation ship to leave, the *Arandora Star*. Many at the Foreign Office [the international experts] did not like the policy of deportation, certainly not in relation to the Italians. An interesting note dated 1 July 1940 on one of their files deals with the deportations of the Italians on the *Arandora Star* ,which had happened that morning, and the *Ettrick,* which was due to depart on 3 July. It reads: "There is nothing we can do, it is a Cabinet decision and it is our policy is to get rid of as many useless [or "dangerous"] mouths as possible." This, of course, indicates that a different test was now being applied – that of "uselessness" as well as dangerousness should the invasion come

It seems that once the arrests had been made, and the internees had arrived in their various holding camps, the machinery for deportation moved into top gear. This was, of course, what Churchill wanted – that the dangerous enemy aliens should be got out of the country as quickly as possible. No time was allowed for the internees to make proper protest, or for representations to be made on their behalf. An example was Achille Cavadini. Cavadini was 49 years of age, a married man from London with a wife and daughter. He had lived in England for many years, worked in a senior post at the Berkeley Restaurant in London, and had applied for British naturalisation. Nonetheless, he was arrested and sent initially to Lingfield. A Captain H Trevor wrote a letter of reference for him, asking for his release, on 4 July 1940, but he was already too late. In the panic, Cavadini had already been deported on the *Arandora Star* on 1 July.

At Warth Mills, on 30 June, there was a roll call. Luigi Beschizza was sunbathing on the roof when he heard names being called, and he came downstairs. Nobody had told the prisoners why names were being called out, and Beschizza thought, like many others, that they would be going to the Isle of Man. It had to be better there than at the Warth Mills camp. Beschizza stepped forward when his number was called. Nicola Cua and his father also both stepped forward when their turn came. There were no identity checks, and it seems that at Warth Mills the record of who was being taken to Liverpool to board the *Arandora Star* was far from accurate. Prisoners stepped forward in place of others when their own names had not been called, because they wanted go with their relative or a friend.

At Leeds, where he was being held, Gino Guarnieri repeated that when the prisoners were called together on 30 June, they did not know where they were going to be taken to next. Gino said that in his camp, the British called out the names of mostly old people, but then added about fifty youngsters to make up numbers. The orders that the guards had received were that there had to be a full compliment of prisoners on the *Arandora Star*, and all the prisoners there had been declared to be "desperate characters." Those who asked whether they could go before a tribunal to prove their loyalty to Britain were told that they could go before a tribunal after they arrived at their destination. The International Red Cross were not notified of the ship's departure. The German-Austrian prisoners who were put onto the *Arandora Star* were more of a mixed bag than the Italians. There were some prisoners of war, crews captured off German civilian ships, and some of these were active Nazis. However, there were also many German and Austrian Jews, refugees who had fled with or without their families to Britain, and who were sworn enemies of Adolf Hitler.

The *Arandora Star* was a ship of the Blue Star Line, which was founded by the Vestey family of Liverpool in July 1911. The *Arandora*, as she was originally named, was built by Cammell Laird as a refrigerated passenger/cargo liner and launched in 1927. She was driven by four steam turbine engines, and was initially designed to carry 164 first class passengers, and cargo. However, before long, the company decided to convert her into a first-class cruise liner. In 1929, the cargo storage was removed, the passenger capacity was expanded to 354 first class passengers, and the ship was renamed the *Arandora Star*.

The *Arandora Star* became a leading luxury cruise liner of her day, travelling the world with her passengers to visit a variety of exotic locations. She carried only First Class passengers, and in that way was unlike most of her competitors. She was equipped with a ballroom, swimming pool and games deck, and her passengers enjoyed the height of luxury. She had six decks. Deck A, known as the Main Deck, was the lowest of the cabin decks, Deck B was known as the Upper Deck, and contained more cabins and the entire forward portion of the deck was occupied by the sumptuous Louis XIV Dining Saloon. Deck C was the Bridge Deck, with the entrance hall, further cabins and the bridge, Deck D was the Promenade Deck, with the Ball Room, Garden Lounge, Smoke Room, Card Room and Music Room Lounge. Deck E contained the Games Deck and the swimming pool. Above that was an Observation deck, which also contained a gymnasium and coits decks. The cabins [known as Staterooms] were spread across the decks A to E. There were 273 in all.

Life on the *Arandora Star* during the 1930s was one of music, dancing, fine dining and above all luxury. The ship was a beautiful environment from which to view and visit some of the most spectacular and fascinating places around the world. The company with which the Captain shared his dinner table was sparkling. It included royalty, members of the nobility, leading men of commerce, and men of letters such as George Bernard Shaw. It was civilisation at its best, and a totally different world to that which the

Captain and crew would experience with the onset of war. The brochure for 1938 described the Arandora Star as: "The World's Most Delightful Cruising Liner", and advertised a winter cruise leaving Southampton on 22nd January, visiting Madeira, Trinidad, La Guayra, Cristobal, Grand Cayman, Vera Cruz, Havanna, Miami, Nassau, San Juan, Barbados and Tenerife, returning to Southampton on16 March, a distance of 13,907 miles.

Under a banner of "Spaciousness…Tranquility", the brochure read: "From grey skies to blue, from England's bleak and chilly winter to the exotic sun-drenched islands of the West Indies, the ancient glories of Mexico and the gay life of Havanna and Miami. This is what the "ARANDORA STAR" has in store for you this winter – A Perfect Holiday. No matter upon which of the Seven Seas the "ARANDORA STAR" sails, she remains by popular acclaim "The World's most delightful Cruising Liner".Your cabin is a state room de luxe, with hot and cold running water, and bedspreads with Vi-sprung mattresses. Throughout the ship the arrangements and decorations combine magnificence with exquisite taste. A strictly limited passenger list of under 400 enables all to be accommodated at one sitting in the Louis Quatorze restaurant. The ballroom, one of the finest afloat, comfortably accommodates every couple on the ship. For the rest, there are card rooms, music rooms, café lounge, smoking room, writing room, garden lounge galleries, to say nothing of the large silent sun deck, main games deck, and the great open-air azure blue tiled pool, with surrounding sun lido. The atmosphere of the ship creates in all passengers a sense of cheerful comfort and ease. All passengers are first class; they are, and feel like, the members of an exclusive floating club, the whole forming such a combination of happiness. Live in a different world next winter…" The fare was advertised as "from 114 guineas".

The *Arandora Star's* cruise calendar was varied. In 1937, there was a Christmas and New Year West African Sunshine Cruise; in January a Winter Sunshine Cruise to the West Indies; in April a cruise to Malta, Greece, Turkey, Syria, Egypt, Algeria and Portugal; in mid-May a Whitsun Coronation Royal Naval Review cruise; in late May a cruise to Madeira, the Canary Islands and Morocco; in early June Greece, Italy, Venice, Yugoslavia and Portugal; from late

June to the end of August, Northern Capitals cruises to Germany, Kiel Canal, Denmark, Danzig and Sweden, and "Land of the Midnight" sun cruises to Iceland, Norway, and Finland. Then from September, cruises again to the sunshine.

The pattern in 1939 had been similar. Between 12 and 31 August, the *Arandora Star* carried her passengers on a cruise to northern Europe. She was due to visit Rekjavik, Stockholm, Helsinki, Bornholm and Aarhus, Danzig and the Kiel canal. However, with the worsening international situation, the last two calls were omitted, and she returned to Southampton on 26 August. The Blue Star office in Regent Street, London, was besieged by Americans desperate to return home, and therefore the *Arandora Star* was assigned to sail from Southampton to New York. She left Southampton on 1 September.

The *Arandora Star's* serving Captain when war broke out on 3 September 1939 was Edgar Wallace Moulton. Captain Moulton was 54 years old, and had been the Master of the *Arandora Star* throughout most of the 1930s. He was tall, courteous, very experienced, respected by his crew, and popular with the wealthy passengers whom the *Arandora Star* always carried. With the outbreak of war, his life, and that of his ship was to change dramatically. When war was actually declared on 3 September, as the ship journeyed towards New York, the crew set about painting her funnels a dull grey and shading her porthole windows dark blue. At night the ship was blacked out, and smoking outside on the decks was forbidden. On 11 September 1939, the *Arandora Star* docked in New York, and discharged her passengers. She left New York on 13 September and sailed to Halifax, Nova Scotia. From there, she was directed to return to England, and to Dartmouth.

The British Government requisitioned a number of ocean-going liners, and the Blue Star Line's *Arandora Star* was one of them. Captain Moulton remained in command. His life, and that of his ship changed. Moulton now commanded an exclusively male civilian crew – comprised mainly of those who had been her peacetime crew. The ship's peacetime finery was stripped away. She was painted grey, and at some stage she had a 4.7inch cannon and a 12-pound anti-aircraft gun mounted, one fore, one aft, to provide her with some defence against marauders.

Having been assessed and found satisfactory by the Ministry of Shipping, in December the *Arandora Star* took part in her first wartime duties – ironically [as it would turn out] acting as a trial ship in Admiralty trials of anti-torpedo nets.

Then she was assigned to serve in Gibraltar as a "Postal Censor Ship". In effect she became for a while a floating office. In late May 1940, as the German *blitzkrieg* rolled across the Low Countries and into France, and disaster seemed about to overwhelm Great Britain and Northern Ireland she found herself assigned as a Troop Carrier. She was ordered initially to Liverpool, and from there she was sent to Greenock on 31 May 1940, bound for Norway. The *Arandora Star* had entered the war in earnest.

On 9 April 1940, German forces had invaded Norway, seizing four of its biggest towns. Great Britain and France responded in support of the Norwegian government, and fierce fighting began. However, on the night of 24/25 May, a decision was made by Winston Churchill and the British High Command in London that the situation in France and the Low Countries had become too critical, and that all British forces must be brought back from Norway to the British mainland. The following day, the evacuation of Dunkirk was to begin. However, one further attack was authorised in Norway on the port of Narvik, which was in the hands of the Germans, in the hope that it could be captured and certain installations destroyed. Narvik was successfully attacked and captured on the night of 27/28 May. There had been Allied concern that Narvik might be used as a source of iron ore by the Germans, but having seized the town, it was discovered that the ore-handling plant had already been destroyed in the fighting, the ore quays were burnt out, and the harbour was full of wrecked ships. The Allied Chief Engineer reported that it would take at least a year to repair.

In total there were some 24,500 Allied troops to be evacuated from Norway, together with the King of Norway and his Government. Britain now needed some of the liners that she had requisitioned to use as troopships. Fifteen, including the *Arandora Star*, were commanded to rendezvous about 180 miles from the Norwegian coast, and to operate under the command of Rear-Admiral Vivian. The *Arandora Star* left Greenock on 31 May 1940, and the troopships sailed to Norway in two groups. As a troop ship, the *Arandora Star* became a much sought-after target for both the Nazi air force -the Luftwaffe - and the U-Boat fleet. The difficulty for the troop ships was that they were invitingly large targets, and since they were passenger liners, it was pretty obvious what their purpose was. They had little defence against U-boats or attack from the air. They relied on their Royal Navy escorts for protection. Initially, the *Arandora Star* was ordered to join a group under the protection of the aircraft carrier HMS *Glorious* and the anti-aircraft cruiser HMS.*Coventry*.

Once the *Arandora Star* and the other troop ships arrived 180 miles off the coast of Norway, they sailed two at a time under anti-submarine protection into the sheltered waters north of Harstad. British destroyers worked up and down the narrow channels outside nearby Narvik, picking up men from smaller craft and from the quayside where possible, and ferrying them to the troopships. The men were evacuated first, and then as much of their equipment as possible followed.

The *Arandora Star* was in very real danger. This was the land of the midnight sun, and in early June there were twenty-four hours of daylight. There was of course a danger from mines, and of attack by enemy surface craft and submarines, but the greatest danger was of attack by air. Thankfully, the days of the final embarkation of the men were cloudy and overcast, robbing enemy aircraft of the good visibility that they needed.

The *Arandora Star*, with Captain Moulton on the bridge, sailed into Narvik Fjord, together with other transport ships under the escort of British warships. The evacuees were delivered to the *Arandora Star*, and Captain Moulton successfully carried away to safety about 1,600 officers and men of the Royal Air Force, together with a number of French and Polish troops. The King of Norway was evacuated from Tromso on 7 June, and the final British troops left on 8 June.

The *Arandora Star* sailed back to Glasgow in a convoy carrying a total of 10,000 troops under the escort of the battleship HMS *Valiant*. She arrived there safely on 13 June, and off-loaded the troops that she had saved. In total some 25,000 men were evacuated from Norway. However, the operation was not without cost. Not all of the troop ships were as fortunate as the *Arandora Star*. The troopship *Arama* was sunk to the far north of Narvik on 8 June 1940, and after the successful withdrawal, the aircraft carrier *Glorious* was attacked and sunk on the way home, with significant loss of life. The work of the *Arandora Star,* her Captain and her crew had become extremely dangerous.

Having disembarked her troops at Glasgow, the *Arandora Star* was given a day's rest and then ordered on 15 June to sail immediately to Swansea. The evacuation of British and Allied troops from Dunkirk had been completed on 4 June, but there were still very many British and Allied troops left in north west France. Between 10 and 13 June, thousands more troops had been evacuated from Le Havre [Operation *Cycle*] and on 15 June, it was decided to evacuate all other troops from rest of France. Operation *Aerial*, the evacuation plan, was officially launched on that day, and the *Arandora Star* was to play a major part in it, as was another liner called the *Ettrick*. Although never publicly acknowledged in the way that the evacuation from Dunkirk has been, Operation *Aerial* succeeded in bringing nearly 200,000 British and Allied troops back to England, together with diplomatic personnel and civilians. The official figures set out in one of the War Office files were: British 139,812; French 17,062; Free Poles 24,352; Free Czechs 4,938, Belgians 163. The total number who disembarked in the United Kingdom was 186,327.

In addition, a large number of vehicles and equipment were evacuated, and demolition of what was left was carried out. The orders were that the evacuation ships, once loaded, should return to Britain as quickly as possible, with one destroyer to escort each convoy or group of ships home.

From Swansea, the *Arandora Star* received orders to sail with other ships to Brest as a part of *Operation Ariel*, to bring out any troops and refugees that she could. This was the second of five evacuation trips that Captain Moulton was ordered to make during the month of

June, as Britain faced total defeat in mainland Europe and struggled to assemble as many fighting troops as possible on the islands of the United Kingdom. On all of these evacuation operations, the *Arandora Star* was under threat. She was a large target, and had very little to defend herself with. She relied heavily on whatever escort she was given, but if a U-boat surfaced to fire its torpedoes or deck gun, the *Arandora Star* could engage it with her own deck gun. However, the most regular threat was from enemy bombers.

The evacuation of Brest took place on 16 and 17 June. More than 28,000 British troops were evacuated, and more than 4,000 Allied troops. A convoy of seven ships, commanded by Captain H.F Fuller, arrived in Quiberon Bay, north of Nantes in the Bay of Biscay, at 0700hrs on 17 June. Apart from the *Arandora Star*, a number of liners were being used in the evacuation, including the *Lancastria*, an ex-Cunard liner, and the *Oronsay*, of the Orient Line. Both the latter ships were bombed. The *Oronsay* was the luckier of the two. Her bridge was hit by a bomb, which destroyed the ship's compass, and all her navigating equipment, but she remained afloat. The *Lancastria*, which was waiting for the arrival of an escort, was very heavily laden with an estimated 6,000-9,000 men women and children. She was hit by bombs dropped by a single Ju-88 bomber off the harbour of St Lazaire, and sank within twenty minutes. The sinking resulted in what was then, and still remains, the greatest single loss of life in naval history. Because of the chaos of the moment, no complete list of those lost exists, but apart from thousands of military men, it included civilians, men, women and children. A heavy blanket of fuel oil escaped from the ship's ruptured tanks, and many of those in the sea were suffocated by that. Eyewitnesses say that the Ju-88 returned twice, once to drop incendiary bombs onto the oil in an attempt to set it alight, and once to machine gun the survivors. Less than 1,800 people were saved, and thousands died. The *Lancastria* was heavily overloaded with evacuees, because the order of the day was that these ships should disregard peace time rules, and to pick up as many people as they possibly could for the journey back to England. The loss of life was so great that Prime Minister Winston Churchill imposed a news blackout – Britain was already experiencing its "darkest hour". However, the news of the tragedy soon reached the United States, and was published there. The "D Notice" restricting press coverage was lifted in Britain the following month, and the Daily Mirror of 26 July 1940 reported that 2,823 lives had been lost. In truth, the loss must have been far greater than that.

Captain Moulton and the crew of the *Arandora Star* simply carried on doing their duty. At Brest, the *Arandora Star* picked up only a few passengers, most had already been lifted off. She carried these back to Falmouth in Cornwall. Having re-fuelled, she was ordered again to Quiberon Bay, where she took off about 300 men, and again carried them back to Falmouth. On this return trip, in daylight hours on 18 June 1940 between 1625hrs and 1752hrs, one war diary records: "*Arandora Star* chased by, but escaped from, U-boat". No doubt the *Arandora Star* posted lookouts at all times, to watch for U-boats or enemy aircraft. The *Arandora Star* was a fast ship, and if a U-boat remained below the surface, she was easily capable of out-running it. Since she carried a 4.7 inch cannon, a U-boat Captain would be loathe to surface in daylight.

The *Arandora Star's* fourth trip was to Bayonne, to try to help troops there to safety. She was escorted on this trip by a Canadian destroyer, *HMCS Restigouche*, leaving a little after midnight on the night of 21/22 June. Arriving off the coast of France, enemy bombers were busy overhead, and Captain Moulton was warned to keep moving, rather than provide a stationary target to the bombers, which made picking up troops difficult. The sea between the ship and the beach was full of overloaded craft hoping for a ship to pick them up. Captain Moulton and his crew did their best, and eventually managed to collect about 500 men, and carry them across to Falmouth.

The fifth and final trip was to St Jean de Luz, the last port where there was any hope of getting troops out. Despite the fact that most of the waters off the French coast were now in chaos, it was thankfully fairly quiet when the *Arandora Star* arrived in the small port on the evening of 23 June. Embarkation of the troops began, but had to be stopped at 2100hrs, because there was too much swell of the sea. This had calmed by the following morning, and embarkation restarted at 0700hrs on 24 June. More than 3,000 Poles, many of them airmen, and a number of British refugees were loaded. Captain

Moulton had managed to lift off most of the Free Polish staff and troops who had been fighting their way down the French coast. Just after the *Arandora Star* got clear of the port, the enemy bombers arrived, but happily paid her no attention. Captain Moulton was ordered to Liverpool on this occasion, escorted by the destroyer HMS *Harvester*, where he arrived at 0725hrs on 27 June, and duly disembarked the evacuees.

On 28 June, Captain Moulton wrote a letter home to his three daughters. After wishing them well, and giving them air raid shelter advice, he mentioned that the previous night, whilst they were moored, an enemy plane had dropped a bomb that had missed them by a mere 12 yards. The night of 27/28 June had been, said Captain Moulton, his first night in bed for 28 days: "I allowed 2 fathers and 2 mothers and 2 children to have my bed on our way back from Southern France. They had been chased for days and had lost everything. We brought back 3,500 Polish troops…the old Germans gave out twice on the radio that they had sunk us…We are all in for a very hard time thanks to the old fools who have control of us, and there is only one thing for you to do and that is try and keep safe…"

During the month of June 1940, the *Arandora Star* and her crew successfully ran the gauntlet of enemy attack on five occasions, and brought to safety thousands of men. She had played a significant part in the evacuation of Allied troops who otherwise might have been trapped in Norway, or would have been trapped in enemy occupied Europe. It is worth bearing in mind that the strain upon Captain Moulton, his officers and his crew, must have been enormous during this period. In total contrast to the luxurious days before 3 September 1939, war had now come to the crew of the *Arandora Star* with a vengeance. Time and time again, their lives had been in danger as they had seen war at first hand. The fatigue of the crew of *Arandora Star* must have been considerable when they finally arrived at Liverpool on the morning of 27 June. After carrying a great variety of exhausted troops and civilians, the passenger accommodation and public parts of the ship are likely to have been in a complete mess. The *Arandora Star*, after its refit in 1929, was designed to carry about 400 first class passengers. On her return from Norway, she had carried 1,600 men in addition to the crew, and shortly afterwards had carried 500 from Bayonne, and then over 3,000 from St Jean de Luz. No doubt all these men had stretched out to sleep wherever they could.

It is to be noted that at 2215 hrs on 25 June, having left the contested waters of St Jean de Luz, the anti-aircraft cruiser, HMS *Calcutta* accidentally rammed a Canadian destroyer HMCS *Fraser*, cutting her in half and causing her to sink. The commanding officer of the *Fraser* was said to be: "labouring under intense fatigue". There can be little doubt that most of the crew of the Arandora Star were in a similar condition. Captain Moulton and his crew of the *Arandora Star* were civilians, used to running a luxury cruise liner. Nothing could have prepared them for what they had been through in the month of June. As they docked in Liverpool early on 27 June, every member of the crew must have been longing for rest and recuperation. However, it seems that most of them had only a day's shore leave before their next expedition. For example, Nobby Fulford, normally a bar steward, who had been with the *Arandora Star* since 1933, was discharged from the ship on 29 June, but returned to duty twenty-four hours later. It was on 29 June that the *Arandora Star* received new orders. The once luxurious liner was to become a prison ship for more than 1,200 "dangerous prisoners".

Captain Moulton now found his once beautiful ship reduced to a most unattractive role for which it was ill-suited. He had spent the last month engaged on dangerous but worthwhile rescue missions, helping British and Allied troops and some civilian personnel to return to the relative safety of Britain's shores. Unknown to Captain Moulton, the *Arandora Star* had been originally scheduled to sail for Canada with a cargo of prisoners on 25 June 1940, but her duties on the French coast made that impossible. Having finally returned to port on 27 June for a well-deserved rest, Moulton was informed with virtually no notice that the *Arandora Star* was to be transformed into a prison ship for a large contingent of dangerous enemy aliens, and was to leave unescorted for Canada on 30 June. He received his orders on 29 June, and the *Arandora Star* was expected to sail the following night. Captain Moulton understood that this was an important task – the "dangerous prisoners" had to be removed from

Britain's shores to the security of Canada, where they would not be able to assist in any way with the expected German invasion.

Physically, there was a lot to be done to convert the ship to suit its new purpose, and everything had to be done in a hurry. On board the ship there were going to be about 1,200 dangerous prisoners, a military contingent of 254 guards [a ratio of about one to five] and a crew of 182. These figures are as accurate as they can be, but even now there is little confidence as to exactly how many in each category sailed from Liverpool on 1 July. As well as the usual dangers from without [U-Boats and enemy aircraft], there would now be potential danger from within the *Arandora Star*, where the "dangerous prisoners" would be held. The *Arandora Star* was already painted grey, and had a gun fore and aft as some minimal protection against aircraft or seaborne attack. The luxury of the ship had been stripped away to make room for numerous exhausted troops, but there was no internal security of any kind. In the time available, something had to be done to guard against a rebellion or a break out by the dangerous prisoners. The main precaution seems to have been the spreading of barbed wire across certain approaches to the guns, life boats and life rafts. The prisoners had to be prevented from swarming over the boat deck and commandeering some life boats to escape in. No extra markings had been added to the ship. She was not a hospital ship. There was nothing to indicate that her cargo was enemy prisoners and their guards.

As already stated, the decision had been taken that the *Arandora Star* would sail across the North Atlantic without an escort of any kind. She would zig-zag at high speed through the most dangerous of waters, from Liverpool, around the coast of Northern Ireland and on towards North America. Captain Moulton was well aware of the threat of U-Boats, or attack by air, and protested at his orders, saying that they would have no chance, on their own, of crossing the Atlantic. His protests fell on deaf ears. The first prison ship to sail to Canada, the *Duchess of York*, succeeded on a similar lonely journey. Tactically, there were always two alternatives: to send a ship in convoy or to send it "independently", i.e. alone. The *Arandora Star* was a fast ship, who had outrun a U-Boat before, and she would hopefully attract less attention alone than in a convoy. Convoys were easier to spot, and were regularly being attacked. Perhaps there were not enough Royal Naval ships to provide an escort to a Canadian bound convoy at the end of June. Perhaps it was part of the general mood of panic – get rid of the dangerous aliens by any means possible before the German invasion comes. France had surrendered to the Germans on the 17 June, and the situation had never been blacker. However the fact remains that the *Arandora Star* was carrying more than 1,600 souls on board, of whom 430 were British, and when she sailed from Liverpool, she sailed unescorted, despite the protests of her Captain. Her guns provided some small defence, but also suggested that she was a military vessel.

The prisoners were loaded onto the *Arandora Star* on 30 June. The ship had been due to sail that evening, but in the event she did not leave until after midnight. Probably, the loading and "stowing" of the prisoners, about 480 Germans and about 710 Italians, took longer than expected. All the cabins were used, with six or seven prisoners in each replacing the married couples of peace time. Most slept on palliases on the floor. The upper saloons were also used for prisoners to sleep. Those in the saloons on the upper decks had an advantage over those in the cabins lower down in the ship, they could get outside more easily. Deck houses had been built on the upper decks to provide extra accommodation, and these gave the same advantage.

There was no lifeboat drill before leaving or on the first day of the voyage. For the German and Austrian seamen who were now prisoners of war, this would not have been a great problem. They were experienced in life aboard their ships, and knew how to cope with most problems that might occur. They would certainly have had training in the launching of lifeboats and life rafts should it become necessary. But for the Jewish refugees, and for the Italians it was different. They were not seafarers. Many of the Italians came from the mountainous regions of Italy, could not swim, and had no experience of the sea. They would not know what to do if disaster struck. Similarly, the military guard were soldiers, not Royal Marines. They would need training for life on board a ship, and there is no evidence at all that they had any. Inevitably, the mindset of the guards on board [and of Captain Moulton and his crew] was governed by the fact that their prisoners were twelve hundred dangerous enemy aliens - so dangerous that they had to be removed from Britain. Security had to be the guards' primary concern. Doubtless the guards thought that to bring large groups of dangerous aliens onto the boat deck for boat drill would simply be inviting trouble. Whatever the reason, no lifeboat drill was held, even though there was a substantial danger of the *Arandora Star* being attacked as she steered herself into the Atlantic and towards Canada. It is difficult to find an excuse for this. Even if they had to be brought up on deck in small groups, the prisoners were surely entitled to know the basics of survival should an enemy torpedo or bomb strike the ship.

Amongst the British guards posted to the *Arandora Star* for the voyage to Canada was Corporal Ivor James Duxbery, a Welshman from Carmarthen. Duxbery had served in the Territorial Army before the war, and was now in the Welch Regiment. He had been sent to France after war had broken out as part of a unit intended to hold German prisoners of war once they had been captured. At Rennes, earlier in 1940, he and his unit had built prisoner of war cages intended for German prisoners, but because of the German *blitzkrieg* the cages were never used. Having returned to England, in late June the unit was told that they were going to Canada, and were ordered to Liverpool to board the *Arandora Star.* Duxbery had no problem with guarding the German prisoners, although he was under the impression that they included U-Boat captains and their crews. He clearly did not know of the numerous refugees amongst them. Duxbery was very unhappy, however, about the Italian prisoners. There was a large contingent of Welsh Italians – some of them Duxbery knew and had been to school with. He knew them as decent men and harmless civilians, and thought that they should not be on the same ship as the Germans.

Duxbery was also unhappy with the barbed wire he found on board – according to his account all the lifeboats were covered in barbed wire, and there was barbed wire everywhere. He also complained later that there should have been Red Cross markings on the sides of the ship which there were not. Duxbery and his section were specifically ordered to guard the wheel house against any possible interference [i.e. an attack] by the prisoners. Duxbery was quartered in a very crowded cabin on one of the lower decks, but chose not to sleep there. He slept on one of the upper decks instead.

Amongst the crew of the *Arandora Star* was a Jewish Liverpudlian Assistant Steward, 25 years of age. His name was Abraham Abrahams. Having no doubt been warned of the dangerous enemy aliens that the *Arandora Star* was about to carry, Abrahams must have been astonished by the arrival of so many Jewish refugees.

Nicola Cua said that the Italian prisoners were treated very well by guards, particularly as they began to realise that their prisoners actually were nothing like the dangerous Nazis and Fascists whom they had been told to expect. The Italians, like the Germans, were a very mixed bunch. Young Cua found himself sleeping next to Dr Gaetano Zezzi, the Harley Street doctor. Dr Zezzi happened to be the personal doctor of the Chairman of the Blue Star Shipping Line, and had accompanied him on cruises on the *Arandora Star* in past happier days, yet here he was imprisoned aboard her as a dangerous potential saboteur. Dr Zezzi had suffered the deprivations of Warth Mills with the other prisoners, and now found himself crammed onto the *Arandora Star* like a common criminal. On 1 July, when Captain Moulton discovered that Dr Zezzi was one of the prisoners on board, he was very surprised. Presuming that a mistake had been made, he offered Doctor Zezzi a cabin to himself. The Doctor declined, preferring to share the suffering of his fellow countrymen, but he did accept an invitation to dine with the Captain that evening. Tidying himself up, Dr Zezzi went off to dine with Captain Moulton at the appointed time – there is no record of where they had dinner, it could not have been in the dining room, since that was now a dormitory. Presumably it was in the Captain's own cabin, or elsewhere in the crew's quarters.

The dinner must have been a strange affair. Captain Moulton, having been warned that he was to transport dangerous enemy aliens under armed guard to Canada, had suddenly found out that one of them was a Harley Street doctor of skill and high reputation. Zezzi no doubt told Moulton the truth about the Italians amongst his human cargo - that he was not the only mistake, that there were skilled chefs from the leading London hotels, and all sorts of ordinary people, who were not dangerous Fifth Columnists at all. He no doubt described the ordeal that they had already gone through at Warth Mills. Moulton must have believed that the British Government had gone mad – sending him on a very dangerous unescorted mission to get rid of dangerous enemy aliens who weren't really dangerous at all. It seems that Moulton responded by telling Dr Zezzi of his fears for the voyage – that they were totally alone in dangerous seas with little or no protection from enemy attack.

It is clear that, at every level, it was quickly realised on board the *Arandora Star* that something had gone very wrong with the selection of the prisoners.

The arbitrary nature of the selection of these "dangerous enemy aliens" can be illustrated many times. Raffaele Rossi from Bardi went to work in Swansea, where he opened Rossi's Café. He had three sons, Luigi, Mario and Joe, but only Mario was born in Britain. Therefore when the police came to call in June 1940, they took away Luigi and Joe, but not Mario, who was a British citizen. A friend of Raffaele's, Michele di Marco, aged 50, had arrived in Swansea in 1910, where he set up eventually three ice cream parlours and had two sons, Gerald and Leslie, both born in Britain and therefore British citizens. When the police came to his home, they arrested Michele – despite the fact that his two sons were already serving in the British forces – Gerald with the South Wales Borderers and Leslie with the Royal Air Force. Luigi Rossi, Joe Rossi and Michele di Marco all ended up on the *Arandora Star*.

When Doctor Zezzi returned to his prisoner's quarters after dinner, he reported to Nicola Cua that the Captain was very worried about the safety of the ship, since they were "all alone". Captain Moulton had warned Zezzi to be prepared for anything, a warning that Zezzi passed on to Cua and his other prisoner companions, even though there was little that they could do. For Nicola Cua, the warning didn't sink in – he and his young friends still didn't appreciate the danger that they were in. As Cua said: "Our community were mostly in the catering line, waiters or cooks, nobody knew any routine about lifeboats."

Meanwhile, Gino Guarnieri had found himself in a cabin on A Deck, the lowest of the accommodation decks. He was one of seven men squeezed into the cabin. All the normal cruise furniture had been taken out to make room for the extra occupants. The cabin door was not locked, but there was a guard outside their cabin. It was overcrowded, hot and stuffy. The prisoners were not allowed matches, and had to ask the guard outside to light their cigarettes for them, which he did. Because it was so stuffy [no doubt not helped by the cigarette smoke] Gino slept just in his underwear.

Ludwig Baruch had been taken from the German camp at Seaton directly to Liverpool to be put on the *Arandora Star*. His first impression as he went on board was that it was a beautiful liner. But inside, the boat was a shambles. He was placed in a cabin with three others.

Luigi Beschizza was also placed in a cabin low down on the ship. He was one of five members of the extended Beschizza family who were on board. Luigi had to share with four other older men, and he slept on the floor – or tried to. His four elder companions snored heavily, and Luigi eventually gave up trying to sleep there, and took his pallias out of the cabin, and went up to an upper deck. The guards did not stop him. Luigi found that people were lying down on the floor everywhere, and in one of the saloons he laid down his pallias to join them. He got talking to an older man called Galante, who took young Luigi under his wing and helped him.

Uberto Limentani was put into a cabin on A Deck, with three other Italians. No-one knew where they were being taken to. Once in their cabins, the prisoners had to stay there. There were armed sentries in the corridor outside. During the daytime of 1 July, they were allowed out only once, for a stroll on the deck lasting three quarters of an hour. Limentani looked at the lifeboats that he could see, and noted that they did not look in a perfect state. That was in fact not surprising - the *Arandora Star* had been working hard in various zones of the war throughout June. Limentani's observation was that it seemed that the whole enterprise had had little proper planning or preparation. Sadly, he was absolutely correct.

On the night of 1-2 July 1940, the prisoners lay on their palliases for the second night of their voyage, still not knowing where they were going, but praying that they would remain safe. Their prayers were not answered.

CHAPTER TEN

GUNTHER PRIEN: THE BULL OF SCAPA FLOW

One of those stalking the North Atlantic at the beginning of July 1940 was German U-Boat *U-47*. Its Captain, Gunther Prien, had been for many months the "pin-up" national hero of the German U-Boat fleet. He had been born on 16 January 1908 at Osterfield in Central Germany. His father was a judge, and the family circumstances were comfortable. Prien was later joined in the world by a younger brother and sister. Whatever relations might have been like between Prien's father and mother, Prien's early life was financially comfortable. In August 1914 World War One began, with Prien a mere six years old. The war lasted until November 1918, when Germany was defeated and dramatically changed as a result. As a boy growing up, between the ages of six and ten, the effect of the war must have been traumatic. Added to this was the fact that at some stage, his father and mother parted, and were divorced. Prien went to live with his mother, brother and sister in Leipzig. Life after Germany had lost the war was hard for the young Gunther Prien and his family. Rampant inflation quickly deprived the family of their savings. His mother rapidly became very short of money, and Prien as the eldest child took on work as a delivery boy to supplement the family budget. Prien had fallen from a life of comfort to a life of real hardship, as had very many of his countrymen.

From an early age, Prien longed to go to sea. It is said that his hero was Vasca da Gama, and that he kept his photograph beside his bed. By 1923, Prien was fifteen, and as a result of a spell working as a guide at the Leipzig Trade Fair, he had a modest amount of saved funds. He decided to leave home and to spend his money on a three-month seaman's course at a seaman's college near Hamburg. He duly qualified as a seaman, and, still only fifteen and now penniless, he urgently sought work. Prien's first job was on a sailing ship called the *Hamburg*, working as a general dogsbody and cabin boy. He sailed to America, the Azores and Great Britain between 1923 and 1925, until he experienced what all seafarers dread, a shipwreck. The *Hamburg* was caught in a violent storm off the Irish coast, she was driven onto the rocks and was so badly damaged that she was later written off as a wreck. Prien and the rest of the crew were rescued in the nick of time by the local Irish lifeboat. Prien was only seventeen when he was shipwrecked. It must have been a terrifying experience, and inevitably it must have shaped his development significantly. He had already experienced enough in his young life to bring him to an early maturity, but now he had experienced the horrors of a ship sinking beneath him.

The wrecking of the *Hamburg* left Prien without a job, and therefore without an income. He and his shipmates travelled back to Germany third class. However, Prien was not out of work for long, finding a position as an officer cadet on a freighter called the *Pfalzburg*. Prien was still very young, but was determined to work towards a master's certificate, which would enable him to look for work as a ship's officer – a significant step up the Merchant Navy ladder. Despite not being very happy on board, Prien worked hard and obtained both his master's certificate and a wireless operator's certificate. Then, in early 1929, he obtained his first junior officer's job, as Fourth Officer on the passenger vessel *San Francisco*. He was 21. However, soon after Prien joined the crew, in March 1929, the *San Francisco* collided with a steamer called the *Karlsruhe* not far outside Hamburg. Happily, there was no great damage done to either ship, but Prien believed that he was to be made the scapegoat for the collision when a court of enquiry was called. After an agonizing wait, during which he believed that all that he had worked to achieve might be lost, Prien, the Captain and the First Officer of the *San Francisco* were all called before the Marine Court, but eventually all three were acquitted of any blame, and the collision was deemed to have been caused by the poor weather. Prien remained on the *San Francisco* for the next three years.

Throughout the time that Prien was working on the *San Francisco*, he became very familiar with life aboard a civilian passenger ship. He knew not only how the ship was run, but also how the passengers passed their time, and where they would be at meal times and in the evenings. They were a part of his responsibility as one of the ship's officers. Thus his work in the Merchant Marine brought him intimate knowledge of the lives not only of those who worked on freighters such as the *Pfalzburg*, but also of civilian passengers on passenger vessels. When some years later, he peered through the periscope of his submarine *U-47* at an intended target, he would have been able to visualise the activities of many of the crewmen and passengers that he was about to kill.

Prien worked hard, studied for his Captain's Certificate, and achieved that goal in January 1932, aged 24. He now sought work as a ship's captain, but failed to find a job. Germany was still suffering from a major recession, and work in the Merchant Marine was in short supply. Prien's life and career appeared to be in ruins, despite his enormous amount of hard work. He eventually returned to the family home in Leipzig, and once his meagre savings ran out, he was forced to go on the dole, queuing up at the local *Mietskaserne* office with other penniless fellow Germans for minimal government handouts. Prien was bitter and humiliated – all that he had worked so hard to achieve over the past nine years seemed lost. The unemployed Merchant Marine Captain soon found himself working as a labourer in a succession of work-gangs in the Vogtland. Eventually, he joined the *Reichsmarine*, with the rank of ordinary seaman.

In May 1932 Prien joined the Nazi party. He was like many others who joined the Nazis: a disillusioned, embittered young man who was desperately looking for a way out of destitution and hopelessness. He was no doubt delighted when Adolf Hitler became Chancellor of Germany in January 1933. With Hitler's rise, so did Prien begin his rise up from his ordinary seaman/ labourer's status. He soon became an Officer Cadet. By October 1935, he had a full commission, and with Hitler and the Nazis in power, he transferred to the U-boat force with the rank of *Leutnant* . He was soon promoted to *Oberleutnant zur See*. He saw service patrolling in Spanish waters during the Spanish Civil War, helping Germany's ally, Generalissimo Franco. On 17 December 1938, Prien was given command of a new type of U-Boat, the Type VIIB *U-47*. He had risen rapidly up the ladder of the U-boat force, and was the most junior officer to take command of this new type of U-boat. In the following year, he married. Thanks to Hitler and the Nazi party, his whole life had changed.

When Germany invaded Poland on 1 September 1939, Prien and *U-47* were already on patrol in the Atlantic. They had left Kiel with four other U-boats on 19 August. There was an international protocol in existence in the late 1930s, called the 1936 London Submarine Protocol, which governed how submarines and their commanders should act towards their civilian targets – it had arisen out of the use of submarines in the Spanish Civil War. The protocol demanded that crews of civilian vessels should be taken off the vessel before it was sunk, and steps should be taken to ensure their safety. Immediately Britain declared war on 3 September, Prien began hunting for targets in the Bay of Biscay. At this time, his orders were to observe the London Submarine Protocol, and he did so for his three "kills", the *Bosnia*, the *Rio Claro* and the *Gartavon* on 5,6 and 7 September. Each was a lone, British registered unarmed cargo ship. The crews were allowed to leave the ships, and then the ships were sunk. Prien and his crew returned to port on 15 September 1939, and shortly afterwards he was awarded the Iron Cross Second Class. He was highly rated by Kommodore [later Grand Admiral] Donitz, the chief of Hitler's U-boat fleet. He was soon to be chosen for a task that would transform him into one of the Third Reich's outstanding heroes.

Britain's principal north Atlantic naval base was at Scapa Flow, Orkney, 525 miles north of the Admiralty in London. Scapa Flow had been the home of the British Navy during the First World War, and had never been successfully penetrated by a German U-boat, despite a number of attempts. Two U-boats had been sunk. Scapa Flow is a huge natural harbour. Its two main entrances are Hoy Sound and Hoxa Sound, but there are other smaller entrances also. Most of the defences put in place during the 1914-18 war had been stripped away after that war had been won. Nothing was left of the land defences except empty gun emplacements and casements for searchlights. At sea, by the 1930s, only rusting blockships in some of the smaller entrances to the Flow remained. In October 1937, the British Admiralty realised that if Hitler was intent on a new war with Britain, Scapa Flow would again be of great use as a base for the Home Fleet. However, as stated, there was virtually nothing still in place by way of defences. Nonetheless, Scapa Flow was declared to be a "Category A Defended Port", and work began to try to remedy the lack of defences, and to prepare Scapa Flow to once again hold a substantial naval presence. Booms were laid across the main entrances to Scapa Flow, oil tanks were built to house the huge amount of fuel oil that the fleet would need, and anti-aircraft guns were dug in to protect them. Coastal guns from the First World War were established overlooking Hoy Sound and Hoxa Sound, the main entrances to Scapa Flow. By September 1939, Hoxa Sound, Hoy Sound and Switha Sound were all protected by booms and submarine nets, and controlled minefields and induction loops were about to be laid across the main entrances to the flow [which would allow minefields to be detonated if a U-Boat was detected]. There was significant anti-aircraft cover, and a resident army garrison.

From August 1939, Scapa Flow was in full use, and 44 Royal Navy ships were anchored there, including several battleships, battlecruisers and aircraft carriers. However, there were still weak points in the defences. There were smaller entrances to the Flow, particularly on the eastern side, which were not yet properly sealed. The World War One block ships no longer provided adequate protection – many of them had been moved by storms or had been salvaged or cleared. Four of the smaller entrances awaited new block ships to seal them off – Kirk Sound, Skerry Sound, Weddell Sound and Water Sound.

Kommodore Donitz had a keen desire to send one of his U-boats into Scapa Flow to attack the British Capital ships at anchor there. He believed, rightly, that if successful, such a raid would have enormous propaganda value, as well as hopefully doing significant damage to the British fleet. Scapa Flow had proved to be impregnable in World War One – now Donitz wished to demonstrate that Hitler's Third Reich could penetrate it and strike right at the heart of the British Home Fleet. He ordered aerial reconnaissance of all the minor entrances to Scapa Flow, and eventually concluded that a daring navigator could take a U-Boat through Kirk Sound despite the blockships, and into Scapa Flow. Of course, if a U-boat succeeded in getting in, once its torpedoes were fired and the alarm was raised, it would be far harder to get out again.

Donitz now had to find a U-boat commander prepared to go on what many would regard as a suicide mission. It was the sort of mission that he did not wish to order any of his commanders to perform. He wanted a volunteer. The crew would, of course, have to follow orders, but the commander must share Donitz' enthusiasm for the enterprise. Donitz knew Prien to be an ambitious and aggressive officer. Prien had performed exceptionally well during the summer manoevres that had preceded the war, and he had just won himself an Iron Cross on his first wartime patrol. Therefore on 1 October 1939, Donitz summoned Prien, and explained the mission, code named "Special Operation P".

He outlined the plan to Prien, suggesting entry to Scapa Flow through the block ships in Kirk Sound. There were three block ships in place there, the *Numidian* and the *Thames* left over from World War One, and the *Soriano*, which had been added to the defences in March 1939. From aerial photographs, Donitz believed that there was a possibility that a U-boat would be able to squeeze through at high tide, either between the bows of the *Soriano* and the shore of mainland Orkney, or between the bows of the *Thames* and the shore of the uninhabited island of Lamb Holm, which bordered the other side of Kirk Sound. The possible use of Kirk Sound as an entry point for the enemy had been considered by at least one senior officer in the British Navy, but a survey carried out in May 1939 by HMS *Scott* had reported that: "no risk at present exists of submerged entry…entry on the surface would be extremely hazardous". Nothing more was done to block Kirk Sound.

Once in Scapa Flow, Prien was to commit the maximum damage that he could to the British Fleet. Once he had fired his torpedoes, and the alarm was raised, U-47 was to make its way out by the same route that it had used to enter, and return home. Midnight on 13/14 October was the suggested optimum time for the raid, at high tide and slack water, with the very beginning of a new moon meaning maximum darkness. Obviously, Donitz wanted the attack to take place as soon as possible, before the British could improve their defences, and this appeared to be the ideal night. Prien was given copies of all the latest photographs and intelligence, and was sent away to consider them for a few days, to decide whether he believed the mission was achievable, and whether he wanted to accept the job. It was a mission fraught with danger, whose most likely outcome was the death or capture of all on board the *U-47*. Prien had dinner that night with his new bride, and accepted the mission the following day.

There can be no doubt that Prien was a very brave and exceptionally talented U-boat commander. He was now 31 and had been selected by his commander as being the most likely to succeed in what was a genuine death or glory mission. If Prien succeeded in sinking one or more of Britain's capital ships, and got away with it, he would become a national Nazi hero overnight. He obviously knew this, and it drove him even more to succeed.

Prien's First Officer was Engelbert Endrass, who was later to gain his own command, and to become Prien's main rival as the top U-boat ace. Endrass was one of the few whom Prien briefed on the purpose of their mission before the *U-47* departed on Sunday 8 October from Kiel. The mission was, of course, top secret. As was the practice, *U-47* travelled on the surface at night, and sat on the seabed during the daylight hours.

As it happened, when they arrived off Orkney on 13 October, most of the British Fleet was away from Scapa Flow at sea, hunting the German battleship *Gneisenau*. Also, a German air reconnaissance plane had been spotted over Scapa Flow on 12 October, and of the Capital ships, *Repulse* and *Furious* had sailed at dusk that day because of the possibility of air attack. Only the First World War battleship *Royal Oak* remained in harbour. There were a number of light cruisers, destroyers and auxiliary vessels, and a seaplane carrier called *Pegasus*. The *Royal Oak*, although still packing a mighty punch with her eight 15 inch guns, was no longer considered a front-line battleship. She had been in service for 23 years, and had a maximum speed of just over 20 knots, too slow to keep up with the more modern ships of the fleet. Many of those on board on the night of 13/14 October were boy sailors under the age of 18.

The daytime of 13 October 1939 passed slowly for Prien and the crew of *U-47*. The submarine sat silently on the seabed, 25 miles to the south-east of the entrances to Scapa Flow. The crew now knew what their target was to be. Throughout their voyage from Kiel, day and night had been reversed for the crew of *U-47*. Most of the crew slept during the daytime. 13 October was no different, save that all now knew the dangers that they were about to face. At 1700hrs, with the crew now all awake, a substantial hot meal was served. With action imminent, Prien recorded in the ship's log: "The morale of the crew is excellent".

At 1900hrs, the submarine rose off the seabed and ascended to periscope depth, about five metres below the surface. The world above the sea was in darkness, although the Northern Lights were flickering across the sky. Prien surfaced and scanned the horizon through binoculars. He saw no other ships, and gave the order to continue on the surface towards the entrance of Scapa Flow. Somewhat later, Prien spotted a ship of some sort, which he was never able to identify, and the submarine submerged again. It continued slowly beneath the surface. Eventually, close to the entrance, Prien surfaced again. It was now about 23.30hrs, and high water was expected at 23.38 that night. The more water there was, the better their chance of squeezing through Kirk Sound past the blockships. As the minutes passed, *U-47* crept forward into what Prien believed was Kirk Sound. However, they could only see one blockship, and there should have been three. Then the water began shallowing fast, and Prien realised that he had mistakenly taken *U-47* into Skerry Sound. He quickly turned the boat hard to starboard, and steered out of that Sound.

His second attempt to find Kirk Sound succeeded, and as *U-47* approached the block ships there, Prien had to decide what course to take to try and get through them. There was no time for a considered assessment, and Prien made the instant decision to pass north of the *Soriano*. He described in the ship's log what happened: "…I recognised the cable of the northern blockship [*Soriano*] at an angle of 45 degrees ahead. Port engine stopped, starboard engine slow ahead, and rudder hard to port, the boat slowly touches the bottom. The stern still touches the cable, the boat becomes free, it is pulled round to port, and brought back on to course again with difficult rapid manoevring". Some historians have doubted whether this could be an accurate account of the manoevre· saying that it was close to suicide. There is other evidence that Prien was capable of exaggerating what happened that night. But however Prien achieved it, his success in getting *U-47* through the blockships and into Scapa

Flow was remarkable. If he did scrape both the bottom of the Sound and the mooring cable of the *Soriano*, then he was extremely lucky not to do significant damage to *U-47*, or to become trapped by the cable.

Prien was in, and still undetected. The ships of the British Home Fleet which remained in Scapa Flow were at his mercy. It was a moonless night, but the sky was bright with stars and the northern lights· There was still much to do, and the situation of *U-47* remained perilous every moment that she was in Scapa Flow. The inland sea is huge – eight nautical miles long and six miles wide. The main anchorage for capital ships was north of Flotta Island, nearly five nautical miles away from where *U-47* had stolen into the flow. The blackness of the night now made Prien's task much more difficult as the U-boat crept forward, hunting for a suitable target. He remained on the surface. Eventually, with the time approaching 0100hrs on 14 October, the outline of a large battleship loomed up about 3,000 metres ahead of the *U-47*. It was HMS *Royal Oak*, although Prien was unable to identify it. He and his crew believed that there was a second capital ship behind and to the north of the *Royal Oak*, but they were wrong.

At 0104hrs, Prien fired three torpedoes from his front torpedo tubes at HMS *Royal Oak*, which was broadside on to him. He was later to claim that he was firing at two capital ships, suggesting that he had also fired at and hit the battlecruiser HMS *Repulse*. However, it is clear that in fact there was only one ship there. The nearest other large vessel was HMS *Pegasus*, the sea plane carrier, but she was more than 1,000 metres away from the *Royal Oak*, and almost certainly out of the view of the *U-47*. However, what Prien did not know was that a steam drifter, Daisy II, was lying moored to the Royal Oak on her port side. She was the duty drifter for that day, and was under the command of a civilian skipper, John Gatt. She was blind side from Prien and the *U-47*.

Only one of the three torpedoes fired by Prien struck a target. It hit the very front of the *Royal Oak's* bow and exploded. The strike was two foot from the front of the bow and about ten foot below the waterline. Extraordinarily, nobody on the *Royal Oak* realised that the ship had been hit by a torpedo. The Skipper and crew of the *Daisy II* felt their ship suddenly shaken, and a deep rumble was heard which to their ears sounded like a depth charge exploding not far away. The Skipper, trawlerman John Gatt, hailed the deck of the *Royal Oak*, but the officer of the watch who replied had no idea what had happened. Rear Admiral Blagrove and his officers on the *Royal Oak* investigated, but a U-boat attack was the last thing anyone expected inside Scapa Flow. There was no obvious damage that the eye could see from on board the *Royal Oak*. The second and third torpedoes seem to have quietly petered out in the expansive waters of Scapa Flow. In the minutes that followed, those in command of the *Royal Oak* came to the conclusion that the explosion had either been an internal one, perhaps occurring in the Inflammable Store near the bow of the ship, or possibly an attack from the air. Hundreds of men came up on deck from their bunks, but since they and the ship were thought to be in no danger, they were ordered below again – as it turned out a tragic decision.

Before there was time to confirm the cause of the explosion, Prien fired again. Prien had seen one of his three bow torpedoes strike, and believed that it had in fact struck the second, or more northern, ship that he believed to be there, rather than the *Royal Oak*. He was amazed by the lack of reaction from the ships and in the whole of the anchorage. He decided to reload his bow torpedo tubes, and whilst his crew were doing that, he swung *U-47* around so that he could fire his stern torpedo at the *Royal Oak*. He did so, but for a third time the torpedo missed its target, and disappeared silently into the waters of Scapa Flow.

Good fortune had provided Prien with far more time than he was entitled to expect. He had now fired four torpedoes, had had one hit, and yet there was still absolutely no hostile reaction to his presence in Scapa Flow. With his bow torpedo tubes reloaded, he turned and at 0116hrs fired another three torpedo spread at the broadside silhouette of the *Royal Oak*. It took three minutes for the torpedoes to run between the *U-47* and the *Royal Oak,* and this time two of them struck the old battleship amidships, well below the waterline, and exploded. There was a third big explosion within the ship, probably as the cordite charges in one of the gun battery magazines detonated. The lights went out, and the power failed, meaning that there could be little communication within throughout the ship. Captain W.G.Benn, the Commander and a few of the men began throwing Carley floats and wood that would float over the side, but there was no time to achieve much. Only five minutes after the second explosions, the *Royal Oak* rolled over onto her starboard side. Fourteen minutes later, the hull sank beneath the waters of Scapa Flow, taking the majority of its crew with it. Admiral Blagrove was last seen on deck amidships, helping the men to save themselves. At least 833 men and boys died with her, either killed instantaneously by the explosions, or trapped below decks as she went down, or drowned in the dark, icy, oily waters of Scapa Flow. The depth of the sea at the point that she sank was 16 fathoms [29.3 metres].

The casualties would have been greater in number had it not been for the actions of Skipper John Gatt and the *Daisy II*. After the first explosion, he had remained on deck. When the three further explosions occurred, the *Daisy II* was still moored to the *Royal Oak*'s port side. As the *Royal Oak* rolled over to starboard, the very much smaller *Daisy II* was immediately threatened. Happily, Gatt and his crew were able to cut their ship free from the *Royal Oak* before she was completely lifted out of the water, and she was able to move clear of her giant neighbour. Gatt's report says that the *Royal Oak* rolled completely onto her starboard side within seven minutes, and sank shortly after that.

Skipper Gatt immediately ordered the acetylene lamps in the wheel house to be lit, so that those from the *Royal Oak* now in the sea could see him, and swim towards his small ship. By making himself conspicuous to those in need of rescue, he also made the presence of the *Daisy II* obvious to whoever was the attacker of the *Royal Oak*, but happily *U-47* immediately turned to flee Scapa Flow. Vast quantities of oil were escaping from the wreck of the Royal Oak, and the oil caused the deaths of many of the initial survivors as they struggled in the water. It was impossible to swim through it. Gatt estimated that in some places the oil was eighteen inches thick, and it was very cold. He and his crew threw everything that could float from the *Daisy II* into the sea to try and help the survivors. Although only 17 feet wide and a little over 100 feet long, the *Daisy II* managed to pick 386 survivors from the sea as she crossed back and forth amongst those desperately fighting for their lives in the sea and the oil. She was helped, once they arrived, by boats from H.M.S *Pegasus*. The boats picked survivors from the sea and carried them to the *Daisy II*. Aboard her, they were squeezed into every available space on the little drifter, the holds, the engine room, the boiler room, the cabins and on the deck. *Daisy II* then carried them to the *Pegasus*, where they were given dry clothes, hot drinks and food. Rear Admiral Blagrove was lost, but the *Daisy II* picked up the Captain and the Commander of the *Royal Oak* – both of them in their pyjamas. Skipper John Gatt was subsequently awarded the Distinguished Service Cross for his courageous conduct on that night, an award never normally given to a civilian seaman.

Understandably, having seen his torpedoes hit the *Royal Oak,* Prien decided that the time had come to leave. He left total mayhem behind him, and headed back towards Kirk Sound. His accounts of his ex-filtration in his War Diary and in a subsequent ghost-written autobiography include a certain amount of exaggeration and invention. Prien painted a picture of a battle against low water as he exited Kirk Sound, and of being pursued by British destroyers as he made his way out of the Flow, saying that after the double torpedo strike on the *Royal Oak*: "The harbour springs to life. Destroyers are lit up, signalling starts on every side, and on land 200 metres away from me, cars roar along the roads." All exciting stuff, but not in line with the facts. There were no destroyers chasing *U-47*, and only the *Pegasus* sent a signal about the fate of the *Royal Oak* to the Hoxa Head communication centre.

In fact, *U-47* and its crew made its way at full speed back towards Kirk Sound, still on the surface in the dark of the night. They were not chased, although there must undoubtedly have been considerable tension amongst the crew who expected that they would be. The tide had turned, and the flow of the sea was with the *U-47*. There was still in fact ample water, and according to Prien's war diary, the *U-47* this time passed through the sound under the bows of the block ship *Thames*. As soon as they were out, the *U-47* headed for the open sea, still on the surface. By dawn, Prien was eighty nautical miles from Scapa Flow, and he submerged the *U-47* down to the seabed, one hundred metres below the surface of the North Sea. The first destroyer to arrive off Kirk Sound did not arrive until some forty-five minutes after *U-47* had passed through. Prien and his crew were free and clear.

Prien's exaggeration of his feat was un-necessary. What he and the crew of *U-47* had achieved was remarkable – both the entry and exit through Kirk Sound were very fine feats of seamanship. They had attacked and sunk a British capital ship, albeit a rather old one, within Britain's supposedly most secure anchorage. Prien claimed also to have damaged the *Repulse,* but that was untrue. By the time that *U-47* returned victorious to Germany, the crew had painted a picture of a raging bull on either side of the conning tower, and Prien had assumed the nickname of "The Bull of Scapa Flow", said to arise from the aggressive, bullish stance that he had adopted when pressing home the attack on the *Royal Oak. U-47* entered Wilhelmshaven on 17 October to a rapturous reception. Prien, First Officer Endrass and Chief Engineer Wessels were immediately awarded an Iron Cross First Class, and the rest of the crew was awarded the Iron Cross Second Class. The presentation took place on the deck of the *U-47*, and the medals were bestowed by the head of the *Kriegsmarine*, Grand Admiral Erich Raeder.

The whole crew was then summoned to Berlin for an audience with Adolf Hitler himself. Driving through the city, the streets were lined with cheering crowds. Prien received the Knight's Cross from Hitler, becoming the first recipient ever of this high award. This was followed in the evening by a presentation of Prien and the whole of his crew at the Wintergarten theatre in Berlin, to which all their families were invited. In short, on his arrival home, Prien was feted as a national hero. He was the man who had penetrated the defences of Britain's most protected anchorage and sunk one of its most important ships [although in fact the *Royal Oak* was no longer a frontline battleship]. He became a symbol of Nazi might and success. He and his wife Ingeborg became idolised as the perfect Nazi couple.

The success of *U-47* was an enormous propaganda victory for Nazi Germany. Scapa Flow had had a reputation as being a fortress, impregnable throughout the First World War. It had an additional significance to Germany, because at the end of World War One, the German Fleet, which had surrendered, was imprisoned in Scapa Flow, until German Admiral von Reuter ordered all the ships to be scuttled. Now, within six weeks of the outbreak of World War Two, Prien and the *U-47* had attacked Scapa Flow, had sunk the *Royal Oak*, and escaped unscathed. He was described at the time as being as popular in Germany as England's great sea-faring hero Admiral Nelson was in Britain. Colour postcards were printed with a picture of his head and shoulders on, and he became a pin-up hero. It was enough to turn any man's head, and it is difficult to believe that Prien was unaffected by it.

Gunther Prien, the Bull of Scapa Flow, was now confirmed as Germany's greatest U-boat ace. He was determined to keep his place as the top U-boat commander, and in order to do so, he and *U-47* had to make more kills than any other U-boat. The U-boats judged themselves by the number of tons of shipping that they sank, and their score on each patrol that they made mattered greatly to them, as many more ships would find out to their cost in the coming months.

The *Arandora Star* before the war

E.S. "ARANDORA STAR" TWO-BERTH STATEROOM.   BLUE STAR LINE.

Ballroom :- ARANDORA STAR
THE WORLD'S MOST DELIGHTFUL CRUISING LINER.

First Class Only

Pre-war guests enjoying the luxury of a cruise

Captain Edgar Wallace Moulton

Captain Moulton in happier times

With daughters Win, Joan and Edna, and [R] his wife Priscilla

Below: the last page of his last letter

The *Arandora Star* on military service

H.M.S. *Royal Oak*

The *Lancastria*

A life boat off the *Arandora Star*

H.M.C.S *St Laurent*

Gunther Prien

The Very Reverend Father

Gaetano Fricassi

Franz Stampfl M.B.E.

Michele di Marco

Luigi Rossi   Enrico Muzio singing in his bath

FIGHT FEAR

by
Dr.
AVON

WORRY   FEAR

THE disease of fear is something which is infectious, gripping, persistent. It is a canker that destroys the body and the soul. Anybody consumed by fear is a demoralised creature.

The Daily Sketch June 11 1940

Mr Gaetano and Mrs Rosaria Pacitto

The Pacittos' ice cream business "G.A.Padgett & Sons" in Hull

Padgett's Ice Cream

The Cura/Sartori fish shop in Cupar, Fife

The *Dunera*

Archibald Maule Ramsay, MP, founder of the Right Club.
Was his organisation the real Fifth Column in Britain?

CHAPTER ELEVEN

THE SINKING OF THE *ARANDORA STAR*

On 16 November 1939, the *U-47* under the command of U-Boat ace Gunther Prien had left Kiel to begin its third patrol. It was at sea for a month before returning to Kiel on 18 December. Prien sank a British freighter, a Norwegian tanker, and a Netherlands based ship. Adherence to the London Submarine Convention had been abandoned, and Prien's victims on these civilian ships were left to fight for their lives as each ship sank. Although Prien claimed a higher figure, the actual tonnage of the three ships was 23,168 tons. His fourth and fifth patrol were unproductive, the only kill that *U-47* made being a Danish steamer, the *Britta*, 1,146 tons [although Prien claimed 5,000]. The German torpedoes were proving to be unreliable, and Prien was becoming extremely frustrated as his status as the leading U-boat ace came under threat. To make matters worse, his First Officer, Endrass, had now been given his first command, and was threatening to become as successful a U-boat captain as his old boss.

In that way, the scene was set for Prien's sixth patrol. This began on 3 June 1940, and it was on this tour that *U-47* eventually found the *Arandora Star*. Gunther Prien and the *U-47* left Kiel and began stalking the North Atlantic for victims yet again. On 6 June, the U-47 passed north of the Shetlands, and on 8 June, Prien was directed to the Inner Hebrides together with U-32, because British warships had been spotted in that area. On 10 June, west of Colonsay, they spotted a target, but an attack was not possible. Prien and the *U-47* had now been at sea for a week, and had yet to fire a torpedo. On 11 June, again they found no targets. On 12 June, there was a change of tactics – *U-47* was ordered to join with six other U-boats and to form a "wolfpack", which was to be named *Gruppe Prien* after *U-47*'s illustrious commander. Its orders were to hunt down an Allied convoy code name HX.48, which had left Halifax, Canada on 5 June, and was sailing to Liverpool. The targets of choice for the U-Boat packs were, of course, ships sailing to Britain with much needed supplies. For three days, the *Gruppe Prien* hunted HX.48 without success. On 14 June, the *U-47* found a different convoy, HX.47, which was ahead of HX.48, having left Halifax on 3 June.

Prien fired one torpedo at a tanker, but missed. The *U-47* then tried to follow and cut off the convoy, which was a juicy target of forty-two ships and five escorts, but the convoy outran them – the *U-47*'s submerged speed was insufficient. Finally, on the evening of 14 June, *U-47* spotted a British steamer, the *Balmoralwood*, 5,834 tons, and sank it with torpedoes. At last, after eleven days at sea, U-Boat ace Prien had added to his score. However, he and the *Gruppe Prien* then experienced another five days without anything to fire at, and the *U-47* survived two bombing attacks on 19 June.

On 21 June, Prien's luck changed. He spotted an unknown convoy, which turned out to be HX.49, which had left Halifax on 9 June. This convoy had air cover as well as five escort ships, but Prien surfaced, fired three torpedoes at three different ships in the convoy, and rapidly dived again. One of the torpedoes struck and sank a British oil tanker, the *San Fernando*, 13,056 tons, which was carrying its much needed oil from Curacao to Liverpool. The other two torpedoes missed their targets.

On 24 June, the *U-47* found a small Panamanian freighter, the *Cathrine*, 1,885 tons. Prien missed with two torpedoes, and so surfaced and sank it with gunfire. On 27 June, U-47 attacked the *Lenda*, 4,005 tons, a Norwegian freighter, and the same thing happened again – Prien missed with three torpedoes, and then surfaced and sank it with gunfire. Later the same day, Prien attacked a Dutch tanker, the *Leticia*, 2,580, and again sank it with gunfire. On 28 June, Prien reported to base that he had sunk 33,130 tons of shipping, plus another probable 7,000 tons. In truth, the *U-47* had sunk five ships totalling 27,360 tons. However, to the Germans, Prien's skills were now legendary, and the Nazi propaganda machine announced by radio on 29 June that their U-boat ace had sunk 40,000 tons so far on his patrol. On that same day, *U-47* came across an empty freighter, the *Empire Toucan,* 4,127 tons, sailing in ballast to the United States. Using gunfire until all her ammunition was expended, and then a torpedo, Prien sank her.

Finally, on the following day, 30 June, *U-47* found a Greek freighter, the *Georgios Kyriakides,* 4,201 tons, and sank it with a single torpedo. Prien and *U-47* had now used all their deck gun ammunition, and all but one of their torpedoes. The last of the torpedoes was believed to be faulty.

On 30 June 1940, the *U-47* was ordered to return to base. The U-boat was out of ammunition and effective torpedoes. In the acknowledging signal, Prien claimed to have sunk nine ships, and a total of 51,086 tonnage. In truth he had sunk seven ships, and a total of 35,688 tons, still an impressive score for his patrol.

However, irrespective of the accurate figure for *U-47*'s kills, it was reported by radio to Prien that another U-boat captain had done better. *U-46*, commanded by his old First Officer Engelbert Endrass, had claimed 53,000 tons. This was a red rag to the Bull of Scapa Flow, and Prien ordered that everything possible should be done to repair the final defective torpedo, in the hope that they could find another target on the way home.

Fortune is a strange lady, playing as she does with the lives of so many, ending some purely on a whim and allowing others to continue. War is her fatal companion. What was to happen to the *Arandora Star* on 2 July 1940 was the result of numerous different factors, but one of them was pure ill-fortune. If the *U-47* had not missed with so many of her torpedoes and therefore had not yet been ordered home because her ammunition was exhausted, she would not have been where she was when the *Arandora Star* passed by. If the defective torpedo had proved to be irreparable, it would not have attacked her. If Gunther Prien's ego had not demanded that he beat his former junior officer's score for the patrol, then perhaps U-47 would not still have been in hunting mode.

As it was, on the early morning of 2 July, *U-47* spotted the large and inviting target of the *Arandora Star* off Malin Head, Northern Ireland. She was painted battleship grey and was carrying guns fore and aft. She displayed no lights, and her rear promenade and lower decks were boarded up. She had adopted a zig-zag course which made it obvious that she was a British vessel seeking to dash across the Atlantic. There were no markings to indicate that she was carrying civilians and prisoners of war. On the other hand, the *Arandora Star* was sailing away from Britain. She was not carrying into that war-torn country a vital cargo of supplies. The fact that she was sailing away from Britain, and that she was a passenger liner, strongly suggested that she was carrying a human cargo, carrying evacuees of some kind.

Prien did not hesitate. He was keen for another kill with his last torpedo, and the *Arandora Star* was an easy target. Prien fired the torpedo, and the repairs to it worked. It sped across the ocean towards its target. It struck the *Arandora Star* in the engine room on the starboard side.

On board the *Arandora Star*, at about 0700hrs, most of the passengers were sleeping in their crowded quarters. When the torpedo struck, there was a large explosion, and the whole ship shook. The natural reaction of all the prisoners on board was to head for the upper decks. It was quickly obvious that the ship was mortally wounded and going to sink. The top decks became very crowded, and this initially hampered the launching of the undamaged lifeboats. The military guard cleared the necessary space to enable the lifeboats to be lowered. The official report, submitted by the ship's surviving officers at Greenock on 4 July, stated that there was little or no panic amongst the internees, although there was a marked reluctance by them to jump into the ocean and use the life rafts, once the lifeboats were full.

The most senior member of the *Arandora Star's* crew to survive was Chief Officer Frederick Bertram Brown. He made a formal written statement about the tragedy on 4 July, two days after the sinking. He said that the *Arandora Star* was flying the Blue Ensign with the Admiralty anchor, indicating that it was on British Government Service. Brown said that the *Arandora Star* had actually sailed from Liverpool at 0400hrs on 1 July, that it was doing a No.10 zigzag, and continued zigzagging all the time at a speed of 15 knots. When Brown came on duty at 0400hrs on 2 July, the ship was steering due west. There were four lookouts posted, spotting for U-boats. Brown said that the *Arandora Star* was struck by a torpedo at 0657hrs. The impact was just behind the funnel on the starboard side, in the rear end of the engine room. The engine room began filling up with water very quickly. Brown put the time of sinking as 0802hrs, just over an hour after the torpedo struck. Brown was an experienced seaman, and his timing is almost certainly reliable, but many of the passengers thought that the time between the initial torpedo strike and the sinking of the *Arandora Star* was much shorter. According to Brown two of the lifeboats were damaged as a result of the explosion.

Chief Officer Brown said: "Immediately we were torpedoed the alarms were rung, and within 2 or 3 minutes all the prisoners and their guard were on deck. We had very little deck space owing to the deck houses which had been built for the aliens. The crew were greatly impeded in their work by this and by the barbed wire entanglements about which we had protested before we left Liverpool. My men were slipping the gripes and the next thing we knew, the boats filled with aliens. We fired a shot and got the men out of the boats, and then the crew lowered the boats into the water.. As soon as this was done, the aliens swarmed down the ladders and down the falls and got into the boats. It was almost impossible to do anything with them."

Brown said that twelve boats were lowered, and about twenty rafts were launched. First Officer Hubert Henry Grace successfully got Number 1 lifeboat away, and then returned to the Bridge. Second Officer Stanley Ranson and Fourth Officer Ralph Liddle did the same thing. All three of them died when the ship went down. The Third and Fifth Officers went away with their lifeboats. Brown stayed on the Bridge, and when the moment came that the ship was about to sink, Brown went over the side and swam away from the *Arandora Star*. He survived. The others on the Bridge, including Captain Moulton, were not so fortunate.

When the torpedo struck, Ludwig Baruch was sleeping on the floor with his life jacket as a pillow. There was a terrific bang, he was lifted off the floor by the impact, the lights went out, and the ship immediately began to list. Happily for Baruch and his companions, their cabin was very near to the entrance to one of the decks. Baruch believed that the ship would not stay afloat for long, and therefore went straight to the entrance to the deck, where he was confronted by a sentry with a bayonet on his rifle. Baruch told him to save himself, since the ship was going down. The soldier replied that they had had no orders, and clearly did not know what to do. Baruch went past him onto the deck, where there were a lot of Italians milling around in confusion. The boat deck was wired with barbed wire, and since the weather was fine, Baruch decided that the best thing to do was to get into the water and swim away from the ship, but first of all he threw overboard anything loose that he could find on the deck that might float into the water – timber benches and so forth. The ship was still making way, despite the torpedo, so once safely in the water, the ship would move away from them and not threaten to drag them down. Baruch, who was a very experienced swimmer used to swimming in the sea, and was a fit 23 year old, took charge of his group of friends and companions, and insisted that they get into the water, swim away from the ship, and get hold of floating debris. He warned them to take off, but carry, their lifejackets, since he knew that to jump into the water wearing one was dangerous. Baruch led by example – jumping first into the sea. Eventually most of the others followed him as he swam away from the ship. Baruch found a floating bench, and was joined by a soldier and two other British men, and between them, they managed to get onto it, and all four sat on it in the early morning sunshine.

Luigi Beschizza was sleeping near to his new friend Galante when the torpedo struck, in a saloon on one of the upper decks. He was awoken by the explosion, and thought that the ship had hit an iceberg. Galante soon put him right, and told him to grab his life jacket and put it on. Beschizza got up, and found that there was confusion and bewilderment all around him, but no panic at that stage. He went up to the deck above, believing that if the ship was crippled, they would be taken off. He saw no sign of any member of the ship's crew, but there were lots of people waiting on the deck below him. Many were bleeding, having been cut because when the explosion happened the mirrors around the walls shattered. On deck, Luigi saw some cases of individual panic, but, contrary to what was claimed later, he saw no fighting between Italians and Germans. He remembered the siren blasting "Abandon Ship", and the ship listing sideways. Luigi Beschizza began to run. The next thing that he remembered afterwards was the shock of hitting the water and going under. Sinking down beneath the ocean, he said his last prayers, and heard two big explosions as the ship went down. Beschizza was lucky, somehow he managed to fight his way back up to the surface. He found dead bodies all around him and debris on the water. He was very weak, but he still had his life jacket on, and he could swim. Later, Luigi Beschizza was told how lucky he had been. As the ship had keeled over onto its side, somehow it had catapulted him thirty yards off the deck and into the sea. At some stage, he suffered a big bump on his head. He was wearing his best suit, which had cost him eight guineas, and it became covered in oil.

The first help he found once he had surfaced were some mail bags, which he rested on until they became waterlogged and sank. He then found a piece of wood and hung on to that. Eventually he saw a raft nearby with two men on it. Beschizza tried to swim to it, but was too exhausted. The men on the raft came to him, and he was able to get a grip on it. Eventually, they hauled him onto the raft, utterly exhausted. The raft was about three feet square, probably a table top, and all its three occupants had to sit on it, back to back, with their legs in the water. The sea was thankfully quite calm, although there was a fairly big swell. When the swell went up, they could see nobody else, nothing but emptiness. Beschizza got terrible cramp in his left leg, but there was nothing he could do except suffer, it was too precarious to move. At least he and his companions were still alive. Hundreds were already dead.

Gino Guarnieri was asleep in his crowded cabin on A Deck when he was awoken by the bang of the torpedo exploding. With the explosion, the lights went off, so that the prisoners were left in their cabins in the dark. Guarnieri was in his vest and pants, and couldn't find his pyjamas, so went out into the corridor as he was. There he found panic. It was very difficult in the dark to find any way up to the decks, but eventually, Guarnieri found a staircase and went up it. He made his way into one of the big saloons on the upper deck. There was no panic here. It was crowded, and everybody was wearing a life jacket, and was waiting his turn to go out on deck. Looking out through the windows, Guarnieri saw people jumping into the water. He decided not to join any queue, but to get out onto the deck through one of the windows, which he did. Everything seemed to be happening very quickly. Looking around him, Guarnieri thought that there were not enough lifeboats and rafts for the large number of prisoners, guards and crew on board – enough perhaps for the passengers and crew of a luxury liner, but not for a prison ship such as this. Gino Guarnieri knew how to swim, and his initial plan was to get into the water, swim away from the ship, and hang onto anything in the water that floated. He did not see any barbed wire, and his route was not obstructed by any.

Once out of the window and onto the deck, seeing a life boat lowered down into the sea, Gino tried to get to it by some rope steps. Guarnieri was short and skinny, and he remembered afterwards that a big man had picked him up and put him into the lifeboat. There were about twenty people in the boat. They rowed 200 yards away from the ship, and then stopped. There was a man in charge who then said that the ship was about to sink, and that had they stayed on board they would have gone down with it. The job now was to wait and pick up survivors. There was no panic on board the lifeboat. Its occupants were a complete mixture of prisoners, guards and crew – British, Germans, Austrians and Italians, all united in disaster. As they watched from a safe distance, the *Arandora Star* sank. At first the ship was slanting, and then in mere seconds it went down. Once the water had settled, Guarnieri and the others in his lifeboat began to pick up survivors. There were a lot of people in the water, which was clogged with oil. They picked up as many survivors as they could until the lifeboat was over full. At times they had to stop rowing because there were too many bodies floating in the sea around them. They would reach into the water and look for any signs of life before moving on.

Nicola Cua was sleeping near to Dr Zezzi in one of the upper deck saloons. When the torpedo struck, he was awake, but still lying under a table on his pallias. There was a tremendous explosion. He leapt up and was outside within ten seconds. The immediate reaction was one of total confusion. It was obvious that the ship had been hit, it was already listing, but nobody could see the U-Boat. There was the danger of a second torpedo strike – nobody knew that Prien and the *U-47* were now completely out of all forms of ammunition. Some people tried to lower the lifeboats, but at first there was nobody there who knew what to do. Cua saw one lifeboat being lowered so that it cracked against the side of the ship. The crew of the *Arandora Star* were, of course, familiar with lifeboat drill, as were some of the German prisoners of war. One of these was

Captain Otto Jacob Heinrich Burfeind, Master of the German passenger and cargo ship SS *Adolf Woermann*. In September 1939, when war broke out, Burfeind and his ship found themselves in Capetown, South Africa. He quickly sailed for South America, stopping in Lobito, Portuguese Angola to refuel. There he joined five other German vessels, but could find no fuel. Nonetheless, Burfeind decided to try to reach South America, burning some of the panelling of his ship, and some of its cargo as substitute fuel. Six days out from Lobito, the SS *Adolf Woermann* was intercepted by the light cruiser HMS *Neptune*. Burfeind had orders not to allow his ship to be captured, and therefore evacuated his passengers and crew, and scuttled the ship, denying it and its remaining cargo to his country's enemies. HMS *Neptune* picked up all 162 who had been on board. Burfeind and his crew were taken as prisoners of war to Britain, and later onto the *Arandora Star*. The German crew of the *Adolf Woerman* helped with the launching and manning of the lifeboats after the torpedo struck the *Arandora Star*.

Eventually, a total of ten of the lifeboats were properly lowered and the life rafts were launched. Nicola Cua could not swim, but he and his companions decided to jump into the water anyway. They saw a life raft on the surface of the sea, and decided to jump for it – they believed it was their only chance. Cua was lucky, the sea was quite close to the level of the deck, and his jump wasn't very high. As he went into the sea he managed to catch hold of a rope from the life raft, and hang on to it. A man whom Nicola Cua described as the *Arandora Star*'s ship's carpenter took command of the raft. Cua said this man's conduct was marvellous – if the *Arandora Star* crew list is correct, he was M. Cummings, forty-three years old and born in Dublin. Sitting on the raft with an unlit pipe clamped between his teeth, Cummings helped and encouraged as best he could all those sitting or hanging on to the raft throughout their ordeal.

Cua and his companions watched as the *Arandora Star* slipped beneath the waves. On the bridge, they could see Captain Moulton, together with the German Captain Burfeind doing what little they could for the ship. The old Roman Catholic priest, Father Fricassi, was also there on the bridge, apparently giving comfort and absolution to the seamen in their last moments. Cua could see that there were a lot of people still left on board, and as the ship keeled over, the guns which had been protected by barbed wire, came loose, and the wire and guns slid down the ship sweeping many people with them. According to Cua, the ship slid slowly beneath the waves and disappeared.

Corporal Ivor Duxbery had got on board a lifeboat. He described hearing numerous terrible anguished cries as the *Arandora Star* sank – the dying calling to their mothers and their fathers in their final moments. After the screams of those unfortunates who had been still on board, there was a deathly silence, until a few moments later the ship's boilers exploded, and oil came up to the surface. Nicholas Cua commented that the oil in the sea kept him warm. The sea was cold, despite it being the month of July. The carpenter Cummings did his best, but as the hours went by some of those hanging on to his raft gave up hope, and allowed themselves to float away to their deaths. The ship had sunk not very long after 0700hrs. Cua remained in the water hanging on to the life raft until noon, when finally he was given a place on a lifeboat. He was to survive the sinking, as was his father.

Ivor Duxbery claimed later to have spotted the *U-47*'s periscope out at sea, but before he could draw attention to it, her torpedo hit the *Arandora Star*. He described that Captain Moulton gave the order to lower the lifeboats, ordering also that the prisoners should be evacuated first. Captain Burfeind was with Captain Moulton on the bridge, and they were joined by Major Christopher Aleck Bethell, the commander of the guard. All three of them remained on the bridge, with Father Fricassi, until the ship sank. Witnesses described them as "stepping into the sea" when that happened, but they were, of course, dragged down into the depths of the ocean as the ship sank. Duxbery had a grandstand view of the disaster. He described the lifeboats as covered in wire, and said that some of the plugs had been taken out of them, but there is no support for this. There was undoubtedly wire blocking a number of the gangways leading to the boats, and this proved a significant problem. The German sailors helped the *Arandora Star's* crew, since they were familiar with lifeboat procedures, but because of the prisoners flooding out onto the decks, and the gangways blocked with wire, it was a slow and difficult process. There was no panic on the upper decks, just total confusion as the crew and the German seamen worked desperately to launch the lifeboats. Duxbery and his section remained by the wheelhouse until Captain Moulton told him that there was nothing more that he could do to help, and to save himself.

Duxbery was a good swimmer – he and his section jumped into the sea and swam to a lifeboat. This was floating upside down, but happily Duxbery knew how to turn it over, and he and his section did so. He then took command of the lifeboat, helping survivors to climb on board. Sixty-four in all eventually managed to get onto it. One of them was the film director Mario Zampi, another of those wrongly accused of being a dangerous enemy alien.

Mario Zampi was born 1 November 1903 at Sora, Lazio. He started his film career in Rome as an actor when he was only seventeen, and moved to London in 1923, shortly after Mussolini had taken power in Italy, at the age of 20. After some further acting experience on the stage and in film, he moved onto the technical side, and in 1930 he began working for Warner Brothers' British arm as a film editor. In 1937, Zampi joined with a fellow Italian Filippo Del Giudice in setting up a new film company called Two Cities Films. Del Giudice was a Jewish Italian, trained as a lawyer, who had fled Fascist Italy for England in 1933. Both Zampi and Del Giudice were well settled in England by June 1940. In 1939, Two Cities had released a film of Terence Rattigan's "French without Tears", produced by Mario Zampi. On 7 April 1940, their film "Spy for a Day" was released into British cinemas. Finally, Zampi and Two Cities Films had made a film called "Freedom Radio", which was about the heroism of an anti-Nazi underground radio station, and was strong anti-Nazi propaganda. Despite this both Zampi and his partner del Giudice had been detained on 11 June. For no apparent reason, Zampi was deported on the *Arandora Star*, whilst Del Giudice interned on the Isle of Man. When the *Arandora Star* was close to her end, Zampi jumped overboard and found a bench to cling to floating in the sea which he hung on to. He shared his bench initially with six companions, but lost all but one of them to the sea as the hours went by. Zampi eventually found his way onto Duxberry's lifeboat, and survived.

The following year, in 1941, when Noel Coward began making the famous war film "In Which We Serve", he demanded the release of Del Giudice, Zampi's business partner, who was still interned on the Isle of Man, and got it. Ironically, the film was made under the banner of Two Cities, even though Zampi remained in custody. Happily, when Mario Zampi had survived his detention and was eventually released, he returned to film making, and after the war produced and directed a series of very popular British comedies, working with many of the great British stars of the day, including Alistair Sim, Margaret Rutherford, Terry-Thomas, George Cole and Sid James.

The two sons of Raffaele Rossi from Bardi and Swansea got into the sea, and Joe hung onto his brother Luigi for many hours, holding him up, but it was to no avail. When help eventually came, Luigi was dead. Michele di Marco, whose two sons were serving with British forces, also died.

Franz Stampfl the athletics coach was another of the deportees. After the torpedo hit, Stampfl found a steel plate blocking his route to the deck, but managed to force it aside, before jumping into the sea. He was mentally very strong, and despite the hours in the water waiting for rescue, he survived.

When the torpedo struck, Uberto Limentani was awoken, got up, and tried to calm his frightened companions. He put on his lifebelt, and managed to make his way up to the outside world from A Deck, not an easy feat since the lights were all out, and there were very many people trying to make the same short journey. On deck, there was confusion. Limentani witnessed various efforts to launch the lifeboats, but initially thought that the ship did not look as if it was about to sink. He did not succeed in getting into a lifeboat. After about twenty minutes, it became obvious that the ship was going down. Already many people had jumped into the sea, and the ocean was full of people and dead bodies. One danger was that if someone jumped into the sea with his life jacket on, the impact might force up the cork filled life jacket and break his neck.

After a while, Limentani heard the blasts of the ship's siren that signalled "Abandon Ship". The ship had keeled over onto its right side, and Limentani, who could swim, decided that the time had come to go. He got into the sea from the right side of the ship, and swam away from it as quickly as he could. He was aware of the great danger of being sucked down with the ship when she eventually sank. The water was covered in oil, some of it burning, and with wreckage. Limentani found a bench and hung onto it with a member of the *Arandora Star* crew. The *Arandora Star* turned completely onto her right side, and went beneath the water at the bow, the people still on her decks pouring into the sea with desperate cries. All of a sudden, with a terrible noise, she sank. Limentani had managed to swim far enough away from the ship to avoid being sucked down, and he and his companion kept swimming with their bench for about an hour. They got close enough to a lifeboat to abandon the bench, and swim to the lifeboat, where they were pulled on board. The lifeboat was heavily laden with about 120 survivors.

A post war account, written in 1960 by the author Alistair McClean and based on his interviews with survivors, emphasised the problems caused by the barbed wire, saying that too many prisoners who did reach the upper boat deck found their way to the nearest fore or aft lifeboat blocked by rolls of athwart-ships barbed wire, and went below to find another way up to boats. The press of people below was increasing, the water was rising, and dozens of those who went below were not seen again. Major Bethell ordered his men to clear away the barbed wire in front of the lifeboats – they did so with their rifles, bayonets and with bare hands. Ivor Duxberry still bore scars on his arms many years later from the barbed wire. Also because of the obstructing wire, trained members of the ship's company were unable to reach their boat stations in time. Some of the internees tried to lower the boats themselves, but didn't know how to, and left them hanging half free [like "turkeys outside a poulterer's shop", according to Ivor Duxbery]. The German skipper, Captain Burfeind, marched a group of his men, in column of two, to a number of the lifeboats and lowered several of them in proper order, before he made his way to the Bridge to help Captain Moulton.

The release of the life raft fastenings required a special tool which the prisoners did not have - they tore desperately at them without success. However, a number of the rafts were eventually set loose, and Mario Zampi was one of those who helped with lowering these into the sea. When the *Arandora Star* finally sank, numerous people dragged down into vortex, including those dragged down because they were caught on the barbed wire. The sea was calm and weather fine, but sea was bitterly cold. There were constant weakening cries of "mother" in various languages as people faded and died, killed by the numbing cold of the water, to which their age had no defence, and also from wounds sustained. Some lay face down in their lifejackets in the water, the floating dead.

A minimum of 745 people died as a result of Prien's torpedo - of whom at least 446 were Italians and 146 were Germans and Austrians. Mr Cavadini of the Criterion Restaurant was amongst the Italians who drowned when she was sunk. When Captain Trevor, who had interceded on Cavadini's behalf, asking for his release, discovered this, he wrote again stating: "It is difficult to understand why evacuation [of enemy aliens] was carried out at such headlong speed, which in this case almost certainly caused this man to lose his life."

In the event, the sinking and the great loss of life did not even put Prien ahead on the score sheet, although he claimed that it did. The *Arandora Star* was a ship of 15,501 tons. Added to the other seven ships that *U-47* had actually sunk on this patrol, Prien had reached a true score of 51,189 tons – still short of his rival Endrass's 53,000. However, when the U-47 returned to port, she had the figure of 66,587 painted on her conning tower, purporting to represent the tonnage that she had sunk, and Prien claimed that they had sent ten ships to the bottom of the ocean. According to the author Dougie Martindale, to whom this author is indebted, if Prien's figures had been correct, this would have been the most successful U-boat patrol of the Second World War. On the true figures, however, Prien is demoted to fifteenth place.

CHAPTER TWELVE

SURVIVAL AND RESCUE

Luigi Beschizza had been sitting on his life raft for hours when he and his companions finally saw a plane. Captain Moulton had sent out an SOS message before the *Arandora Star* sank, and eventually a Sunderland plane arrived overhead, hunting for survivors. The plane was carrying emergency supplies: rations, first aid outfits, cigarettes and matches in water-tight bags, which it dropped into the chaos and confusion on the surface of the water where the *Arandora Star* had been, and also messages giving the encouraging news that a ship was on its way to rescue the survivors. Beschizza saw something drop from the Sunderland, and then it flew off again. News soon got round amongst the men floating in or on the sea that help was on its way. One of the lifeboats had a motor, and was circling around amongst the survivors with shouts of encouragement to keep everyone's spirits up. It attempted to distribute the emergency stores, but none reached Beschizza or his companions. Some hours later, a ship came into sight, which proved to be the Canadian destroyer *St Laurent*. Luigi Beschizza believed that he had been in the water for between eight and nine hours by the time she arrived, but it was probably about six hours.

Chief Officer Brown was a fairly good swimmer, and younger than many at 38. He swam first to a piece of timber, and hung on to that with others. He then swam for a life boat, but became exhausted, and happily the lifeboat was able to come to him and pick him up. Each lifeboat was designed to carry 84 persons, but the one he was pulled into had at least 105 on board. At 1400hrs the *St Laurent* arrived. Brown said that the German survivors, many of whom were seamen, had behaved very well indeed. Referring to allegations of panic that appeared in the morning newspaper reports on 4 July, Brown said: "There is absolutely no truth in the statement that German prisoners were pushing the Italians out of the way, nor did I notice any fighting between Germans and Italians."

Ludwig Baruch sat on his bench with his companions until the plane arrived overhead, and then waited confidently for rescue. The significant difference between Baruch and many of the other survivors was that he had no fear of the sea, and was a confident and experienced sea swimmer. Having survived the sinking, he knew that it was only a matter of time before they were rescued, and it was a fine July day.

H.M.C.S.*St Laurent* arrived at the scene between 1300 and 1400hrs. She was guided over the last sixteen miles to the area by a Sunderland flying boat, which then remained on the scene, guiding the St Laurent to the survivors. On reaching the position, the *St Laurent* reported that ten lifeboats, all fairly well filled, were gathered together in a group, whilst westward of them for two or three miles the sea was littered with rafts and small wreckage, to which were clinging many survivors, singly and in small groups. The survivors in the water or clinging to wreckage were covered in fuel oil. The *St Laurent* faced a difficult and dangerous task. She had to sort out those still living from the dead in the sea, and to rescue the living from the lifeboats, the rafts, and the sea. At the same time, she had to remain alert to the fact that the same U-Boat that had sunk the *Arandora Star* might still be lurking beneath the water, waiting to pick off any vessel that came to the rescue. The *St Laurent* initially kept moving as she lowered her own boats to rescue the survivors. Eventually she stopped, because of the sheer numbers of survivors in the sea around her. The work was painfully slow, and few of the survivors in the sea had any strength left to help themselves. In many cases it was necessary to put a man from the *St Laurent* lifeboat into the sea to pass a line around a survivor and pull him bodily inboard the lifeboat. Some were very heavy, with soaked clothing and covered in oil. Once fully laden, the *St Laurent* lifeboats made their way towards the ship, where those that they had saved were taken on board. Rope netting was thrown over the *St Laurent's* sides, for the survivors to climb up if they were able. Hundreds of survivors were being brought on board, and very quickly, every corner of the ship was crowded with wet and exhausted men. The lifeboats returned time and again to rescue more survivors. They continued working until 1555hrs, when the Sunderland flying boat finally reported that it could find no more survivors in the sea.

Gino Guarnieri was in his lifeboat when the plane came over – at first they all thought it was a bird, but were delighted when soon they realised that it was a plane, and a British one. They waited for rescue, and eventually the *St Laurent* appeared. Guarnieri described how the destroyer threw down nets on the side of the ship for them to grab onto, but getting on board was not easy. It was necessary to make at least a yard in distance up the net when you grabbed it, or the climber would get crashed against the ship, which was still under way. Guarnieri had nothing but praise for the Canadian crew. Once aboard, he and his companions had to wriggle down through a manhole, one at a time – he was still dressed only in his underpants. They were given a ration of rum and chocolate to revive them as soon as they arrived. Guarnieri got talking to a member of the crew of the *St Laurent*, who dampened his spirits a little by telling him that the danger of the *St Laurent* being torpedoed was about 50/50. The ordeal was not over yet. Guarnieri was given some temporary clothing, and at Greenock, he was given a military uniform, with a red mark on the back to indicate prisoner of war – which he was not.

Baruch was picked up by lifeboat, and then managed to climb up a rope ladder onto the destroyer. Once aboard, like Beschizza he was sent below to get food and get a drink. Baruch met the helmsman from the *Arandora Star* on board, and discovered that he was a member of the Liverpool communist party whom in fact Baruch knew. Baruch rightly felt that made a nonsense of his own situation – he was being deported because he was an active communist, and yet one of those taking him there belonged to the same political party.

Once on board the *St Laurent*, Luigi Beschizza ended up in the boiler room. By the time he got there, the ship's supply of rum was already exhausted, and Luigi was given some hot broth. All of the survivors described the crew of the *St Laurent* as being marvellous to them – they treated all the survivors the same, whatever their nationality, giving them rum, hot soup and dry clothes. Having begun to warm up, Luigi and the other survivors started to look for their friends and relatives. Very many of them were missing. Happily, Signor Galante, who had befriended Luigi Beschizza on the *Arandora Star* had survived, and was able to tell Luigi what had happened to him when the *Arandora Star* had sunk. The ordeal was not yet over, however, since the very crowded *St Laurent* had yet to deliver them all safely to dry land. Prien and his *U-47* might have gone, but there were many other U-Boats preying on British and Allied vessels in the North Atlantic.

Nearly all the survivors were stowed below, filling all the messes, the Officers' Quarters and one boiler room, but a number were obliged to remain on deck and were made as comfortable as possible. Some of the surviving cooks from the *Arandora Star* worked alongside those on the *St Laurent* to provide a hot meal for the survivors, who had last eaten the evening before. Two of the survivors turned out to be doctors: Dr Ruhemann from Germany and Dr Otvos from Austria. The report from the *St Laurent* paid tribute to their efforts. They worked throughout the night attending the sick and injured, giving the greatest possible assistance. The survivors, including four who died on board, were successfully landed at Albert Harbour, Greenock, on the morning of 3 July.

Safely arrived at Greenock, Baruch and the other survivors were disembarked. Those who needed hospital treatment were taken to hospital, and the other prisoners were put into a warehouse, which Baruch described as cold and dark. He was grateful to a Salvation Army clergyman who came and gave everybody postcards, so that they could notify their loved ones that they were safe. Baruch described their guards as first class - very sympathetic to the dreadful experience that the prisoners had been through. From Greenock, Baruch was taken to Edinburgh. There, he was held in a tented camp, very well fed, and given a British army uniform, marked with the appropriate flashes to indicate that he was a prisoner. Baruch was held there for 9-10 days. He commented that he was exhausted, and slept a lot.

Uberto Limentani's feet had swollen, and when asked if he needed to go to hospital, he said yes. That proved to be a good decision. The other prisoners were taken away, but Limentani, together with about 60 other Italian survivors and some 70-80 Germans were sent to the Mearnskirk Emergency Hospital, in Newton Mearns, Glasgow, where they received good medical treatment. After eight days at the hospital, most of the prisoners, including Limentani, were transferred to a camp in West Coates, Edinburgh. Limentani stayed there from 11-31 July. They were the lucky ones.

Poor Limentani was reported as dead by the War Office when they drew up a very inaccurate list of the missing and the survivors. They could not even get the camp at which he had been detained right, stating that he had been brought to the *Arandora Star* from Southampton. Nor did they have any prisoner number for him. For more than 250 of the Italian prisoners that they had sent off on the *Arandora Star*, the War Office apparently did not know their camp of origin.

In fact more than four hundred Italians had been lost. Many of them were from Scotland, and at Greenock, Guarnieri said that all the Scottish relatives came to the quay in a state of distress and were asking about their relatives. At this stage, everything remained very confused, and even the surviving prisoners did not know how many had been lost. Even today, the figures for the loss of life on the *Arandora Star* are not entirely certain. The most accurate figure for those Italians lost is probably 446. In addition, 146 Germans and Austrians died, 58 of the *Arandora Star*'s crew, and 95 of the guards. Guarnieri explained the heavy loss of Italian lives by saying that most of them had been at the bottom of the ship i.e.in the cabins on A Deck, and that they were mountain farmers by origin, couldn't swim and didn't want to go into the water. They had wanted to chance their luck on the ship in the hope that it wouldn't sink.

CHAPTER THIRTEEN

LOSSES FROM THE ARANDORA STAR:

The total loss of life that resulted from the sinking of the *Arandora Star* has always been difficult to calculate. No accurate manifest of the number of prisoners on board was prepared before the *Arandora Star* left Liverpool. Nor does there appear to have been a definitive list of the guards, and estimates of their number vary. Many bodies sank with the *Arandora Star* to the bottom of the North Atlantic, and were never recovered. Others were borne away by the sea. Over the months that followed the sinking, bodies from the *Arandora Star* were washed up on the Irish coast, and as far north as the Hebrides, in particular on the island of Colonsay. Some were identifiable, even after weeks in the sea, from their possessions, others were not. A number of lists of the casualties have been drawn up, initially by the British Government, and later by various other bodies and historians. Nearly half of those on board died. The most reliable figures are given in the previous chapter. The worst casualties were amongst the Italians. Two thirds of the Italian prisoners died - for every three Italians who was marched up the gangplank onto the *Arandora Star*, only one survived. Prisoner Mariano di Marco, whose café in Hamilton was one of those that had been smashed up on the British *Kristallnacht* was one of them. He had been arrested, given the number 14702, and held in the internment camp in Edinburgh. From there, he was taken to Liverpool. During the days that he was held prisoner following his arrest, Mariano di Marco was no doubt extremely anxious to know how his family was, but it is very unlikely that he heard anything of them, or they of him. He was shipped off on the *Arandora Star* as a dangerous enemy alien, and lost his life when that ship was torpedoed on 2 July 1940. He was 42 years of age.

In total, one hundred and forty-six of Prien's fellow Germans and Austrians died. Four of them, Rolf Baruch, Rudolf Gellert, Eduard Rudolf Gumplowicz and Heinrich Holmes, were only seventeen years of age. The oldest were in their sixties. Although many of the Germans and Austrians were refugees from the Nazi regime, mostly Jewish, there were also German prisoners of war such as Captain Burfeind and his crew, and some genuine Nazis on board. Captain

Burfeind died trying to save those on the *Arandora Star* from the effects of the torpedo that his fellow countryman Prien had fired. Five others of his crew, including a musician and a ship's cook were lost.

Another of those who died was the unfortunate Frank Hildesheim, the British passport holder who had been arrested under Regulation 18B, and then sent to Seaton internment camp. Having briefly been re-united with his wife in Brixton Prison before he was relocated to Seaton, Hildesheim was never to see his wife again. Despite being a British citizen, he was unlawfully sent from Seaton onto the *Arandora Star* for deportation, and died when it was sunk. His wife Helga received a letter from him at Seaton dated 29 June 1940, saying that he was about to be moved, but didn't yet know where to. She never heard from him after that, and it was months before she knew his fate. Any protest that Hildesheim may have made was not heard, and he sailed from Liverpool on the night of 30 June/1 July. At best, his deportation resulted from chaos at a time of national panic. His fate was not very different to that of his sister Martha, who was a teacher. She died in a Nazi concentration camp at Theresienstadt, Czechoslovakia in 1943.

Other losses included documented enemies of the Nazis. One was Bertold Bloch, a refugee German whose 40th birthday would have been three days later on 5 July. There can be no doubt that he was an enemy of the Nazis, because his name appeared in the *Sonderfahndungsliste,* more commonly known as the Nazi Black Book or Most Wanted List. In preparation for an invasion of Britain, the Nazis had prepared a booklet which listed the names of those in Britain who were to be arrested following the German invasion. This list was discovered in Berlin at the end of the war. It is believed to have been prepared between 1937 and September 1939, and updated in the months before the intended invasion. All those listed were to be immediately arrested following the German invasion, and it is likely that few would have survived. Many of those in the "Black Book" were refugees from Germany and Austria who had arrived in Britain– either Jews, or those believed to hold anti-Nazi views. The idea of the list was to purify Britain of all those believed to be anti-Nazi. The information upon which the list was based apparently came from a variety of sources. Some of those in the Black Book had made public statements against the Nazis, some featured in newspaper articles as anti-Nazis, some reportedly held views which clashed with Nazi culture. But also, the Nazis used information obtained through their own intelligence sources. That included information that they received from British Fascists.

Another of those in the Black Book who died on the *Arandora Star* was Professor Dr.Curt Sigmar Gutkind. Gutkind had been born in Germany in 1896, and had done military service for Germany in the First World War, which left him permanently disabled. He had fled Germany in 1933 as a result of the Nazis rise to power. He went first to France, and then to Britain in 1935. Gutkind was a Jew and an academic. He was a Doctor of Philosophy from Heidelberg University, and a Doctor of Literature from London University. He had held an Italian passport until 1938 as a result of a period of academic work in Italy. Then, because he was Jewish, he lost his passport as a result of Mussolini's anti-Jewish laws, introduced that year.

Upon arrival in Britain in 1935, he had obtained an academic post at Oxford University, and by the time that war broke out, he was the Head of the Italian Department at Bedford College, London. He had applied for British naturalisation as soon as he was able to do so, January 1940, supported by excellent British referees. In the confusion in Britain that followed Italy's declaration of war on 10 June, Gutkind was treated as an Italian, and was swept up in the mass arrests that Churchill had ordered. He was sent to Warth Mills Camp, and despite his representations and those of Bedford College, he was marched onto the *Arandora Star* on 30 June. He did not survive its sinking. Thus Gunther Prien's torpedo brought about the deaths of two of the Nazis most wanted men.

Amongst the hundreds of prisoners who died, three others were also British citizens who should never have been on the ship in the first place. One of them was Antonio Mancini, who was aged 54. Mancini had arrived in Britain at the age of 12, 42 years earlier. He was married with six children. He had been naturalised British in 1938. Despite all that, he was unlawfully arrested on 15 June 1940, and was unlawfully deported on the *Arandora Star*. He had had no chance of a tribunal hearing, and all protests that he may have made were in vain. It is inconceivable that Mancini did not mention his British citizenship when he was arrested, but he was clearly ignored. There was no hesitation in sending him to Canada, despite the fact that he had a wife and large family in Britain. He was taken from them, and deported alone, and did not survive the sinking. A Home Office memorandum later described his deportation on the *Arandora Star* as a "most regrettable mistake". The Home Office was forced to accept that Mancini was illegally arrested, illegally detained and illegally deported and lost his life as a direct consequence of those illegal acts. Six British born children were illegally deprived of their father.

Gaetano Antonio Pacitto was another British citizen. He was seized from his home in Hull on 10 June, and, despite being a British citizen with a wife and nine children who had lived in Britain for 45 years, he was illegally deported. He died when the *Arandora Star* sank. To add to the suffering of his family, his whereabouts and his fate were still not known by 8 October 1940, when his MP asked a question in the House of Commons. Only then was it finally confirmed that he had been deported and lost on the *Arandora Star*. Nine British born children were illegally deprived of their father.

There was a third British citizen aboard the *Arandora Star*, a younger man called Giuseppe Parmigiani, who was 27. He had been born in London on 9 July 1912, and his address was 42, Old Compton Street, Soho. He was unlawfully interned on 15 June 1940 as a part of the wave of arrests, and was unlawfully deported on the *Arandora Star*. He too died when she sank. He left a wife and two young children.

As far as the author has been able to discover, only the Pacitto family received any compensation from the British Government. They took action for the sum of £4,500 in compensation, plus costs. The Government's policy was that they would not offer compensation to anyone, but would settle a claim if it was brought. Only Pacitto's family brought a legal claim.

There were many others who died whose detention and deportation had been lawful, but unjust. Decio Anzani, the veteran anti-Fascist

Italian for whose freedom and protection Mr Gillies of the Labour Party had been campaigning, was one of them. The famous tenor, Enrico Muzio also died. His body was eventually washed up on the Hebridean island of Barra. The long time resident of Hamilton, Scotland, Silvestro D'Ambrosio, 67 years of age, also died. He had five British born sons.

There were numerous chefs and hoteliers amongst the Italian prisoners, and many of them died. The West End of London lost Italo Zangiacomi, 61, the general manager of the Piccadilly Hotel, who had opened the hotel in 1910, and therefore was a resident of 30 years, who should not have been interned and deported; Cesare Maggi, 53, the restaurant manager of the Ritz Hotel; Carlo Borgo, 43, the manager of the Café Anglais in Leicester Square; Ettore Zavattoni, 57, the banqueting manager of the Savoy; Giuseppe Benini, 59, the co- manager of the Hungaria Restaurant; and Giovanni Sovrani, 57, the owner of the Normandie Restaurant in Jermyn Street, who was Vice Consul for the independent state of San Marino, and therefore enjoyed diplomatic immunity and had been illegally interned and deported.

Fifty-eight of the crew had died, many of them seamen who had served on the *Arandora Star* in her pre-war role as a luxury liner. They were all civilians, and, as one would expect in the Merchant Navy, came from a number of different countries, including Australia, Canada, Denmark, New Zealand and neutral Eire. Since she was a civilian vessel, some of the crew were very young. D.Nicholls, a Deck Boy from Liverpool was only 15; Frank Pike, a Pantry Boy from Newcastle, was 16, as was L.Taylor, a Scullion, from Brecknock Water. Thankfully, those three survived the sinking. Three of their young workmates, Pantry Boy Henry Davies from Liverpool, Steward's Boy J.Firth from Birmingham, and Sailor Leonard Ernest King from Southampton, all aged 18, were lost. Two brothers from Portsmouth also died: William Halson, aged 28, and Jack Halson, 19. No doubt there would have been a family celebration when young Jack Halson joined his elder brother on the *Arandora Star*, but Prien's torpedo turned celebration to tragedy. The Master, Captain Edgar Wallace Moulton [54] went down with the ship, and the First Officer, Hubert Henry Grace [51], the Second

Officer Stanley Ranson [41], and the Fourth Officer Ralph Liddle [27], were also lost. After the tragedy, all these four were posthumously awarded a Lloyds Medal for Bravery at Sea, awarded by Lloyds of London, together with the Third Officer W.H.Tulip, 29, who survived.

A good indication of the confusion which prevailed as the *Arandora Star* left Liverpool is the fact that there appears to be no clear record of how many British guards were on board. Various figures have been mentioned in reports of the tragedy, and it seems that the most likely one to be accurate is 254. This figure is mentioned by two of the crew survivors, Chief Officer Frederick Bertram Brown and Chief Engineer R.C.Connell. Captain H.G.de Wolf of *HMCS St Laurent* recorded that he landed 5 officers of the guard and 157 men at Greenock after the rescue. If those figures are correct, 92 of the guard perished when the *Arandora Star* went down. However, the generally accepted total of deaths is now 95. The Commander of the Guard was Brevet Major Christopher Aleck Bethell. Born in Greater London in April 1893, he had been commissioned into the Royal Scots Fusiliers on 15 August 1914, shortly after war had broken out. He was a First World War veteran, having served with his regiment in France. He was twice wounded, and as a result he was medically downgraded, and was transferred to garrison duties in India. By 1921, Bethell had recovered sufficiently from his injuries to transfer to the Tank Corps with the rank of Captain. He retired in 1936, but remained on the reserve list, and was recalled to arms when the Second World War broke out. He was given the rank of Brevet Major, and was placed in command of a unit whose duty would be to escort detainees and prisoners of war to new camps in Canada. In July 1940 he was 47, apparently the oldest of the military guard, as well as its commander. He died as he stepped off the bridge of the *Arandora Star* as she sank, together with Captain Moulton and Captain Burfeind. Before going to the bridge, he was seen to give his lifebelt to a deportee who had not got one.

The men under Bethell's command came from a variety of different regiments, and some had been rescued from Dunkirk only a few weeks before the *Arandora Star* left Liverpool. The youngest of them was 17year old Private Peter Clarke of 4 Battalion, the Devon

Regiment, who had grown up in the lovely village of Kentisbeare in Devon. He lost his life when the ship went down, and his body eventually washed up on Keadue Strand, in County Donegal in late August. Peter Clarke was the youngest of nineteen soldiers from the Devonshire Regiment who died on the *Arandora Star*. Since he was only seventeen, it is probable that he lied about his age when joining up. It was a sad fate for those who had survived Dunkirk, and for the others, some of whom most probably died in the service of their country without ever firing a shot in anger.

The total loss of British and Irish lives on the *Arandora Star* was therefore one hundred and fifty-three, more than the German/Austrians, but only about one third of the number of Italian lives lost. Arguably, the ninety-five British servicemen were the only legitimate casualties on Gunther Prien's scoresheet. All of the rest were civilians or prisoners.

Sadly, when the sorry story of the loss of the *Arandora Star* was reported in the press on 4 July, the truth was deliberately distorted for propaganda purposes. Lurid stories appeared, alleging that the Italians and Germans had fought each other for a place in the lifeboats, and that there had been mass panic on the behalf of the Italians. There was a celebration of the fact that this was an attack by a German U-Boat on fellow Germans, and there was no mention of the fact that there were more British casualties than German. The Daily Express of 4 July 1940 was perhaps typical. The headline read: "Germans torpedo Germans" and an allegation followed that 1,500 aliens had panicked [there were only 1,200 on board]. The press suggested that the panic and fighting amongst the aliens led to the heavy loss of life.

CHAPTER FOURTEEN

REACTION AND AFTERMATH

The reaction of the British Government when it heard of the loss of the *Arandora Star* was not one that did them any credit. The Admiralty would have known of its sinking soon after it happened, an SOS message had been sent out, a search plane had been sent, and the *St Laurent* raced to the rescue of the survivors. The Government must have known well before the end of the day. On the day after that, 3 July, the same day that the survivors of the *Arandora Star* were landed at Greenock, the British Government, despite knowing the fate of the *Arandora Star*, sent another deportation ship out from Liverpool, overloaded with prisoners.

21 year old Joe Pieri, from Glasgow, who had witnessed the smashing up of his family's café, had not been sent on the *Arandora Star*, but he was amongst those selected for the next prison ship due to leave. It was the S.S.*Ettrick.* which had been working alongside the *Arandora Star* on the evacuation of North West France. The *Arandora Star* having been torpedoed on the early morning of 2 July 1940, the *Ettrick* set out on an identical journey on the following day. Joe Pieri was on it. He described the ship as being badly over-crowded [as the *Arandora Star* had been]. There were 2,600 prisoners on board – a mixture of internees and prisoners of war. The *Ettrick's* crossing to Canada was very rough, and lasted two weeks. It had apparently been a complete lottery as to which ship the Italian detainees went on. Poor Joe Pieri's parents, back in Glasgow, did not know whether he had sailed on the *Arandora Star* or another ship, and for a month did not know whether he was alive or dead. Happily, the *Ettrick* reached Canada safely, and Joe Pieri survived. He was to remain a prisoner in Canada for three years, however, and did not see any of his family during that time. The S.S.*Ettrick* safely returned from Canada, but she was sunk on 15 November 1942 by U-Boat 155, in the Atlantic.

A memorandum dated 2 July from Neville Chamberlain, now Lord President of the Privy Council, to the War Cabinet, made recommendations for continuing the policy of deportations. It was issued after the first news of the sinking of the *Arandora Star* had been received. A meeting of the War Cabinet was due to take place the following day. Chamberlain began by reminding his colleagues that it was Prime Minister Churchill's impetus that was behind the rush to deport as many enemy aliens as possible. He stressed that since 11 June, every effort had been made, on the direction of the Prime Minister, to arrange for as many of them as possible to be sent overseas. Chamberlain argued strongly against a memorandum that had been previously submitted by Sir John Anderson, the Home Secretary, who had adopted a far more humane view. The Home Secretary had suggested that proper care should be taken in the selection of the candidates for deportation, and expressed the view that no internees should be sent overseas if they fell into one of three categories: [i] Men required for war production; [ii] Men interned in error; and [iii] Married men with wives and children in this country upon whom special hardship would be imposed by separation [this would apply to the large majority of Italian restaurant and café owners]. Anderson also expressed the view that special care should be taken not to mix Jews with Nazis or Fascists in the contingents sent overseas. The Foreign Office agreed with his approach.

In his 2 July memorandum, Neville Chamberlain urged that there was no time for such niceties – inferring, although not saying in plain words, that fairness and humanity must take second place in Britain's hour of need. Summarising the present situation, Chamberlain said that by now, practically all Category A and B Germans and Austrians had been interned, and that the Category Cs were in the process of internment. 4,000 Italians had so far been interned. Chamberlain supported Churchill's view that the enemy aliens should be cleared out of Britain as soon as possible. He argued that it would be quite impossible to vet the internees selected for shipment if the deportation sailings already fixed were to be adhered to. The next sailing was to be the *Ettrick* to Canada on the following day, 3 July, with the intention that she should carry 858 Class B Germans, 1,348 German prisoners of war and 405 young single Italians. A fourth ship, the *Sobieski* was due to sail for Newfoundland and Canada on 7 July, carrying 450 German prisoners of war, and 1,000 single Germans between the ages of 16 and 40. The latter would be mainly Class B, but would also include some Class C – those who had been found by tribunals to be of no threat whatsoever. A fifth ship, the *Dunera* was due to sail for Australia on 7 July, and two other ships were due to follow her there later in the month. Chamberlain argued that, apart from the need for speed, if all the categories suggested by the Home Secretary were excluded, it would be impossible to fill the accommodation on the deportation ships. In reality, the *Duchess of York* and the *Arandora Star* had been grossly overcrowded, and so were the ships that followed.

Ironically, on that same day, 2 July, Mr Shakespeare, the Deputy Secretary for the Dominions told the House of Commons about the efforts being made by those responsible for the Children's Overseas Reception Scheme – this was a scheme to transport thousands of British children aged between 5 and 16 to the safety of the Dominions on a series of ships. These were, of course, to be evacuations, not deportations, but there were obvious parallels between the two operations. Mr Shakespeare emphasised the need to avoid being panicked into overhasty and disorganised action, saying: "The Committee will have noted comments from certain quarters that we should proceed at the speed of Dunkirk. My view is that if, in our eagerness to proceed as quickly as possible in this task, we dispense with all provision for the welfare and safety of our children, sending them overseas without selection or medical tests, rushing them to the ports and herding them like cattle into any ship we may find, we shall be guilty of a gross breach of trust. So long as my Board and I are administering this scheme, we shall not countenance anything of that kind." Mr Shakespeare, perhaps aware of the panic in relation to the deportation of enemy aliens, but probably in ignorance of the loss of the *Arandora Star*, was stating the obvious – this sort of operation required careful execution including proper selection and medical checks. That was exactly what the panic to deport enemy aliens did not have.

The War Cabinet met on 3 July. After discussing Chamberlain's memorandum, they over-ruled the view of the Home Secretary Sir John Anderson, and decided that the current shipments of internees to Canada and Australia, should go ahead, even if this meant the deportation of some in Anderson's proposed categories for exclusion from deportation. The War Cabinet decided that the fate of the

Arandora Star would change nothing. They did however agree to delay the shipment of internees to Australia for a few days to enable these internees to be more carefully selected. The Foreign Office was not happy. Endorsed in the margin of their copy of the War Cabinet's conclusions, alongside the word "selected", is the comment: "selected by whom, when and under what principles?" The War Cabinet specifically approved the sailing of the *Ettrick* to Canada that same day, 3 July. The Cabinet was reminded that the *Ettrick* was due to sail unescorted. Despite the fate of the *Arandora Star*, the War Cabinet confirmed that the *Ettrick* would proceed unescorted.

As an illustration of the impossible burden on Winston Churchill, it was on this day too, 3 July 1940, that the Royal Navy attacked and eliminated the fleet of its erstwhile ally France, thereby causing the deaths of very many Frenchmen. Now that France had surrendered, Britain simply could not risk the French ships falling into the hands of the Nazis.

On 7 July, yet another deportation ship sailed for Canada. This was the *S.S. Sobieski* carrying 450 German prisoners of war and 1,000 "single Germans", chiefly Category B but "possibly" C. The major clear out of aliens which Churchill was pressing for was continuing. In truth, numerous non-dangerous refugees were now being exported across the North Atlantic as quickly as possible.

The *Dunera's* departure was delayed until 10 July. However, as we will see, it appears that following the War Cabinet's decision, absolutely nothing was done to sort out the all important question of selection i.e. who was rightly or wrongly being deported.

The Home Secretary, Sir John Anderson, was understandably cross that his recommendations for a fair and balanced approach had been ignored. He wrote later, on 15 July, to the Foreign Secretary Lord Halifax that: "the plans agreed between us and our respective departments were, in fact, swept on one side by subsequent directions given under Cabinet authority which I, for my part, had no full knowledge of until after the event." Anderson confirmed that his enquiries had shown that the Italians who were sent on the *Arandora Star* were selected by M.I.5 as persons whom they wished to get rid of on the ground that they were potentially dangerous. The 405 Italians who were sent to Canada on the *Ettrick* were selected from the camps by the War Office who regarded themselves as covered by the Cabinet decisions of 3 July. Anderson and Halifax both agreed that the arrangements for dealing with these Italians had been most unsatisfactory.

Once any internees were arrested, they were handed over to the military, who were under the control of the War Office, and who ran the internment camps, and provided the guards when the prisoners there were transported or deported. Thus once M.I.5 had pronounced which Italians were dangerous and directed the arrests, the War Office were responsible for their future. It was the War Office who arranged for their accommodation, and then supplied the prisoners for deportation.

Anderson went on in his letter of 15 July 1940 to Lord Halifax to emphasise that he was still trying to avoid further injustice, saying: "In order to avoid further muddle, I have taken or am taking, the following steps, namely:

[1] I have given orders that no more Italians should be sent overseas except with my express concurrence.

[2] I propose to take steps at an early date to appoint a small Committee of Enquiry to visit camps in which Italians are detained and to classify them on some systematic basis. Such a Committee should, I think, consist of representatives of the Foreign Office and of reliable anti-Fascists recommended by the Foreign Office…When this classification has been completed we shall then, and then only, be in a position to decide which of the Italians could be properly released from internment, which could be properly sent abroad, and which could be repatriated to Italy."

Anderson was trying to ensure a fairer selection process, and that at least some justice was done. However, his approach had been overridden on 3 July by a War Cabinet driven by Churchill and Chamberlain, the two most powerful men in the Conservative party, and this letter of 15 July came too late to save the survivors of the *Arandora Star* from further grievous suffering.

Following the sinking of the *Arandora Star,* the immediate duty of the British Government was to supply details of those who had been lost, and those who had survived, both to their families in Britain, and to the enemy nations whose citizens they were. Word of the sinking got out quickly, and as previously stated, when the *St Laurent* arrived in Greenock on 3 July, there were worried relatives waiting on the quay for news of their loved ones.

What followed was either an unbelievable display of incompetence, or deliberate sabotage. The War Office prepared two official lists, one of those believed lost and one of those believed rescued. Each list was divided into two sections: one for Germans and Austrians, and one for Italians. On 6 July 1940, Major General Sir Alan Hunter, on behalf of the War Office sent out the list of the missing. Each section was headed: "Casualties: First List of Missing". Those "missing" were undoubtedly dead. 292 Germans and Austrians appeared on one section of the list – the first on the list being Ludwig Baruch. 225 Italians appeared on the other section of the list – the last on page one being Gino Guarnieri. Both Ludwig Baruch and Gino Guarnieri had in truth been rescued and brought back on the *St Laurent* to Greenock. The lists had the wrong heading – those announced as dead were in fact saved.

A copy was of the list of missing was sent to the Foreign Office, and a copy was given, unofficially at this early stage, to the Swiss Red Cross. A copy was then sent to the Brazilian Embassy, who represented Italy's interests now that a state of war existed between Italy and the United Kingdom. It would be their duty to inform the relatives.

The Foreign Office knew at once that the list was hopelessly wrong. Apart from anything else, the numbers could not be right. The Foreign Office had already got a good idea of the scale of the disaster. The telephone was probably red hot as the Foreign Office and the War Office spoke. On the following day, 7 July, Major General Hunter wrote again to the Foreign Office "cancelling" the list. New lists were then issued, with the proper headings. They were still inaccurate, as we shall see later.

Had the false lists been openly circulated, it would have caused extraordinary distress.

It soon became obvious that even after 7 July, there was no accurate list of those who had been lost on the *Arandora Star*, one reason being that in the panic to get rid of as many dangerous enemy aliens as possible, there was no reliable list of those who had embarked i.e. those who had been on the ship when it was sunk. The inaccuracies went far further than just the headings - for example, when the headings had been corrected and the new lists prepared, on those new lists the BBC broadcaster, Uberto Limentani, who was on the ship was shown as lost, although he had in fact survived. Later, when the new, "corrected" War Office lists were properly checked by police from Scotland Yard, the disgraceful extent of their continued inaccuracy was exposed. Scotland Yard reported on 23 July that on the corrected War Office list, twenty-four Germans and Austrians shown as lost had in fact survived. Thirty-seven Italians shown as lost had survived but three Italians shown to have survived had been lost. Thus there were 64 significant mistakes in the original list. In addition, there were eight Germans named as having survived the sinking who had not even been on board the *Arandora Star*, and three Germans were not named who had in fact been on board, but had survived.

A tragic example of the effect of the inaccuracies was the case of Antonio Belli. He was born in Bardi on 11 November 1885. Many families from Bardi were establishing businesses in Wales, and Antonio arrived in the town of Maesteg at an early age. He was established in business in the town before the beginning of the First World War in 1914. There was an Italian community in Maesteg, of which the Belli family were a part. Antonio's wife was called Ida, and he had at least two sons, Frank and Angelo. The family established a café in Talbot Street, Maesteg, where all the family worked. The Bellis were described as early as May 1914 as a respectable family. Antonio visited Italy in 1922, and re-entered the United Kingdom on 20 November that year. Thereafter the evidence is that he remained in Wales.

In June, therefore, Antonio Belli had lived in Britain for at least thirty years, and had not visited Italy for nearly eighteen years. He clearly could defend himself against the threat of internment by proving his length of residence – the cut off point was 20 years. His brother also ran a café in Maesteg. It appears that at least one of Antonio's children had been born in Britain, since he served in the British Army as a Bombardier in the Royal Artillery. Antonio Belli was 55, and described on his medical card as obese, perhaps the price of his chosen path in life. Despite all of this, once Mussolini declared war on Britain, Antonio found himself under arrest. So did at least one of his children, his son Frank. Antonio was despatched with two friends from Maesteg, both born in Bardi, Giovanni Sidoli and Antonio Spagna, to Warth Mills Camp. After two uncomfortable weeks there, he and his two friends were marched onto the *Arandora Star* for deportation as "dangerous characters". Tragically, when the ship was sunk, all three of them died.

The sinking of the *Arandora Star* was on 2 July 1940. For the Belli family, the news that the *Arandora Star* had been sunk, and that hundreds of Italian internees had died, caused enormous anxiety. When the first lists were published [the new lists] of Italian internees who had survived and those lost, Antonio Belli was listed as lost. The Belli family began to grieve. Then, nearly three months later on 20 September 1940, Mrs Ida Belli received a letter from the Red Cross telling her that her husband was now listed as a survivor. The Red Cross had been informed by the Brazilian Embassy, representing Italy, that they had been informed that Antonio Belli had survived. The Brazilians had been supplied with the list of survivors by the British Government. The Belli family celebrated. Antonio was alive. A search then began to try and find out where he was being held. The search proved fruitless. On 31 October, Mrs Belli was again told that her husband was alive, and that every effort was being made to find him. Still he was not found.

Finally, on 15 January 1941, Mrs Belli having believed that her husband was alive since she had been so informed on 20 September 1940, the Alien's Department of the Home Office wrote to the Brazilian Embassy to inform them that Antonio Belli was dead. The Home Office letter gave a pathetic excuse: "The mistake in the shipping lists arose through the name of a survivor Cibelli being so badly written that it had the appearance of being Abelli, and as no such person as Abelli sailed, it was presumed that it must have been intended for Belli A. The result was that Belli A. was shown as a survivor and Cibelli shown as lost, whereas we know that Cibelli is alive and walking about in Glasgow today. A further complication was that Cibelli's name in the shipping list was printed as Cibrella, but we have confirmed that this is intended for Cibelli."

In truth, the entry in the Embarkation List was Cibrella G. Mr Cibelli's Christian name was Guy. It is difficult to believe that anyone could confuse Belli A with Cibrella G.

The real Cibelli had in fact been in hospital receiving treatment for his injuries from 3-12 July 1940. It seems extraordinary that nobody bothered to check who was in hospital before declaring him dead and Belli alive. Hopefully, Cibelli's family did not have to suffer in the belief that he was dead for too long. No doubt, Cibelli himself could have announced from his hospital bed who he was.

The Home Office letter concluded by saying to the Brazilian Embassy: "…unless I hear from you to the contrary, I will assume that you will communicate the distressing news to the family." There is no apology for the horrors that the Home Office had put the Belli family through, and they left it to the Brazilian Embassy to break the news to them, even though the deceased had a son, Angelo, who was serving in the British Army.

When taken into internment, Antonio Belli had had his gold watch with him. Following the procedures of the Warth Mills Camp, he had to surrender his gold watch when he arrived there. After Belli's death was confirmed, his son Bombardier Angelo Belli asked for its return. It was never returned. Warth Mills Camp had, of course, been under the command of Major Braybrook – a thief.

Another sad, bad case was that of Efisio Remo Vitale Azario. Azario was 54 years old. He had come to England in 1899 at the age of fourteen, and by June of 1940 he had lived in England for 41 years. He had only returned to Italy once – in 1919, three years before Mussolini came to power. No-one could suggest that he had lived anywhere but England over the past 41 years. His family understandably regarded themselves as British, and almost certainly some or all of his children were born in England and were therefore

British citizens. Azario was not a fascist, and did not belong to any clubs.

Not withstanding all of that, at 07.00hrs on 11 June, police arrived to arrest Azario as a dangerous enemy alien, and by 19 June, he was a prisoner in Warth Mills Camp. On 30 June, he too was marched aboard the *Arandora Star* and he did not survive its sinking. His family heard nothing from the British Government about his fate, and eventually they were informed of his death by the Brazilian Embassy. As British people do, the Azario family wrote to their MP, Lt Colonel George Doland, asking that they be told what had happened and why their father had been arrested. They said:

"It seems utterly foolish that he has been classed amongst the most dangerous aliens in this country, if it is true that the men aboard the *Arandora Star* were all such, and we desire that his name should be publicly cleared from any suspicion of disloyalty toward the country in which he had for so long made his home."

Lt Colonel Doland passed on their letter immediately to Mr Peake, MP, the Under Secretary of State at the Home Office, but they received no reply. A second letter dated 16 August 1940 complains: "...still no word from the people who took our father away...Surely sir this is no way to treat British people, to take their father from them, send him, unwittingly it is true, to his death, and never give a word about him to his family..."

This sad case, of course, highlights another problem for the deportees families – the British Government was claiming publicly that their loved ones were or had been dangerous spies and saboteurs, a very serious allegation in war-time Britain. Those who were dead had little means of defending themselves.

The first press reports of the *Arandora Star* tragedy were crudely distorted to suit propaganda purposes, but in a democracy, even in wartime, the truth can never be supressed for very long. The demand increased to know what had actually happened, and why. Unlike its enemies, Great Britain and Northern Ireland remained a democracy, and it was through its parliament that democracy continued to operate. Many relatives of the deportees were trying to discover the truth of what had happened to their loved ones. Their concerns were passed on to British members of parliament – both in the House of Commons and in the House of Lords. Little by little the outcry grew. On 9 July 1940, the Minister for Shipping, Robert Cross, MP, was asked a question in the House of Commons as to whether there had been refugees on the *Arandora Star*. He replied: "The Germans on board were Nazi sympathisers and none came to this country as refugees." That answer was untrue, and the information given to Cross upon which he based his answer must have been untrue. Why?

The next question in the House of Commons was asked on the following day, 10 July. This time the question asked about the Italians who had been sent to Canada aboard the *Arandora Star*. Mr Peake, MP, the Under Secretary for the Home Office, replied to the question on behalf of the Government, simply saying: "The Italians who were included for sending to Canada had been interned for security reasons." Not surprisingly, bearing in mind the truth that was slowly emerging, Mr Peake's reply was not accepted. It was already realised that there were many deportees on board the *Arandora Star* who should not have been on board. They were not "dangerous enemy aliens" at all.

Despite the answers of Mr Cross and Mr Peake, the whole question of the internment and deportation of aliens was raised in an adjournment debate of the House of Commons on the evening of 10 July, the same day that Mr Peake had given his reply. It was now eight days since the *Arandora Star* had been sunk. Major Cazalet, MP [Conservative], and Miss Eleanor Rathbone, MP [Independent], raised the question. The Under Secretary of State for War, Sir Edward Grigg, MP, and Mr Peake, again sought to defend the Government's position. Mr Peake made clear, when challenged, that: "The question of sending refugees and internees overseas is a decision that is not taken either by the Secretary of State for War [Anthony Eden], or the Home Secretary [Sir John Anderson]. It is a decision taken by a Committee of the Cabinet [in fact the HDSE and the War Cabinet], presided over by the Lord President of the Council [Neville Chamberlain]." By intent or accident, Neville Chamberlain was not in the chamber – nor did he visit the Commons during the debate. Thus, the most informed person made no contribution at all to it.

During the wide-ranging and sometimes heated debate, Mr Peake outlined the procedure that had been used for admitting refugees into Britain in the first place, long before any tribunal stage was reached: "Apart from the vouching of character [of the refugees] by the organisation or the individual [the sponsors], there was then an examination by the British Consul abroad of the bona fides of the individuals who wished to come. Then there was a scrutiny by the immigration officer when the alien came into this country. After landing, every alien had to report and register with the local police…" Thus there was a three stage vetting process before the refugee was admitted. Mr Peake then referred to the sinking of the *Arandora Star* as a "tragic disaster". He referred to the answer given by the Minister of Shipping Mr Cross on 9 July that all the Germans on board were Nazi sympathisers, and that none were refugees, saying that it should be some relief to the relatives of refugees in this country to know that. The official lie was still being perpetuated. Mr Peake, on 10 July was saying: "Refugees admitted to this country were very carefully checked. No refugees were on the *Arandora Star*."

Mr Wilfrid Roberts, Liberal MP for Cumberland, Northern, was later to point out that in Holland, where a Fifth Column had undoubtedly played an active part, there was a treaty obligation on the Dutch to allow Germans to enter and live in their country – a total contrast to the British position.

One of those who spoke in the debate was Mrs Mavis Tate, Conservative member for Frome. She supported the government line of wholescale internment, saying "our first consideration should be for our own people…we should err on the side of interning the innocent…In the case of certain members in this House, one has only to say the word "Jew" and they lose all sense of reason. I sympathise with the Jews, but Germany has learned to make skilful use of them…" Mrs Tate claimed that her name was on the Nazi black list. That was untrue – when the Nazi "black book" was eventually discovered, Mavis Tate was not on it. It will come as no surprise for the reader to know that Mrs Tate's name was found in the membership book of the Right Club.

Viscount Wolmer, Conservative MP for Aldershot replied to Mrs Tate, saying: "I profoundly disagree with a great deal that she has said…The view on which the speech of my Honourable Friend is based is what may be shortly called the "panic" view." Viscount Woolmer added that the Home Office had a thick dossier of information about practically every refugee [as was to be expected following the vetting process that Mr Peake had outlined]. Viscount Woolmer emphasised that there was a great fund of ability amongst the refugees which was at the service of the United Kingdom, and should be utilised. He concluded: "We should treat this matter in a common sense way and not in the spirit of panic."

Colonel Wedgwood, Liberal MP for Newcastle-under-Lyme, who had been instrumental in bringing 222 refugees into Britain, described Mr Peake's performance in the debate in the following way: "His heart was in the right place, but he felt bound to defend an administration which is too easily swayed by the Daily Mail and by the agitation of uneducated, panicky people…I see in this wave of internment cum "Daily Mail" panic from which we have been suffering lately a wholly incorrect view of what this war means and is…This war is not a matter of nationality at all. It is a war of religion, the religion of freedom as against the religion of dictatorship. We are no longer divided, as we were in the last war, between English and Germans and Austrians and French…"

Mr Sidney Silverman, Labour MP for Nelson and Colne, questioned the role of the War Office in the decision to intern all enemy aliens. Mr Peake had said that the War Office had pressed the Home Office to act as it had done, but Mr Silverman posed the question: "What did the War Office know about aliens?" It was the Home Office who had detailed information on them, and yet allowed themselves to be persuaded to adopt a policy of wholesale internment. Mr Silverman said that it was not unfair to describe such a policy as a policy of panic, adding: "People do unjust and cruel things when they are afraid."

Mr Reginald Sorenson, Labour MP for Leyton, West, commented that the country was governed by Parliament and not the Army, and that there were some matters in which the Army was not perhaps well qualified to offer advice, and that refugees was one of them. "It is true that at a time of difficulty and apprehension moods of panic are generated, but it does not follow one should give way to such moods. Some people, when the mood of panic is on them, assume that the only thing is to splutter out hatred, to become insensitive and more inhumane. I am not sure that there were one or two in this House who gave way to panic in that fashion. I am glad that now an attempt is being made to counter-balance that mood of panic."

Mr Maurice Petherick, Conservative MP for Penryn and Falmouth, objected to the suggestion of panic, and accused those who opposed the Government's decision on internment as having taken a point of view of total complacency. He thought that it was impossible to be too careful. Mr Hubert Beaumont, Labour MP for Botley and Morley, agreed saying: "In these grave and critical times, we cannot afford to take any modicum of risk." Mr David Logan, Labour MP for Liverpool, Scotland Division, who had actually been on the Liverpool landing stage when the *Arandora Star* had sailed, said: "Why should we waste time with the problem of aliens instead of dealing with the protection of our own land?...Why should we trouble if one, two or a thousand suspects are interned if this land of ours is safe...Look after Number One first, giving protection to those who come to our shores only when we know they deserve it". Mr Logan's comments, however, represented the views of those said to have panicked, since the refugees had only been admitted to this country on the basis that they were genuine refugees and deserved safe shelter. The reader may conclude that those who advocated mass internment were following the Machiavellian principle that the end justifies the means, and that whatever infringement of human rights occurred did not matter.

Mr Graham White, Liberal MP for Birkenhead East, dealt specifically with the *Arandora Star*, saying: "The relatives of everybody who was on the *Arandora Star* ought to be informed immediately. In many cases there is great anxiety at the present time...the *Arandora Star* comes into the last letter which I received just before I came to the house today. A son writes of his father: "My mother and I are British born, and my sentiments are all with this country. My father, an Italian, came to this country as a young man, and fought for the Allies in the last war, he was badly wounded in the head…he had no political ideas and did not belong to any association…My parents had never been apart for a single day during the whole of their married life. On 11 June he was taken away and interned…We found out that he was on the *Arandora Star* and posted as missing. Up to the present we have not had any news from the authorities…"

Mr White, MP, continued: "I would ask that all the facts concerning the Arandora Star should be cleared up without delay…It was stated in the House yesterday by the Minister for Shipping that there were no German refugees on board the *Arandora Star*, I am assured by those who have been in contact with survivors that there were at least 200 German refugees on board." Mr White went on to emphasise again that this war was not a war between nations, but between ideals – democracy versus nazi/fascism, and he added that the way in which the aliens question was being dealt with was one which would do Britain's national cause the maximum amount of harm. He referred to the damage being done to Britain's image by the policy of internment and the headlines that had appeared in the English Press. "The utmost use is being made [of this] in Germany, with the object of showing that the enemies of Hitler in Germany are now the enemies of England. They ask: "Where are the much vaunted cultural values of democracy?"…There has been cruelty. Cruelty was to be expected from the Nazis because they adopted a policy which ruled out any considerations of common humanity. We expected cruelty there, as a type of disease and there was in fact sadistic cruelty, which could be understood, but the kind of cruelty which comes from bad administration, from disorganised procedure between one Department and another, or from sheer stupidity, is intolerable."

Mr White's accusation of British cruelty was based on what he believed to be bad administration, disorganised procedure and sheer stupidity. Little did he know that on that very same day that he uttered that protest in the House of Commons, all of the survivors of the *Arandora Star* who were fit enough were marched onto another prison ship, the *Dunera*, and despatched on a long voyage to Australia in appalling conditions. After the horrors of the sinking of the *Arandora Star*, they had been allowed a mere seven days to recuperate before being again imprisoned aboard ship and sent out into the perilous seas of the North Atlantic. Undoubtedly, none of the MPs who spoke against the Government's actions knew about this new act of cruelty – the government ministers, Sir Edward Grigg and Mr Peake probably didn't know either.

Remarkably, and emphatically demonstrating that Britain remained a democracy where freedom of speech and criticism of the government were allowed, two books were published in England before the end of 1940 – both strongly criticising internment and deportation. One was "Anderson's Prisoners" published by Victor Gollancz Ltd and written under the pseudonym "Judex" [Judge], the other was "The Internment of Aliens" by Francois Lafitte, published by Penguin Books. Although neither author had the luxury that this author has enjoyed of viewing the numerous once secret records of M.I.5, the Foreign Office, the Home Office, the War Office and the War Cabinet, each author made a strong case. "Anderson's Prisoners" is an interesting contemporary source. The author of "Anderson's Prisoners" cites numerous obvious miscarriages of justice, where distinguished enemy aliens already working for the British state were interned. Some of them ended up on the *Arandora Star* and the *Dunera*. The author protects the identity of those involved in many of the cases he cites, but states that twenty German announcers and translators working in the Enemy Propaganda department of the BBC, all of whom had been very carefully vetted because of the nature of their work, were suddenly arrested and whisked off into internment in May 1940, when the panic began to spread to the British Government. He does name a number of well-known anti Nazi/Fascist authors who were interned – Rudolf Olden, Heinrich Frankel, Paolo Treves and Sebastian Haffner. Haffner's book: "Germany – Jekyll and Hyde" was published two days after his internment, and was subsequently widely used by the Ministry of Information.

"Judex" also writes of the terrible anguish that the very prospect of internment wrought amongst refugees, in particular those who had been imprisoned in German concentration camps. Professor Frederich Leopold Meyer was a leading chemist, aged 62. He had been imprisoned in Buchenwald Concentration Camp for many months by the Nazis, and when released, for a long time was refused permission to leave Germany. He eventually escaped to England, and took up work for an English chemical firm. When he heard that he was soon to be interned, he took his own life. His was far from being the only suicide – others shared the view that if their "friends" were now turning on them and were intending to imprison them, life was no longer worth living. One of the saddest of the cases of suicide listed by Judex is that of Alfred Rosenberg. His wife rang him one afternoon, suggesting that they should go out to dinner that night, because he was going to be arrested and interned the following morning. When she got home that evening, she found that her husband had committed suicide by poison. Another married couple, the Austrians Josef and Teresa Blumel, decided to commit suicide together, rather than be separated by Josef's impending internment.

This author is not aware of any official statistics as to the number of suicides brought about by the threat of internment, or by internment itself. However, if Judex was right, suicide as an alternative to internment was not uncommon.

CHAPTER FIFTEEN

THE HELL SHIP – HIRED MILITARY TRANSPORT
DUNERA

When the surviving prisoners awoke on 4 July 1940, the morning
after the *St Laurent* reached Greenock, the situation was that 592 of
their fellow countrymen who had left Liverpool on 1 July were dead
– 446 Italians and 146 Germans and Austrians - and 52 Italians were
known to be in hospital. The author has not discovered the number
of Germans and Austrians who were hospitalised. The survivors did
not, of course, know the figures – they simply knew that hundreds of
their friends, family and fellow prisoners had died when the
Arandora Star sank. They had seen many of their bodies floating in
the sea. The survivors themselves had had the most horrifying of
experiences. In the modern world, they would automatically have
been offered counselling, and careful examinations would have been
made for signs of Post Traumatic Stress Disorder. Even in wartime
Britain in 1940, basic humanity demanded that the survivors be
given some time to recover from their ordeal, that they be allowed to
see the families from whom they had been torn away, and that their
individual cases be considered, to discover whether they had been
wrongly arrested and deported. None of that was to happen. The
impetus remained, driven by the Prime Minister, to get all potentially
dangerous aliens out of the country as quickly as possible.

Surprisingly perhaps, bearing in mind Australian history, the
Australian government had agreed to accept a shipload of
"dangerous aliens" from Britain. Australia had experienced the
unhappy arrival of many British prison ships in the previous century.
However, the request that Australia should take these men was
expressed upon the basis that they were dangerous, that the retention
in the United Kingdom of such dangerous men would impose a
serious burden on the authorities responsible for their custody, and
would prevent the considerable number of soldiers who would be
necessary to guard them from performing other duties to resist the
imminent German invasion. In the event of a serious attack on the
United Kingdom, there was the danger that the internees would
assist the enemy. Faced with that plea for help at what was a

desperate time for Britain, the Australian government agreed in early July 1940 to accept a total of 6,000 internees and prisoners of war.

Although it was beginning to emerge publicly in the days following the sinking of the *Arandora Star* that the selection of the "dangerous characters" on board had been hopelessly flawed, the official line remained that the survivors of the *Arandora Star* were dangerous enemy aliens. The War Office had its orders to deport them as soon as possible, and the same false categorisation that had justified their initial hurried deportation on the *Arandora Star* was no doubt the basis of the decision to send them off on the high seas again. Neither the Home Office nor the Foreign Office were informed that this was going to happen.

452 of the survivors of the *Arandora Star* were therefore marched aboard the *Dunera,* just a few days after the horror of the sinking. They were 250 Germans and Austrians and either 201 or 202 Italians, accounts differ. This was done by the War Office, without the knowledge of either the Home Office or the Foreign Office. They were taken from their temporary accommodation back to Liverpool, and on 10 July they were put onto H.M.T. *Dunera*, another troop carrier adapted as a prison ship, for deportation this time to Australia. Again, they were not allowed to know where they were going. With the 452 survivors of the *Arandora Star* went a little over 2,000 other Germans and Austrians who were categorised as Bs and Cs. The vast majority were refugees. Of them, most were Jewish.

The British officer who was in charge of the guard that marched the Italian survivors to the ship, Lieutenant Merlin Scott, was so distressed at what he had been ordered to do that he was almost in tears. An extract from a letter written by him on 12 July to his father, who was an Assistant Under Secretary at the Foreign Office, later found its way onto a Foreign Office file. It said: "The last two days I've spent guarding the Italian survivors of the *Arandora Star*. I thought they were treated abominably badly – now they have all been sent to sea again to Canada [in fact Australia] – the one thing nearly all were absolutely dreading, having lost their fathers, brothers etc the first time. Many valuable men, I think, have been packed off. We had a certain Martinez, who had been the head of the Pirelli Cable and Tyre factories, and who knows more about armaments production than most – there were many others, who had just been rounded up without any enquiry."

"When they got down to the ship, their baggage was naturally searched, but what I thought was so bad was that masses of their stuff – clothes etc was simply taken away from them and thrown in piles out in the rain, and they were only allowed a handful of things. Needless to say, various people, including policemen started helping themselves to what had been left behind. They were hounded up the gangway, and pushed along with bayonets, with people jeering at them. It was, in fact, a thoroughly bad show, I think largely due to some of those useless hard-bitten bogus Majors who were standing around in large numbers. Masses of telegrams came for them [the deportees] saying: "Thank God you are safe" and they were not allowed to see them."

If this account is true, and it is supported in various ways by the accounts of the deportees, then Mr White MP's accusation of British cruelty was inaccurate. The cruelty was not the result of negligence, it was deliberate.

A damning account was given in a remarkable application dated 11 November 1940, made by over five hundred of the Jewish deportees, and addressed to the Under Secretary of State at the Home Office Aliens Department. It described their arrival on the *Dunera* as follows: "When boarding H.M.T *Dunera*, we were searched and deprived of almost all our valuables and documents, no receipts being given and no records of any sort ever being made. Some of our documents were destroyed before our eyes. Our luggage was similarly seized. Confined below deck in rooms crowded at twice their capacity, we travelled for two months through tropical and other climates without such necessities as soap, towels, tooth brushes etc, or a second shirt or garment to change into. Also during the voyage, we were repeatedly searched and whatever valuables had not been previously taken were taken off us – again no receipts being given as before. We also had the shock of being suddenly informed that the transport was going to Australia instead of Canada. Further, our luggage was forced open and a considerable part of it was destroyed before our eyes. The loss of documents such as Birth Certificates, Marriage Certificates, Certificates of Good Conduct which were issued by the German authorities and are essential for our emigration, confronts us with a difficult problem because they cannot easily be replaced." To destroy such things was again pure cruelty on the behalf of the guards. These Jewish refugees, as all the other prisoners on the *Dunera*, would arrive in Australia penniless and deprived of their documentation.

The prisoners, Germans, Austrians, Italians and Jews, were subject to the abuse of their guards for the whole of the long voyage to Australia. They rarely saw any member of the crew, only occasionally meeting them in the kitchens. They were kept below decks for all but half an hour each day. For that half hour, they were allowed to go onto a confined deck area in small groups, where the guards would make them run round in a circle in bare feet. A game that the guards used to play was to break bottles on the deck, so that the prisoners had difficulty in not cutting their feet. Gino Guarnieri commented that throughout the two months of the voyage, he did not meet a single sympathetic guard.

The German and Austrian survivors of the *Arandora Star,* together with their fellow countrymen and the Italian survivors, made up a total of 2,542 prisoners on board the *Dunera*. It later became clear that the Home Office had not even been accurately informed of how many prisoners were taken on board. The figure that they gave to the Australians who were to receive them was 2,368 dangerous men. In fact a further 174 were loaded. The cruelty was combined with staggering incompetence.

Since permission to send deportees had only been granted by Australia in the first few days of July, the voyage of the *Dunera* was put together at great speed. As the official Australian report later put it: "Embarkation in England had been effected under trying conditions: speed was essential owing to the collapse of France, and it had been impracticable to give adequate attention to questions of accommodation and conditions of the vessel. As a result, the internees suffered a most uncomfortable trip......No basic documents were supplied [to us] in respect of the internees and some considerable time was required to document them after their arrival at internment camps in Australia."

Article 26 of the Prisoners of War Convention required that the destination of travel should be known to prisoners. This right had been denied to the prisoners on the *Arandora Star*, and was again denied on the *Dunera*. Also, the Convention specified that prisoners should be allowed to take with them their personal effects. This was permitted on the *Arandora Star*, although most personal belongings were lost to the sea when she sank. On the *Dunera*, this right was to be badly abused.

The *Dunera* was grossly over-crowded with prisoners, a situation made worse by the fact that all of them were categorised as dangerous aliens and "desperate characters", and therefore demanded maximum security. The survivors of the *Arandora Star*, both German/Austrians and Italians found themselves on board with a much larger number of other Germans and Austrians. As on the *Arandora Star*, some of the German/Austrians were prisoners of war, and some genuine Nazis, but the majority were Jewish refugees who had fled from Hitler's evil empire. The 202 Italians from the *Arandora Star* were the only Italians aboard. The prisoners were segregated, but only by nationality. The Italians were kept in a separate hold to the Germans and Austrians. The Germans and Austrians were imprisoned together, Nazis and anti-Nazis, in two connected holds below sea level. If the ship was torpedoed, they would have little chance of survival. Quarters were required for the guards, who numbered 309, and in addition there was the crew. When the *Dunera* had been working as a troop carrier, its capacity was put at 1,000 men, and that was regarded as an absolute maximum. Now it carried 2,542 prisoners, plus guards and crew.

Presumably, the survivors of the *Arandora Star* were still having nightmares about their very recent experience when on the night of 9/10 July they found themselves marched on board the *Dunera*, bound for another unknown destination. Compared to conditions aboard the *Arandora Star,* the conditions that now greeted the prisoners were far worse. The prisoners were held in cargo holds, and there were not enough toilets to be shared amongst more than 2,500 prisoners. Luigi Beschizza recalled that the ten toilets in the Italian hold were the only toilets available for one of the German holds, who had to use them as well as the Italians. During the voyage there was an outbreak of dysentery amongst the prisoners, and conditions became indescribable, with some of the toilets becoming blocked. It became necessary for the prisoners to set up a system of toilet monitors, who would call on the next sufferer in the queue when a toilet was free. Beschizza confirmed that, apart from the Italians, the vast majority of the other prisoners were Jews. The German/Austrians who had been brought from the *Arandora Star,* like the Italians had little or had no luggage, but others were ordinary internees, mainly Jewish. They arrived with many of the possessions that they had taken from their homes when they had first been arrested – often in good quality suitcases with valuable items inside.

The 309 guards, and their officers, were of the very worst kind - low quality troops, mostly from the Pioneer Corps, who could be spared from the defence of Britain. They behaved disgracefully towards their prisoners. There is no doubt that the deportees found themselves in the hands of the dregs of the British military. It has been suggested that many of these guards were "Soldiers of the King's Pardon" i.e. men who had been let out of prison on a pardon in order to fight for Britain, but the author has been unable to find any proof of this. The Pioneer Corps generally gave good service. Many refugees joined it once they were allowed to do so, and later went on to give distinguished service. However, early in the war, it contained many "undesirables". By way of example, in March 1941, 28 members of the Pioneer Corps were tried, convicted and sent to prison at the Old Bailey for looting – stripping lead from slightly damaged buildings when they were ordered to clear damage from the railway, and selling it. Sergeant George Gallan, aged 58, was found to be the instigator, and before being sentenced to 3 years imprisonment, it was revealed that he had 17 previous convictions.

The Australian report later gave no excuse for the bad behaviour of the guards. However, it said: "It is reported that officers and men allotted to the vessel for escort duties were given only two hours notice, and in many instances their wives did not know of their departure." This no doubt must have been a source of much unhappiness amongst the guards – the voyage of the *Dunera* out to Australia would last the better part of two months through dangerous seas, and then they had to survive a return journey too – but it was no justification of the way they treated their prisoners.

Descriptions of the brutality meted out to the prisoners come from both German/Austrian and Italian sources. A statement dated 2 December 1940, signed by three well-educated refugees Dr Alfred Wiener, Paul Auerbach and Dr K.J.Joseph [who was a member of the English Bar] details various examples of the violence used. However, their letter starts with this paragraph:

"We have refrained up to now from describing our treatment aboard HMT *Dunera* as we were afraid that these facts might be used for enemy propaganda. We are now - three months after our arrival – giving this statement for the use of the authorities only, and it is our wish that if the authorities should think that the treatment of these facts during the war might prove detrimental, this statement should not be regarded as a complaint, but that the matter should rest."

The authors were obviously aware that the Germans might say: "Look – the British treat the Jews in the same way as we do!" They confirmed that the huge majority of the prisoners on the *Dunera* were either political or racial [Jewish] refugees, many of whom had gone through the hardships of the Nazi concentration camps, and were the bitterest enemies of the Nazis. Despite this, the treatment that they received from the guards on board the *Dunera* was brutal. Incidents of violence towards the prisoners were common. The statement itemised various examples – Moriz Chlumecki suffered a rifle butt slammed against his foot when he tried to protect his son's violin, the violin was torn from his grasp, and Lieutenant O'Neill VC manhandled him away. Chlumecki's foot was bloodied and his nails torn as a result of the assault. A Dr Edgar Elbogen suffered his ears being boxed because he tried to explain that an attache case that he brought on board contained only toilet utensils. If any other refugee tried to protest at the violence and theft that was commonplace, he too would be threatened or beaten. Dr K.J.Joseph, a signatory of the statement, was one of those who was badly knocked about. According to the statement, Lieutenant O'Neill regularly supervised the violent assaults on the prisoners, and used violence on the prisoners himself. On one occasion, he punched a 19 year old called Hans Kronberger in the face whilst Kronberger's hands were tied.

For the Germans and Austrians, the conditions in which they were kept were extremely bad. The quarters were excessively crowded, the washing facilities were totally inadequate, they were allowed no change of clothes and there was no fresh air, since the portholes were always locked shut. There was no natural light in their quarters. Many had to sleep on or under tables because there were too few hammocks. In consequence of the lack of cleaning and washing facilities many skin diseases occurred, such as impetigo and furunculosis. The food was exceedingly poor, and diarrhoea was almost universal.

Nothing could justify the dreadful treatment meted out by the guards to the prisoners, who were brutalised, bullied, and robbed of anything valuable that the guards could find over the fifty-six days of the voyage. Their suitcases were taken on to the deck, cut open with bayonets, looted, and then thrown over the side. The saddest case was of one of the Jewish prisoners, Jakob Weiss, who saw his passport, which contained his visa to enter Argentina, taken, torn up and thrown overboard. This was an invaluable set of papers to a refugee. Weiss had been told that even though he was being deported from Britain, he could use his visa for Argentina when he arrived in the new country to which he was going. So distraught was he when he saw his passport and visa destroyed that he threw himself off the ship into the sea, committing suicide. Surprisingly, he was one of only three prisoners who died during the voyage – the others were recorded as dying of natural causes, although there is a suggestion that one of these had in fact been shot dead by an officer. Nicola Cua's father, who was with him on the *Dunera* as he had been on the *Arandora Star,* believed that the guards behaviour towards them was so bad that they would not be able to afford to let their prisoners live at the end of the voyage, and would kill them all.

The commander of the guard contingent, Lieutenant Colonel W.P.Scott allowed his men to abuse the prisoners, often physically, and held a particularly poor opinion of the Jews and Italians. In his first report back to the War Office during the voyage, dated 18 July 1940, Scott emphasised the excellent behaviour of his own men, saying: "An extremely friendly atmosphere prevails between my Command and the ship's company. Concerts and games have been organised, and the men are not only doing their duties to very best advantage but are an extremely happy company." In truth, his men were robbing and abusing their prisoners.

After they had arrived in Australia, Constance Duncan, Director of the Victoria [Australia] Refugees Society, submitted a detailed report of what she had learned to Bloomsbury House in London, blaming two of the officers, "Captain" Neil, VC [presumably Lieutenant O'Neill], and "Captain" Scott [presumably Lieutenant Colonel W.P. Scott] as being the most abusive. In her report, she said: "The men arrived at Tatura and Hay [Internment] camps [in Australia] in a ghastly condition – unshaven and unwashed, with all kinds of makeshift clothing, and some so weak that they could hardly walk. The Commandant of the Hay camp told Bishop Pilcher [Bishop Coadjutor C.V.Pilcher of Sydney] that tears came into the eyes of his officers when they watched the internees arriving. When they received their luggage, it had been pilfered of everything worth taking..."

Duncan continued: "The things that happened on the *Dunera* are almost beyond belief...The two military officers on the Dunera who were the chief offenders were Captain Neil VC and Captain Scott, the former being particularly brutal. When they were ill-treating the men on the *Dunera*, the English guards would say to their prisoners: "Oh, this is nothing to the way the Australians will treat you." To cover their own misdeeds, the guard of the *Dunera* announced on their arrival here [in Australia] that the men had mutinied and that their behaviour had been very bad indeed."

It is sad to see John O'Neill named as being particularly brutal to the prisoners. He had won his Victoria Cross when a sergeant in 1918, at the age of 21. His brother had been killed on the same day. When World War 2 broke out, O'Neill, now aged 53, was commissioned into the Pioneer Corps. Deprived of any real fighting, if the reports received by Duncan are true, O'Neill chose to brutalise his prisoners – said to be dangerous enemy spies and saboteurs.

In a report submitted at the end of the voyage to justify the brutal treatment that he allowed his men to mete out to the prisoners, Lieutenant Colonel Scott described the Nazi Germans as: "a fine type, honest and straightforward, and extremely well-disciplined..." but went on to say that the German and Austrian Jews, who were anti-Nazi and had fled for their lives from Germany and Austria, were: "subversive liars, demanding and arrogant, I have taken steps to bring them into my line of thought..." Scott did not say what the steps were that he had taken, but they presumably included physical abuse. Scott dismissed the Italians [all of whom had suffered the sinking of the *Arandora Star*] as: "filthy in their habits, without a vestige of discipline, and cowards to a degree."

It is obvious that Scott's sympathy was with his Nazi prisoners, and that he shared their views of the Jews. Inevitably, the question arises as to whether Scott was associated with the Right Club, or one of the other British Fascist organisations. His name does not appear in the Right Club secret ledger.

In addition to the suffering inflicted on them on board, the prisoners lived in constant fear of being attacked by U-Boats. Gino Guarnieri said that the morale of the prisoners was extremely low. The guards robbed him of his cigarettes, even taking a half cigarette out of his pocket. He commented that they were absolutely different to guards that they had had on the *Arandora Star* - they seemed a different race. They took everything that the prisoners had, which in Gino's case was extremely little. Guarnieri thought that they were low-life riff raff. They looked rough, as though they had been selected from British prisons. When the *Dunera* stopped for supplies en route to Australia, some of them deserted.

Those prisoners who tried to resist their property being stolen suffered physically. Everything of any value went – one prisoner talked of seeing a guard walking off in his raincoat. A lot of the older prisoners gave up all hope. There were plenty of them who were aged between 60 and 70. Many had sons who had been born in Britain, some of whom were now serving in the British army. It made no difference to the way in which they were treated.

Abrascha Gorbulski, who changed his name after the war to Alexander Gordon, was a young Jewish Polish-German, who had come to Britain with the *Kindertransport* in 1938. His father had died when he was three years old, and his mother had had to go out to work, so that Abrascha was looked after in a Jewish orphanage. When his mother was subsequently deported, he was left alone in Germany. Born on 31 January 1922, he was sixteen at the time of *Kristellnacht.* Gorbulski was told in the orphanage about the *Kindertransport* scheme, signed on for it, and was welcomed into Britain still aged only 16. The upper age limit for refugee children was 17. He had had every reason then to be grateful to Great Britain for its charity in accepting him as a refugee when many countries, including the United States, had refused the refugee children access. By June 1940, however, everything had changed, and Churchill's government was in a state of panic over the enemy aliens it had within its shores. Gorbulski, now aged 18, was arrested in late June, and was included on the list of deportees to be sent on the *Dunera* to Australia. When interviewed for the excellent Warner Brothers documentary film "Into the Arms of Strangers" in 2000, Gorbalski said that his memory would not allow him to describe the horrors of his voyage on the *Dunera*, saying only that he and his fellow prisoners had been treated like pigs throughout the voyage, and starved of any decent food.

Nicola Cua confirmed that some British guards had deserted in ports on the way – Capetown, Freemantle, and then at Melbourne. He said that he did not know where the soldiers came from, but that they were definitely rough types. When they had taken things off the prisoners, they would play dice amongst themselves to see who got this and who got that. He said that his friend Luigi Beschizza lost his gold hunter watch, but the ones who really lost everything were the Jews. He described seeing the guards ripping open beautiful suitcases, made of really good leather, and throwing everything over the side, or getting some of the Italian prisoners to throw them into the sea. The guards would come down regularly into the Italian prisoners' hold, and take rings and other small valuables off the prisoners. It got so bad that the leader of the Italians, a Colonel G. Borghi, who had been with them since Warth Mills, went to an officer that Nicola Cua referred to as "the Captain", and was probably either O'Neill or Scott, and reported to him what his soldiers were doing. Borghi received a promise that he would do something about it. Later "the Captain" came down to the hold, and invited the prisoners to gather their valuables together, and give them all to him for safe keeping. He said that they would be returned when they reached their prison camp. Therefore, most of the Italian prisoners gathered their remaining valuables together into a bag, and gave them to "the Captain". They never saw their valuables again. Cua was one of those who refused, and hung on to what he had still got. Any personal documents were stolen, and even their false teeth, which were frequently thrown overboard in acts of pure cruelty. For the Jews, anti-semitism was rife amongst their guards.

Gino Guarnieri described the conditions in which the Italians had to live. He said that they were at sea level, and could see the waves. The two hundred Italians were absolutely cramped together. There were only a few hammocks, most of the prisoners had to sleep on the floor, or benches or the tables which were used for meals. He felt suffocated. They worried constantly about another torpedo attack. At the beginning of the voyage, they did not know where they were going, but it obviously wasn't to the Isle of Man. They were locked into their hold, and were frightened that in the event of another attack, they would not be able to get out. Underneath them were the Germans, equally secure.

Somewhere off the coast of Ireland, two days out from Liverpool, the U-Boat U-56, under Oberleutnant Harms spotted the *Dunera*, and the moment that they had all been fearing came. Two torpedoes were fired at them. Although the calculations on the U-Boat suggested that both torpedoes missed, those on board the *Dunera* told a different tale. They said that one hit the *Dunera* with a bang, but mercifully did not explode, scraping along the side of the ship and passing on its way. Abrascha Gorbulski, in the hold beneath the waterline, remembered that the lights went out after the noise of the impact, but thankfully came on again after a short time. A second torpedo apparently passed underneath them, either because the ship was not carrying anything but human cargo and was therefore light in the water, or possibly simply because the *Dunera* rode up on a wave as the torpedo passed beneath. The Germans in quarters below them broke open the locked door that held them in, but were confronted by an armed sentry prepared to fire. The Italians were unable to break out of their hold. To get out, they had to go up a flight of steps which had barbed wire all round. When the bang of the torpedo came, there was a rush up the steps, but the trapdoor which was the exit was also covered in barbed wire, and they could not get out. Had the torpedo exploded, and the *Dunera* been sunk, it is highly likely that all the prisoners would have died.

A little later, a British officer came round to confirm that the ship had been attacked, but was undamaged. For the prisoners stuck below decks, particularly the survivors of the *Arandora Star,* it must have been a day of pure terror. They now knew that there was a U-Boat out there that was hunting them, but there was absolutely nothing that they could do about it. Was history to repeat itself within a period of no more than ten days? On the *Dunera,* like the *Arandora Star*, no boat drill was allowed for the prisoners.

Thankfully, the U-Boat did not attack again, and the voyage continued. It was to last more than 56 days and the attack had come on only the second or third day. Each waking hour brought the fear of another U-Boat attack. Gino Guarnieri put their fears into words, confessing that he was more afraid on the *Dunera* than the *Arandora Star.* As the journey went on, day after day after day, the prisoners kept asking where they were going, but were told repeatedly that it was classified information which they were not allowed to know. Only at a late stage were they told that they were going to Australia.

Nicola Cua, one of the group of youngsters who had been at Warth Mills, said that any attempts to have fun on the *Dunera* were impossible. The accommodation was really terrible, made worse by the dysentery amongst the prisoners. In the hold occupied by the Italians, there were ten tables for twenty Italians each to eat at, benches and a few hammocks. Many slept on the floor. In the middle of the hold was a big staircase, down which hundreds of people came every day to use toilets. The food was terrible. Life for a youngster such as Cua and his friends was difficult, for the older people it was simply terrible. Apart from the effects of dysentery, the sea was very rough in the Indian Ocean, and many of the prisoners were sea sick, vomiting onto the already filthy deck. The staircase was unsafe in the very rough weather, and the food would fall off the table. Nicola remembered scrabbling around on the floor to pick up pieces of meat for his father and himself.

The *Dunera* stopped at Sierra Leone, and then at Cape Town. From there, despite some guards deserting, the *Dunera* sailed on. The food remained of very poor quality and it was sparse. Conditions improved somewhat when the ship docked at Freemantle, the first Australian port, where a number of Australian troops came on board, but by this time all the prisoners had lost considerable weight. The *Dunera* eventually reached Melbourne on 3 September 1940. Nicola Cua's father had to be carried off on a stretcher, he was too ill to walk.

The Australians had agreed to take internees from Britain, but on 16 July 1940, six days after the Dunera had left Liverpool, the Australian Government telegrammed to ask for details of who the internees were. Hitherto, they had only been told that they were to be dangerous Fifth Columnists. In a reply on 17 July, the British Government stated: "Persons already sent consist of 2,164 Germans and 202 Italians, all males and practically all single…" The latter was simply not true. Many of the prisoners were leaving their families behind, and had been promised that their families would be allowed to follow them wherever they were sent. Furthermore, there were 2,542 prisoners on board, not 2,366. However, the Australians having been told that dangerous prisoners were to be placed in their care, made the appropriate arrangements. Camps were prepared which were secure, and a substantial armed guard was paraded to meet the *Dunera* when it arrived in Melbourne. As a result, when the *Dunera* finally docked in Melbourne and its prisoners disembarked, the Australians were stunned. As Nicola Cua later put it: "The Aussies had been told we were dangerous, Fifth Columnists, spies etc. The docks were heavily fortified to greet us. They saw this dishevelled, skinny crowd, old, and they thought that there must be a mistake." Gino Guarnieri described the same reaction: "I had nothing when I arrived in Australia. The Australian soldiers who greeted us on our arrival were heavily armed, and said: "We are here to pick up a Fifth Column, who are you?"

The *Dunera* had been at sea from 10 July until 3 September, a total of fifty-six days. Confined in the most appalling conditions, and regularly abused, it is no surprise that most of the prisoners arrived in Australia in a much-weakened condition.

Sixteen of the deportees were taken back on board the *Dunera* before she left Melbourne on her return voyage to England. During her voyage out, some of the worst mistakes of the selection were realised, and orders had been sent from London that these sixteen "mistakes" should be sent back immediately. Eventually, something in the region of a staggering seventy-five percent of the deportees were designated for release and offered passage back to Britain, or on to the countries to which they wanted to emigrate.

Nicola Cua's initial attitude to his internment, as with most of the young Italian men, was one of understanding and acceptance. As he put it: "We, the younger ones, understood it, because we were of military age." In fact, many of them, before they experienced the horrors of the *Arandora Star* and the *Dunera,* were thankful that they would not be called upon to fight for either side. British born Italians, who were British nationals, faced the possibility that once conscripted, they would be called upon to fight against Italian troops who might include their conscripted Italian cousins. Cua commented on the fact that amongst those deported to Australia were a number of older Italians who had sons serving in the British army – one of them had three sons serving the King.

Cua said that they did not suffer in the camp in which they were held in Australia. The food was good, and, of course, was prepared in their own kitchen by expert Italian chefs. Cua explained that one of their chefs had worked in Buckingham Palace, one had worked on the *Mauritania*, and his own father was chef at the Criterion. They were all head chefs. In total, Cua said, they had fourteen of the best chefs in London in their Italian group.

After the shocking trip on the *Dunera*, their lives improved. The deportees were divided into different camps or compounds by the Australians – one for Italians, one for Jews, and one for other Germans and Austrians. In the Italian camp, Cua described a rounded life: a Dr Marzocchi gave lessons in Spanish, Fortonino

Mantagna used to paint "all the details for big occasions"-presumably theatrical shows or concerts - and his brother was a musician. Franz Stampfl, the athletics coach, organised numerous different sporting encounters, driven by: "an inner desire to survive and remain sane for myself and my friends in the camp". Dr Zezzi, from Harley Street, turned out to be a champion tennis player. As previously stated, Dr Zezzi was the European Director for Elizabeth Arden, and he wrote to her to tell her of his plight. She sent out some of her products to the camp.

In April 1942, Franz Stampfl escaped from internment by joining the 8th Australian Employment Company of the Australian Army, with whom he served until January 1946, obtaining the rank of Corporal. After the war he became a well-known international athletics coach, and played a significant part in training the English squad for Roger Bannister's first four minute mile.

Contact with home was difficult for the deportees, mainly because of the distance involved. Gino Guarnieri recalled that it was only after about six months in Australia that the deportees were able to send any communication to relations in Italy, and then it was simply a postcard saying that the prisoner was alive and well. For the United Kingdom, they could write a letter once a fortnight, but their letters took a very long time to arrive. The Italians were held in an adjoining compound to some of the German deportees, amongst whom there was a group of Nazis. Guarnieri sometimes saw signs of violence on the Nazis, which suggested that they were not popular amongst their fellow prisoners.

CHAPTER SIXTEEN

A CHANGE OF POLICY

The *Dunera* was dispatched to Australia on 10 July, the same day as the adjournment debate. The suffering of those on the *Dunera* continued into September, but meanwhile things were developing in Britain, and the outcry at the government's internment policy, in particular at the deportations, was increasing day by day. Six days after the departure of the *Dunera,* on 16 July, the Secretary of State for War, Anthony Eden, answered questions about the *Arandora Star* tragedy from five MPs in the House of Commons. As Secretary of State for War, he was the head of the War Office, which was responsible for everything that happened to internees after their initial arrest. The five MPs who asked questions were from across the House - Colonel Josiah Wedgwood [Liberal], Mr Rhys Davies [Labour], Mr George Strauss [Labour] , Sir Herbert Williams [Conservative] and Miss Eleanor Rathbone [Independent]. Four of them asked about German and Austrian deportees. Only one, Miss Rathbone, asked about the Italians. The questions complained that anti-Nazi Jews, refugees from Nazi oppression, and anti-Hitler aliens should not be deported in company with Nazi prisoners; married men should not be deported without their wives and families; and that when the prisoners arrived in the new country, their relatives should be informed of their addresses. Mr Rhys Davies specifically asked the Secretary of State for War to bear in mind the "terrible agony of parents, and especially of wives."

Anthony Eden's reply was, presumably, based on what he had been told by his department. It was, in the circumstances, extraordinary. He started by saying: "The interned enemy aliens on the *Arandora Star* were Italian Fascists and Class A Germans. It is understood by my Department that none of these Germans were refugees." He added that he was making enquiries on the latter point, and asserted that there were no prisoners of war on board the *Arandora Star*. It is quite clear that the Head of the War Office had no idea of what his department was doing.

As a striking contrast, the Foreign Office, which had no control over the arrests and deportations, remained very concerned that something had gone badly wrong. A Foreign Office memorandum dated 14 July 1940 [two days before Eden's replies in the Commons] and headed "Shipment overseas of Interned friendly Aliens of enemy nationality - different categories of persons who have been [a] interned, [b] sent overseas", showed their concerns. The memorandum includes a one page document also dated 14 July. That states: "It appears from various published documents and from statements made in parliament that the passengers of the *Arandora Star*, which was recently torpedoed in the Atlantic, included in addition to known Nazi and Fascist sympathisers, the following:

[i] Some Germans and Austrians of anti-Nazi sentiments who were nevertheless put in Category A [i.e. ordered to be interned] by the Home Office tribunals which were operating before Christmas [1939] on the ground that they were persons of left sympathies, or on other grounds which the Tribunals thought sufficient [it will be remembered that the instructions to the tribunals permitted them to direct internment on grounds other than hostile sentiments].

[ii] A number of German and Austrian refugee youths who attained the age of 16 [at which the jurisdiction of the Home Office tribunals, and with it a liability to internment, begins], after the first set of tribunals had ceased functioning, and who accordingly had not been classified into any category.

[iii] Numerous Italians not known to be Fascists

[iv] The Vice-Consul of the Republic of San Marino [who had diplomatic immunity]."

The memorandum went on to request that the Prisoners of War department of the War Office confirm to the Foreign Office whether enemy aliens other than those of hostile sentiments had been included in the transports, and whether the Foreign Office was suggested to have agreed with this, or to have intimated approval in any way [which it had not!].

Eden's reply in the House of Commons two days later was therefore known to his opponents to be untrue. Colonel Wedgwood fired back: "Are we to understand that there were no C category Germans – anti-Nazi aliens – on the *Arandora Star*? How does the Right

Honourable Gentleman account for the fact that some of these are known to have been saved? Did the War Office really not know who were on board the ship?"

Eden stuck to his script, saying "What I said was that these were all category A"

Colonel Wedgwood asked: "Surely the right honourable Gentleman must know by now – he has the names of those who were saved – that they were not category A but categories B and C"

Mr Strauss added: "Is the right honourable gentleman aware that some of the men on the *Arandora Star* were sentenced to terms of imprisonment by the Nazis, and others beaten up by the Nazis..."

Eden, obviously beginning to realise that he was on doubtful ground, began to back down, saying: "I have gone into the question very carefully, and that is the assurance that I was given. In view of what the right honourable Gentleman says, I will go into it again."

Miss Rathbone then asked: "Is the right honourable Gentleman aware that there were on board several very distinguished anti-Fascist Italians, of whom at least one was drowned?" She received no satisfactory reply.

Anthony Eden was apparently not aware of the awful truth of what had happened. The chapter of unpardonable "errors" had been concealed from him. The author feels bound to ask why? Could this have just been further muddle on the behalf of the War Office, or was the covert hand of the Right Club in evidence? If the Foreign Office knew what had gone on from the evidence that was emerging, why did not the War Office? Two comments appear on the Foreign Office file on the subject after Mr Eden had given his reply – one from Mr Farquhar read: "If I were the Secretary of State for War, I should be rather angry with certain people in the War Office. He evidently had a rough passage in the house." An unattributed Foreign Office source commented: "I agree with Mr Farquhar. Mismanagement of this kind is bound to shake public confidence in the efficiency of the Security Service." What it amounts to is that by 16 July, the Foreign Office and a number of others were well aware that serious mistakes had been made, but the War Office, which was responsible, continued to deny them.

All this time, the *Dunera* continued to sail towards Australia, with its prisoners suffering under horrendous conditions.

Two weeks later, on 2 August, Mr Farquhar of the Foreign Office, who was trying to secure the release of some detainees still in the United Kingdom who should never have been arrested, wrote: "The whole situation as regards these and other internees strikes me as thoroughly unsatisfactory. The Home Secretary on his own authority and on the advice of our famous Security Services, proceeds to lock certain people up; when asked whether he can release them we are given evasive replies. Surely, the authority which has the authority to lock people up also has the power to let them loose. If not, I should like to know why not."

Another comment on the Foreign Office file, dated the same day, reads: "the continued delays and the persistent appearances of administrative ineptitude is discreditable, and calculated not only to bring us to ridicule and contempt, but also to make enemies of those who have been our friends. The more who are aware of these facts, the less likely are misfortunes to befall innocent people in our country again." The Foreign Office was quite clearly furious with the Home Office and the War Office.

Parliament continued to pursue the Government to try and obtain a true picture of what had happened. On 6 August, with the *Dunera* still at sea, it was the turn of the House of Lords, some of whom were well briefed. Lord Faringdon led the debate, and began by asking for the Government to make a statement with regard to the internment and transportation of aliens of enemy and other nationality, saying: "I hope to show your Lordships that such abuses have arisen in the treatment of enemy aliens in this country that the more of us who are aware of these facts the less likely are such misfortunes to befall innocent people in our country again." He then set out a number of examples of leading anti-Nazis who had been deported.

Lord Faringdon began by naming two Germans: Karl Olbrish and Louis Weber. Karl Olbrish was born in 1902 in Essen. He was a former member of the Reichstag, the German parliament, but was expelled by Hitler when he took power in 1933. The same year, Olbrish was sentenced to three years in prison followed by a year in a concentration camp. When released, he fled to Czechoslovakia, and then came to Britain in 1938 on a temporary Czech passport.

Louis Weber was a member of the International Transport Union, and was a seaman. After Hitler's accession to power, he signed on as a seaman on to neutral ships. He came to Britain on a neutral ship as an anti-Nazi, but was interned nonetheless. Held in Warner's Camp in Seaton, Devon, he organised an anti-Nazi trade union against the Nazis who were being held in the same camp.

Lord Farringdon stressed that both men were clearly anti-Nazi and should never have been interned. Both men lost their lives on the *Arandora Star*, and Lord Farringdon said: "I consider that whoever was responsible for these men and, after their internment, for their transportation, is answerable for their deaths."

Farringdon also named four Austrians: Kurt Regner, Karl Mayerhaefler, Ernst Seeman and Michael Glass. Kurt Regner was born 4 August 1912, in Baden near Vienna. He was a lawyer, and as a student had been one of the most active members of the Socialist Student Movement. He was one of the instigators an anti-Nazi demonstration in Baden, and was beaten up for it. He fled during the night into Czechoslovakia, and was brought to safety in England by the Czech Refugee Trust Fund. He was regarded by them as one of the most endangered refugees. Karl Mayerhaefler was born on 21 December 1911 in St Peter Freiensten, Austria. He was another Austrian Socialist, who fled to Britain as a refugee on 22 January 1939, not long after Kristallnacht. His fiancée was a Jewess, and he wanted to marry her in England. Ernst Seeman and Michael Glass were hunted by the Gestapo in Vienna, but managed to escape and flee to Britain.

Another German who Farringdon named was Valentin Wittke, born in 1904 in Marienburg, who was a cabinet maker and later a ship's joiner. He was a leading official in the workers' organisation, or Trade Union. He fought for the rights of anti-Fascist workers, and in 1933 organised the collection of money for political prisoners of the

Nazis and their families. He was forced to flee to England. When the time came, not only Valentin was interned, but also his wife. Lord Farringdon ran through an extensive list of complaints about the conditions of internment, the lack of defence lawyers at Tribunals, the separation of families, the difficulties in sending and receiving post, and other matters.

His speech was followed by one from the Lord Bishop of Chichester. He had recently returned from a number of days visiting the internment camps on the Isle of Man and at Huyton. The Bishop said that he knew many of the internees whom he met in the camps because he had helped them in escaping oppression, and some were his intimate friends. Beyond the palisade at Huyton camp, he had seen crowds of men, useful men, able men, distinguished looking men walking aimlessly about with nothing to do. They were shut off from their families, and from the world, and as the months passed were losing all hope. Many of the prisoners had experienced life in German concentration camps. The Bishop emphasised that refugees were, or should be, in a different category to enemy aliens, and that they had rights as refugees. He emphasised his astonishment at the quality of the refugees Britain was holding in the internment camps – doctors, professors, scientists, inventors, chemists, industrialists, manufacturers and humanists – all wanting to work for Britain, freedom and justice.

Lord Mottistone urged the creation of a new body to supervise and advise on interment. He said that the regular police simply did not have time to do the job properly, and a special Home Office force should be created.

The Duke of Devonshire, replying for the Government, emphasised what a difficult time it had been in May when the overall order for internment had been agreed. He sought to minimise the tragedy of the *Arandora Star*, saying that of the Germans and Austrians, all were Category A. He said there had been fifty-three refugees on board, but that they had all been placed in Category A by Tribunals. He did not mention the Italians at all. He claimed that working under great stress, mistakes had been made.

The extent of mis-management had become increasingly clear as the days went by. A memorandum from the Foreign Office, dated 18 July 1940 reads: "Monsieur Preiswerk told me this morning that the German Government are pressing to have as soon as possible details of those missing from the *Arandora Star*, and also survivors. He remarked that amongst those on board were internees from Seaton, most of whom were Communists and who would not wish to have their names notified. So strongly are these people opposed to the Hitler regime that 50 of them refused to accept a payment of £1 from the Special Division, although they were completely destitute. He thinks that they are all Jews…I would be much obliged if you could kindly let me have the lists of the non-Nazis who were on board the Arandora Star so that I can communicate the names to Monsieur Preiswerk. He will then delete from the lists sent to Germany those names."

Sir George Warner of the Foreign Office liaised with Moylan at Scotland Yard. Moylan replied on 9 August 1940, three days after the debate in the House of Lords. He said that he had now received from Wormwood Scrubs [which was where M.I.5 were now based] an analysis of Germans and Austrians on the *Arandora Star* embarkation list. The summary of the list asserted that out of the 460 Germans and Austrians on board, only 175 were categorized as Nazis. Of them, 72 had lost their lives. There were 65 classified anti-Nazis, of whom 31 had died. There were also 220 assorted seamen and civilians, whose affiliation was apparently unknown, of whom 45 were lost. Thus, the truth was beginning to emerge. By 9 August, the official position was that only 38% of the German and Austrian prisoners on the *Arandora Star* had been known Nazis.

Three days later, on 12 August 1940, Winston Churchill appointed an ex-Cabinet Minister to chair an enquiry into the *Arandora Star* affair, Lord Snell. Snell's brief was: "to inquire into the method of selection of aliens to be sent overseas in the *Arandora Star*; whether the actual selection of individuals was in accordance with the method determined, and generally the action taken." Lord Snell eventually reported on 24 October, and the author will come to his report later.

However, the secrecy attaching to the HDSE [the Swinton Committee] and the activities of M.I.5 behind it remained very unpopular with MPs. On 15 August 1940, Winston Churchill felt forced to make a statement to the House of Commons, saying: "I submitted to the House some time ago the view that it was not in the public interest that Questions should be asked and answered about this Committee or other branches of Secret Service work, or about measures to deal with Fifth Column activities....Now why is it that we have thought it right to plead public interest against the discussion of the Swinton Committee and its work? Not assuredly because we have anything to conceal which would reflect upon the loyalty, impartiality and good faith of the Government, or anything that would do the Government harm as a Government if it were all explained in the utmost details. The reason is simply one of principle, namely that matters of this kind, and Committees of this kind, are not fitted for public discussion, least of all in time of war. The House has recognised this principle for many years...I am sure that the House would wish the rule to be respected in the case of a Committee which, as I said, deals with Fifth Column activities and other cognate matters....about ten weeks ago, after the dark and vile conspiracy which in a few days laid the trustful Dutch people at the mercy of Nazi aggression, a wave of alarm passed over this country, and especially in responsible circles, lest the same kind of undermining tactics and treacherous agents of the enemy were at work in our Island...I felt in that hour of anxiety that this side of the business of National Defence wanted pulling together. I therefore asked Lord Swinton to undertake the task...I am glad to tell the House that a very great improvement has been effected in dealing with this Fifth Column danger. ...I am satisfied that it has been reduced to its proper proportions, and is being gripped and looked after with very high efficiency...I can assure the House that the powers that Parliament has given to the Executive will not be used consciously in any unfair, oppressive, or, if I may use the expression, un-British spirit." Presumably, Prime Minister Churchill, when using the words "very great improvement" and "gripped and looked after with very high efficiency" was referring to the mass internments and deportations that he had ordered, which had in fact been handled, at the best, with gross inefficiency, and were unfair, oppressive and un-British.

In late August, as a result of the continuing political outcry, the Home Secretary, Sir John Anderson, set up a tribunal and an advisory committee to consider the possible release of Italian internees. It was called the Loraine Committee after its chairman Sir Percy Loraine, the ex-British Ambassador in Rome. Its purpose was the same as that of the German and Austrian tribunals: to consider whether an individual internee had been justly detained, whether there was a good reason to release an internee, and whether such a release would cause a risk to the security of the nation. Each case was to be judged separately and on its merits. The Loraine Committee was supplied with the M.I.5 and police files upon which the decision to intern had been made.

The Home Office issued a memorandum indicating that as of 19 August, 4,100 Italians had been detained, of whom 1,100 had been deported overseas, and that the purpose of the Loraine Committee review was to divide the Italians into two classes – those who were regarded as friendly to Britain, and those about whose sympathies and attitude there was some doubt [or who were shown to be genuine Fascists]. The memorandum stated: "It is hard to lay down any hard and fast principles for determining whether or not any individual Italian can be regarded as friendly towards this country. It will be the duty of the advisory committee to base their view on such information as is obtainable about the individual alien, and not on any general assumption that the mere possession of Italian nationality will by itself justify the conclusion that the Italian is a source of danger." The memorandum went on to acknowledge and emphasise that membership of the Fascist Party might be of much or little importance, since many Italians had been forced to join the Fascist Party under pressure, through fear of the consequences that might flow from refusal, or because membership of the party was a condition precedent on their ability to return to Italy. At last, common sense seemed to be entering the equation, and Churchill's "collar the lot" approach was being abandoned.

The memorandum noted that there were 390 persons in detention who were of joint Italian and British nationality. However, as is endorsed on the Foreign Office copy of the memorandum, whilst they might be detained under Regulation 18B, British or dual nationals could not be deported. The Foreign Office, who included many Italian experts from the Diplomatic Service, consistently took a very different and better informed view to that of M.I.5. A memorandum in their files dating from August 1940 confirms this. It was apparently written by F.L.Farquhar and reads: "I also attended a meeting convened by Lord Swinton last Saturday, from which it was apparent that our "security services", i.e.M.I.5, were [still] firmly fixed with the idea that the *Fascio* organisation in this country [as distinct from the British Union of Fascists] was a dark and sinister Camorra, that every member was actively engaged in sabotage and Fifth Columnist activities, and that it was sufficient to say that any individual Italian was a member to justify his detention until the end of the war. Under cross-examination, however, they admitted at this meeting that they were largely influenced in their attitude by fear of invasion. They also admitted that in the majority of cases they have practically no evidence of subversive activities beyond mere membership of the *Fascio*. Others at this meeting talked a good deal about "the necessity of adopting a policy of general internment in view of the imminent danger of invasion" etc etc. In short, I got the impression that it has been a case of "the wind up" on the part of the government and ignorance on the part of the experts, as far as our treatment of the Italians in this country has been concerned. At the end of this meeting the M.I.5 representatives handed to Lord Swinton a lengthy memorandum which none of us have seen, but which purports to prove that the Fascist organisation in this country is a danger and a menace."

Also in August 1940, the Foreign Office circulated the memorandum already referred to, written by Professor Foa, on the significance of membership of the Fascist party, and upon Italian Jewish refugees. Foa had been prompted into writing his memorandum by a statement made to the House of Commons by the Home Secretary, Sir John Anderson, on 23 July 1940. The Home Secretary had said that there were few or no Italian refugees in Britain, which simply was not true. The Right Honourable Viscount Swinton was sent a copy of Foa's memorandum in an attempt to defeat the prejudice of M.I.5. Swinton remained unmoved. He responded by accepting that Foa's report was probably true of conditions in Italy, but that the situation in Britain was different. He stood by the MI5 report, and their list of 1500 dangerous Italian aliens.

Once the Loraine Committee started to do its work, the truth of what had happened became increasingly clear. Brigadier Harker, now head of M.I.5, responding as late as 16 October 1940 to a Loraine Committee decision that four Italian men and an Italian woman should be released from internment, vehemently opposed the release of one of them, a certain Romolo Antonelli who was a member of the Manchester *Fascio*, upon the basis that: "the case against Romolo Antonelli is the case against the Italian Fascist Party, as outlined by our notes on the subject. The same consideration applies in the case of the majority of members, and if he is to be released from internment, it seems probable that something like 70% [of the Fascio] may be released on similar grounds. In our opinion, wholesale release of the members of the *Fascio* would constitute a serious danger so long as there is a possibility of an invasion of this country." It was a concession that M.I.5 had indeed built its list of "dangerous Italians" simply on the basis that they were members of the *Fascio*. Against 70% of them, there was no other evidence of ill will against Britain.

The Loraine Committee totally rejected M.I.5's approach in the clearest of terms, saying that they would always consider the individual cases, as was their duty. Sir Percy Loraine wrote to Brigadier Harker on 29 October saying: "My Committee feel so strongly on the point that membership of the Fascist Party is not necessarily condemnation, *ipso facto*, in all cases, that I feel bound to mention it again, and to insist that each case must be judged on its individual merits.

"In many cases these police reports have been drawn up carelessly, and have been found to bear little relation to the facts. This is particularly true of the Manchester Police, whose reports have been found to be particularly tendentious. So far we have had to deal with four female appellants [internees seeking release]. They have all come from Manchester, and in all cases we have recommended release for the simple reason that they were said to belong to an organisation – the *Fascio Femminile* – which, in fact, is non-existent in Manchester. In the case of Mrs Alessandria Montalbetti, the

Manchester police went so far as to suggest that she was living with a man and had changed her name accordingly. This was found to be totally incorrect, and the Committee cannot but suspect that the allegation was made to create a prejudice against the appellant *ab initio*. Their faith in the impartiality of the police has, as a consequence, been shaken, and we consider that the Home Office ought to consider the advisability of inviting the attention of the competent authorities to this aspect of the matter."

There were two significant issues therefore with the material which M.I.5 held, and which had been used to justify arrests: [a] it was not enough that an individual had joined a *fascio* club, and thereby the Fascist party; [b] the police reports on individuals in many cases bore no relation to the facts.

CHAPTER SEVENTEEN

THE SNELL REPORT AND THE LORAINE COMMITTEE

Lord Snell's report was completed on 24 October 1940. The terms of reference of his enquiry were strictly limited to the selection of the aliens who had been deported on the *Arandora Star*, and he stuck to those terms. Snell emphasised that: "the need for speedy action, and for sending aliens overseas in large numbers, was repeatedly emphasised in Minutes from the Prime Minister calling for periodic reports on the progress achieved."

In relation to German/Austrians, Snell said: "All the Germans and Austrians on the *Arandora Star* had been classified as Category A, and I see no reason to question the machinery of classification." A casual examination of the German/Austrian death list from the *Arandora Star* reveals many easily recognisable Jewish names. Was Snell assuming that they were all dangerous communists? Snell did not deal with the question of who decided that the Germans and Austrians who had not been before tribunals were members of the Nazi party or Nazi sympathisers, or why well-known anti-Nazis and at least one British citizen were included. He concludes this section of his report by saying: "All the Germans and Austrians on the *Arandora Star* were therefore persons who had been individually ordered to be interned on grounds of national security and accordingly could properly be regarded as coming within Category A."

In relation to Italians, Snell concluded: "In the case of Italians, no classification by Tribunals had taken place, and there was no alternative but to work on such material as was already available, i.e. the material in the possession of M.I.5…as time did not permit of further scrutiny, these lists were accepted as being the equivalent of Category A Germans and Austrians. The lists were largely based on membership of the Fascist party, which was the only evidence against many of these persons. M.I.5 apparently took the view that those who had been only nominal members of the Fascist party, and those who were ardently Fascist, were equally dangerous. The result was that, among those deported, were a number of men whose sympathies were entirely with this country. I cannot regard this lack of discrimination as satisfactory, and I think that M.I.5 must bear some of the responsibility for the results which followed their decision."

Snell continued: "A copy of the M.I.5 list of dangerous Italians was sent to each of the five camps concerned and the Camp Commandants were instructed to mark for deportation any person named on the list who might be in their camp. The lists, which contained about 1,500 names, could not be delivered to the camps until about 21 June. A period of only about 24 hours was therefore available for identifying Italians for deportation. The difficulties were increased by the fact that a number of Italian names have alternative spellings. There is, too, reason to believe that in one or two cases an Italian who wished to get out of the country impersonated a man whose name appeared on the M.I.5 list.

"In the case of Italians appearing on the embarkation list of the *Arandora Star*, the names of 28 did not coincide with the names on the M.I.5 list. In about a dozen of these cases, however, the names are so similar as to suggest that the persons embarked were in fact persons whose name appeared in the M.I.5 list."

Lord Snell referred to the case of Decio Anzani, perhaps the best known of the anti-Fascist Italians, saying that he had lived in England for 20 years before his arrest. He was not even a nominal member of the Fascist party, was known to be strongly anti-Fascist, and was the Secretary of the Italian Section of the League of the Rights of Men, an early Human Rights organisation. Snell simply commented that Anzani's name had been placed on the M.I.5 list "in error", and does not suggest whose fault that was, or how such an error came about. Decio Anzani died when the *Arandora Star* sank. Having mentioned the fact that Anzani should not have been on the *Arandora Star* [but not mentioned his death], Snell ended his report with the following words: "In compiling the embarkation lists of Italians it seems likely that errors occurred in about a dozen cases. These errors were due largely to the fact that the work was carried out under great pressure. Taking the broad view of the programme of deportation, I do not consider that this number of errors is a cause for serious criticism."

The Loraine Committee took a different view. It had been set up at the end of August 1940, not long after the Snell enquiry had been ordered, to arrange for tribunal hearings for those who had not had them. As we have already seen, its Chairman, Sir Percy Loraine soon became very unhappy with the actions of M.I.5 and the War Office. By the autumn of 1940, parliamentary opinion had swung firmly against deportation, and it had been stopped. A multitude of failures in both internment and deportation was gradually being uncovered, and in certain cases, the British Government was forced to accept that it had acted unlawfully.

Unlike Lord Snell, the Loraine Committee discovered much that had gone wrong. A Treasury file makes the confession that a total of twelve British subjects had been deported illegally to Canada and Australia, including the four already mentioned in this book: Hildesheim, Mancini, Pacitto and Parmagiani had all died when the *Arandora Star* was sunk. For those still alive, the Treasury file reveals that, on 7 October 1940, a remedy was in hand: "Steps are being taken to bring back to this country as quickly as possible those who have reached Canada or Australia. However, the question of compensation to the relatives of those drowned is complicated by the fact that if compensation is given it may give rise to claims for compensation in respect of the illegal removal from this country of those who were not drowned." No claim was apparently received on behalf of Parmigiani, but the families of Mancini and Pacitto had taken legal action, and the British Government were, perhaps not surprisingly, keen to settle their cases out of court, to avoid publicity and the likelihood of punitive damages. In relation to the hundreds of non-British citizens who died – the correspondence includes the concession that: "there were other people who got put on the *Arandora Star* because of departmental errors" but goes on "as these others were aliens, no question of illegal action arises…"

Hearing that a question was likely to be asked in the House of Commons about the death of Pacitto, a statement was prepared saying that: "The Government deeply regret this tragic error and are prepared to offer proper compensation." When the question was asked in the House on 8 October 1940, Herbert Morrison, now the Home Secretary, said: "I very much regret that by an unfortunate series of mistakes Mr Pacitto, who was a naturalised British subject of Italian origin, was interned on the outbreak of war with Italy, at a time when a large number of persons of Italian nationality or origin were interned. Immediately afterwards it was decided to send to Canada a number of internees, and Mr Pacitto was amongst those placed upon the *Arandora Star*. He was not amongst the known survivors, and it must be presumed therefore that he lost his life when the ship was torpedoed by the enemy. The Government fully realise that no expression of regret or sympathy, and no offer of compensation, can repair the loss which the relatives have suffered. The Government deeply regret this tragic error and are prepared to pay proper compensation."

Following this, at a meeting between the Treasury Solicitor's Office, the Home Office, the Lord Advocate's Department for Scotland and the Treasury on 2 December 1940: "It was agreed that the various mistakes made were not such as to necessitate settlement of the claims on a "hush money" basis i.e. that the Home Office must pay anything rather than have the case go to court…As regards the case of Pacitto, the original error was made by the police authorities in Hull, but the Home Office has also assumed liability in respect of internment for 20 days, and by reason of the man [Pacitto] being put on the *Arandora Star*."

The only specific figures that the author has found for the compensation paid to those who had been unlawfully deported and either died on board the *Arandora Star*, or spent time in detention far away from British shores, are in relation to Gaetano Antonio Pacitto. The Government eventually settled the case brought against them by Pacitto's family by paying the sum of £2,000 damages and 400 guineas legal costs. In the early 1940s, a labourer's wages were about £6 a week, or £312 a year, so that the award to Pacitto's family amounted to between 6 and 7 years income for a labourer. However, it must be remembered that Pacitto was not a labourer, but a successful businessman. The settlement was therefore far from generous. In any event, financial compensation could, of course, never make up for the emotional loss of the family. The Pacitto family remained rightly outraged and embittered at what had happened. They continued to run their ice cream business, Padgett's, and in the early 1950s, still feeling a prejudice against them because of their Italian name, they changed their name of Pacitto to Padgett.

The work of the Loraine Committee was intended to correct, in so far as it could, the many wrongful internments and deportations that had taken place. The evidence included in this book has already shown the high level of injustice involved. The author has already referred in the last chapter to the remarkable letter [or petition] dated 11 November 1940, and signed by 545 of the Jewish prisoners who had been deported to Australia on the *Dunera*. It described some of the bad treatment that they had suffered on board that ship. The letter was of great assistance to the Loraine Committee. It began with the following paragraph:

"We are the racial and political refugees who were interned in May, June and July 1940 under the general orders of the Home Secretary, and, on 10 July, sent to Australia. Although the policy of the Home Office changed shortly after our departure, we did not learn about this until the end of October, and many of us feel lost and forgotten as a result of the fact that we are so greatly separated from the authorities dealing with us. We are, in many directions and to a substantial degree, worse off than our fellow internees who remained in the United Kingdom. To avoid misunderstandings, we would like to state at the outset that we have been received and treated by the Australian Camp Authorities with great fairness and kindness which we acknowledge with gratitude."

The letter went on to state: "we suffer from the separation from our families" – a clear contradiction to the British Government assertion by telegram to the Australian government that most were single men. The letter explained that in many of the camps in Britain, before they left, the deportees had been told that their families would in due course be allowed to join them wherever they were to be sent. "Many of us were even promised that our wives and children would be able to follow immediately." That had not happened and was not going to. Australia had not given permission for the families of these "dangerous aliens" to follow them to Australia.

The letter speaks of their very harsh treatment on the *Dunera* and the wanton destruction of their property. All 545 signatories to the letter asked for their cases to be reconsidered by a tribunal, and for their release. They stated: "We have been classified as "Enemy Aliens" entirely from consideration of our origin. But we are fugitives from the country of our origin, many of us have suffered in concentration camps, our relatives have been treated brutally, we have been deprived of our rights of citizenship and nearly everything that was our own – above all, we hate that system of tyranny, violence and mendacity. We are the inveterate and bitterest enemies of Nazi Germany."

By 20 January 1941, the British government had decided that the Home Office was to investigate losses of the deportees on the *Dunera*, and to compensate them. The British military authorities were to investigate the misconduct of guards. Deportees still under the age of eighteen were to be brought back to the United Kingdom as soon as possible. Julian Layton was despatched to investigate the situation in Australia, and to hold tribunals there to judge the cases of the individual deportees. A similar mission to Layton's was sent to Canada, to review the cases of all the deportees held there.

One of the many difficulties, however, was that those who were approved for release would first have to be taken back to the United Kingdom and then released there. Australia had stated that although they were content to lock up the deportees in camps, if they were to be released, they could not stay in Australia, but had to be returned to Britain.

Many of those who had been so brutally deported on the *Arandora Star* and then the *Dunera* were obviously not Fifth Columnists. They were transient refugees, hoping to get to the United States or elsewhere as soon as possible. The *Dunera* application of 11 November 1940 had referred to these cases as "transmigrants." It complained that some on the *Dunera* had been tricked into volunteering for the ship at their internment camps, where they had been told by military officers that the *Dunera* was destined for Canada, and that it would take those who wished to emigrate to the United States much closer to their destination. They then found themselves unwilling prisoners on a voyage to Australia.

In an emotive paragraph, the deportees asked that once released, a pronouncement of their release immediately be made public, even if there had to be a delay before they could actually be released from their camp. They said: "It is of the greatest moral importance for us…we are fugitives from our country of origin, many of us have suffered in concentration camps, our relatives have been treated brutally, we have been deprived of our rights of citizenship and nearly everything that was our own – above all we hate the system of tyranny, violence and mendacity. We are the inveterate and bitterest enemies of Nazi Germany…we feel it against our honour to be interned by a country whose cause is our cause, and whose victory we pray for…"

The letter further asserted that many of the men had wished to join the Pioneer Corps, and had already applied to join the Corps before their internment. Nonetheless, they had been both arrested and deported.

Julian Layton knew before he set off for Australia in January 1941 that the policy of deportation had gone badly wrong. Layton's instructions were [i] to send home any deportee who should be in Category C, [ii] to make arrangements for those who wanted to enlist in the Pioneer Corps so that they might do so; [iii] to help those who want to emigrate to the US or elsewhere.

When Julian Layton investigated the 545 signatories to the *Dunera* letter, he concluded that 428 were eligible for immediate release. The remainder might be eligible, but required specialised consideration before a decision could be made. Further, of the 545 signatories, 256 wanted to emigrate from Britain, and 172 wanted to join the Armed Forces.

The British Government was quite happy to allow those deportees who were to be released, and who had been awaiting immigration into the United States, to go there. Four hundred of the *Dunera* deportees were registered with the US consulates, and were waiting for visas to travel there. However the process of furthering their applications from Australia was not easy. There were now three governments involved [Australia, Great Britain and the United States] and a letter or application form would take about two months to reach Britain, and at least another two months for a reply to be received. Existing registration files had to be transferred from London to the US consulate in Sydney. Also, many applicants had lost their essential documents on the *Dunera*. A ship carrying other personal documents belonging to the deportees was sunk on its voyage to Australia. Of course, for those who were to be returned to Britain, another long and dangerous sea journey was necessary. The Australian deportees who had been on the *Arandora Star* [which included all of the Italians] had already been torpedoed twice, and sunk once.

Layton's task turned out to be an enormous one. The individual claims for compensation for property lost on the *Dunera* were carefully compiled, they were considered by the Camp Leaders in the camps, and then each was sworn before an Australian magistrate. If the Magistrate was unhappy with the content of any claim, he would refer it back to the Camp Leader, or to Major Layton for further consideration. The full details of the claims reached the War Office in London on 6 August 1941. There proved to be 1,607 claimants. The total value of the claims was £38,225, including cash, jewellery, watches, typewriters, stamp collections, spectacles, fountain pens, musical instruments, scientific instruments, dentures, surgical appliances, and many other things. The guards on the *Dunera* had stolen everything of any possible value, and destroyed much else. At this time, the witnesses were still in Australia, but at least their sworn witness statements were available for careful consideration.

Legal action had been taken against those believed to be responsible for what had happened on the *Dunera* long before the detailed claims for compensation were received. As a result of reports from Australia, a Court of Enquiry was held in England in March and April 1941, and Courts Martial followed. Unfortunately, in those proceedings the value of the thefts was greatly underestimated, and it was decided that the loss suffered by the prisoners had only amounted to "several hundred pounds". It was found that a considerable amount of this property was later disposed of by military personnel in pawnshops in India and Australia. Only three members of the guard were court martialled: Lieutenant Colonel

W.P. Scott [who after the voyage had reverted to his substantive rank of Major], Acting Regimental Sergeant Major Charles Albert Bowles, Military Medal, and Sergeant Hellewell. Scott was convicted of "Having reasonable grounds to suppose that an interned prisoner had been treated with violence or neglect, failed to ensure that a proper enquiry was held." He was severely reprimanded. In effect, he was convicted of turning a blind eye in a single case of abuse. Bowles was found to be the main culprit in relation to the thefts and receipt of stolen property. He initially blamed Lieutenant O'Neill, V.C, for giving him some of the stolen property found in his possession. O'Neill however was called as a witness for the Prosecution and denied this. Bowles changed his plea to Guilty on two charges, and was acquitted of nineteen others. He was sentenced to twelve months imprisonment, and was dismissed the service. Sergeant Hellewell was convicted and severely reprimanded. Apparently, only one internee who had been on the *Dunera* gave evidence. Hundreds of others who clearly wished to do so were still in internment in Australia.

As the numerous "mistakes" of the internment and deportation process became publicly known, other action was taken against some of those responsible. As a result of "crimes and irregularities" in connection with the process, a total of three officers were imprisoned, two receiving eighteen months [presumably one of them Major Braybook], one receiving twelve months. In addition, the Director of the Prisoners of War Directorate of the War Office, the Deputy Director, the Inspector of Camps and a Staff Captain were all sacked on the grounds of: "unsuitability through age and inefficiency". The Deputy Director was one of those prosecuted and imprisoned for crime.

There are many sad individual stories of the suffering that the deportation of internees to Australia, and their lengthy detention, there caused. As already stated, the Australians had been told that the internees were almost entirely single men, which was simply not true. One example of the effects of deportation was Dr Alan Kurt Beck, born on 15 January 1892, who lived with his wife on a small farm in Devon, known as Cosy Neuck, Stockland. Having been deported on the *Dunera* on 10 July 1940, Beck eventually arrived home in Devon on 10 February 1942. During his absence his wife had had three operations, and could no longer work outside on their chicken farm. Nonetheless, she was looking after two evacuee children, aged three and four. Beck returned to find that his livestock had died or wandered off, and many of his tools and equipment were gone. He asked for £45 for losses on the *Dunera,* and stated that with that money, he hoped to start again on his farm.

On 26 September 1941, Major Layton in Australia was notified by London that it had been decided that it was desirable to settle the claims promptly, and on a broad basis without subjecting the claims to further individual scrutiny. The compensation payments were made ex-gratia and without any admission of liability, and they were to be accepted in full settlement of all claims present or future. It should be remembered to her credit that at this time Britain was still embroiled in a war that was far from its conclusion, and that she remained likely to lose. The Japanese attack on Pearl Harbour, which brought the mighty United States into the war on Britain's side, did not occur until December 1941.

Deportee Kurt Scheinburg was one of those who had suffered considerable loss on the *Dunera.* He was compensated in the sum of £165, 3 shillings and 8 pence for his loss, and wrote on 3 November 1941 to thank the Under Secretary of State for Home Office for the payment, saying in his letter: "May I also express my deepest gratitude for the peculiar fairness in dealing with the *Dunera* affair and the happenings on board the steamer en route to Australia in July 1940. The debate on this matter in the House of Commons in the middle of an appalling war redounds to the greatest honour of this country and would not have been possible anywhere else in Europe."

Thus, after a period of panic in the months of May, June and July 1940, thanks to her inherent fairness and democracy, the United Kingdom had returned to the basic principles that it was fighting for.

CHAPTER EIGHTEEN

THE LOSS OF *U-47*, THE *ABOSSO* AND THE *WAROONGA*

Despite Britain's return to fairness and democracy, it was very difficult for her to undo the injustice that she had done to the clear majority of the deportees. A large proportion of the deportees in Australia were approved by Major Layton's tribunals for release. However, the Australia Government did not change its view that, if discharged from custody, they had to return to Britain. Australia had been misled into taking them, and felt that it was a British problem that the British should solve. Therefore, the British must transport them back to Britain and process them there, with the only exception being those who had been accepted for entry to other countries such as the United States of America.

The problem was that a return to Britain by sea [the only realistic option] was as dangerous as the outward journey had been. Both those who had been sunk by torpedo on the *Arandora Star*, and those who had heard a torpedo strike the *Dunera* had every reason to fear a return passage. However, the choice was stark – either to risk another lengthy sea journey back to Britain or to remain a prisoner in an internment camp in Australia. Only a small proportion accepted the offer of a return ticket to Britain. The oceans were still stalked by killer U-Boats - Gunther Prien's success as a U-Boat commander had continued throughout the rest of 1940 and into 1941. If he ever learned the full horror of the sinking of the *Arandora Star*, it does not seem to have dulled his enthusiasm for his job. On four further patrols, he and *U-47* sank fifteen further ships and damaged others.

Then, on 6 March 1941 *U-47*, together with *U-70* and *U-99*, was as usual in the North Atlantic, off Ireland, one of their fruitful hunting grounds. At 1800hrs, *U-47* and *U-99* were caught on the surface whilst their two commanders were having a discussion over megaphones. Two British destroyers, HMS *Wolverine* and HMS *Verity*, equipped with radar, found them and attacked. Both U-Boats crash dived, *U-99* found deep water, but Prien and *U-47* were pounded with depth charges. For the time being, they survived. Once night had fallen, Prien surfaced, and managed to re-establish contact with a convoy that he had been stalking. At about 0500hrs on 7

March, all three U-Boats, *U-47, U-70* and *U-99*, began their attack on that convoy. Prien attacked a whaling factory ship, the *Terje Wilken*. The convoy fought back. *U-70* was rammed by a Dutch tanker, the *Mildrecht*, and was then sunk by the escorting Royal Navy corvettes HMS *Arbutus* and HMS *Camellia*. *U-99* came under a sustained depth charge attack from HMS *Wolverine* and HMS *Verity*. During these battles, *U-47* disappeared down beneath the ocean. Prien's last radio signal was timed at 0454hrs on 7 March, and neither Prien or *U-47* were ever heard of again. The cause of the sinking is not known – *U-47* had been heavily attacked the day before and might have sustained some unreported damage then, and the actions of *Arbutus, Camellia, Wolverine* and *Verity* may have compounded that damage on 7 March, or caused new, fatal, damage to *U-47*. However, there is no doubt that *U-47* was sunk, and that Prien and his crew joined the victims of the *Arandora Star* in that watery grave that is the North Atlantic. However, *U-47* and *U-70*, the U-Boats sunk on 7 March 1941, were only two amongst the many U-Boats that stalked the seas.

Some deportees successfully returned to Britain in 1941 and 1942 having been "cleared" by Layton's tribunals. For example, 16 Germans and Austrians travelled on a ship called the *Gleniffer* and survived the long journey. However, in 1942, tragedy was to strike again at some of those who had successfully survived the voyages of the *Arandora Star* and the *Dunera*. Forty-three returning deportees were shipped from Australia to Capetown aboard the SS *Westernland* in the autumn of 1942, and at Capetown were transferred to the MV *Abosso*. They found themselves on 29 October 1942 in the Atlantic, on the Capetown – Liverpool leg of the journey. The *Abosso* had left Capetown on 8 October, and was due to arrive in Liverpool on 31 October. All went well until 29 October, when the ex-deportees were only two days from the end of their journey

The *Abosso* was a relatively small passenger, mail and cargo liner, capable of carrying 656 passengers, 250 of them First Class. At the outbreak of war, the *Abosso* had been commandeered by the British Government and converted into what was known as a Defensively Equipped Merchant Ship. She carried 20 gunners to man her defensive guns. On this voyage, she was carrying 210 passengers: 149 military and 61 civilians. With a crew of 183, her full complement was 393. There were ten women with children, and forty-three of the *Dunera's* returning deportees. The latter had accepted the offer to return to Britain. They no doubt had good reasons for doing so, probably a strong desire to see the families whom they had left behind. Of the forty-three deportees, thirty-six were Germans and Austrians, most of them Jews, all of them veterans of the *Dunera* and some of the *Arandora* Star. Seven were Italians who had survived the sinking of the *Arandora Star*. All of the forty-three had been found by the Layton tribunals to be harmless, and/or had volunteered to join the Pioneer Corps. Seven of the Germans and Austrians gave as their address Bloomsbury House, London confirming that they were returning Jewish refugees. Bloomsbury House, and its predecessor Woburn House, had provided shelter and support for refugees fleeing penniless from Nazi Germany and Austria before and in the early months of the war.

In addition to the detainees, the ship was carrying to war torn Britain an important human cargo. She had on board 44 newly trained pilots from Bulawayo, Southern Rhodesia, and 84 Dutch servicemen, many of them Free Dutch submariners who were scheduled to be the crew of a new U-Class submarine, the rest were soldiers. She also carried a cargo of 400 bags of mail and 3,000 tons of wool.

The *Abosso* was not a fast ship, having a top speed of only 14.5 knots. Despite having an important human cargo, the ship was ordered to sail alone and unescorted. Lieutenant 1st Class Henry Coumou, of the Free Dutch Navy, protested at this, since the seas off West Africa were known to be a major U-Boat hunting ground, but his objection was over-ruled. The *Abosso* sailed alone. She successfully reached the Azores, but there, on 29 October 1942, a little before 2230hrs, she was torpedoed by *U-575*, a U-Boat under the command of Gunther Heydeman. Of the four torpedoes that Heydeman fired, one hit the *Abosso* abaft of the bridge. The ship stopped, her lights failed, and she began to list. The ship had twelve lifeboats, but few of them were successfully launched. As the *Abosso* settled herself in the water, she temporarily righted herself, and the crew got the emergency generator going and switched on her floodlights to help with the evacuation. This gave the *U-575* a perfect target, and Heydeman fired another torpedo into the *Abosso*. Half an hour later, she sank bow first beneath the waves. Although Heydeman reported that he saw about 10 lifeboats and 15 to 20 life rafts carrying survivors of the sinking, he said that he did not surface and try to question them or assist them in any way, because the weather was too poor. *U-575* left *Abosso's* survivors to their fate and continued her patrol.

The author Ulrich Boschwitz had been deported on the *Dunera* as one of the "dangerous Jews" that she carried. He had survived the ill-treatment of his guards and the harshness of the conditions, and duly arrived in Melbourne. He was then interned for two years, before finally being given permission to return to England. It is unclear whether he was one of those who had volunteered to join the British army, or whether Major Layton had simply found him to be one of the many who should never have been interned in the first place. Ulrich was keen to go back, and accepted a berth on the *Abosso*. He knew the dangers that he faced, and wrote to his mother before he sailed, telling her that he had sent some of the edited text of "The Man Who Took Trains" for a new edition to her via a passenger on another ship, in case, as he put it: "he took his chance and failed".

Only 31 persons off the *Abosso* survived. One lifeboat, No.5, was found on 31 October by HMS *Bideford*, which was escorting a convoy as a part of Operation *Torch*, destined for an invasion of North Africa. The occupants were 12 crew, 2 gunners, and 17 passengers. Of the 43 deportees being returned to Britain, only one survived, an Italian called Ugo Achille Bonelli. He finally reached England on 12 November, via Gibraltar. He arrived by sea, aboard the S.S.*Otranto*. Bonelli had been torpedoed on three separate ships, and had survived them all. News of the loss of the *Abosso* duly reached the camps in Australia, and was an obvious deterrent to any others who were thinking of trying to return to Britain before the war had ended.

The journey back to England continued to be a dangerous one. However, some of the deportees were still prepared to take the risk of enemy attack on their journey. Eleven of them travelled on the S.S. *Waroonga*, sailing from Australia on 30 January 1943. By now, they had been prisoners for more than thirty months, and knew that if they successfully got back to England, they would finally be released. The *Waroonga* was carrying foodstuffs, much needed in the UK, and she travelled in convoy. Two of the deportees were Austrians – Stefan Vadja, a 39 year old Company Director from Ashtead in Surrey, and Lazarus Ressler, who was 62 years old, and had most recently worked as a House Decorator.

Ressler was a Jew who had come to England many years before the First World War. He married his first wife in England, and by the time that he was left a widower upon her death in 1910, he had four children, all born in England. Ressler had married again in 1921, and had a son in 1922 by his second wife, Lance Bombardier Soloman Ressler. Soloman Ressler was born in London. At the time of his father's voyage back from Australia, Soloman was serving in the Royal Artillery. Ressler was a long time British resident, and should never have been interned or deported. Despite that, in 1940 Lazarus Ressler was arrested and interned, and he was selected for deportation on the *Arandora Star*. He survived the sinking of that ship, only to be placed on the *Dunera* and deported to Australia. He survived that hellish journey, and was then imprisoned in an internment camp for more than two years. Ressler's return to the United Kingdom for the purposes of his release was authorised on 25 August 1942 as a result on Layton's enquiries, and he was eventually offered a passage home on the *Waroonga*. He was brave enough to accept that place.

The *Waroonga* sailed across the Pacific, through the Panama Canal, on to Cuba and up to New York. From there, she faced the perilous task of crossing the Atlantic to reach England. On 4 April, a little more than two months after leaving Australia, the convoy in which the *Waroonga* was travelling was attacked, and she was struck by a torpedo on her starboard side. All the passengers made their way to boat stations, but after inspecting the damage, the Captain concluded that all were safe on board, and that the ship could continue in convoy. At this stage there were no casualties. The *Waroonga* succeeded in keeping pace with the convoy until 0400hrs on 6 April, when she suddenly started to go down at the stern. The Captain gave the order to abandon ship. The weather was stormy, and there was a very high sea running. The lifeboats were lowered, and those on board had to jump into them to save themselves. This was not an easy manoevre in the high seas, and when poor Lazarus Ressler tried to climb down a rope ladder in order to lessen the jump that he had to make into the lifeboat, he misjudged the force of the waves, and the movement of the lifeboat that he was trying to get into. In the words of Stefan Vadja, who had already jumped into the lifeboat: "The lifeboat swung in towards the ship on a wave, and he was crushed between the lifeboat and the ship before he had the opportunity of alighting in the lifeboat. The crash was severe, we heard the bones in his body crush, and I am certain he was killed instantly. He fell into the sea and I saw him swept away." Lazarus Ressler had survived twice, but not the third time.

The death of Lazarus Ressler in April 1943 is the last of the casualties that the author has identified resulting from the initial decision to deport enemy aliens. However, the imprisonment of enemy aliens in Australia continued until 1945.

CHAPTER NINETEEN

THE ACCIDENTAL FIFTH COLUMN

As we have seen, Churchill's "Collar the Lot" policy was motivated by a fear that a German, Austrian or Italian "Fifth Column" had infiltrated the United Kingdom and would help Germany's invading forces to overwhelm Britain. The events which followed the panic of the summer of 1940 proved how misguided and un-necessary the policy was.

The German and Austrian nationals in Britain were mainly refugees from their home countries, fearful of persecution and extermination if they returned. They wanted to see Nazi Germany defeated. Most hoped that they could contribute to Britain's war effort, and, once the threat arose, strongly desired that Britain and her allies would succeed in resisting an invasion by the Nazis. One of the escape routes from internment was to volunteer for the Pioneer Corps. Although a military unit, historically the Pioneer Corps had been little more than a labour force under military command. However, for aliens in Britain in World War Two, it became a stepping stone to other branches of the British Armed Services. Many Germans, Austrians and Italians joined the Pioneer Corps, and went on to give distinguished service.

Those who had been deported to Canada or Australia could find a way back to Britain by enlisting in the Pioneer Corps. Three examples will perhaps suffice. Abrascha Gorbulski, deported to Australia, had always hated the Nazis, and was longing to fight against them. After the arrival of Major Layton in Australia, Gorbulski was released from internment and successfully travelled back to Liverpool, where he signed up to the Pioneer Corps, and by November 1941, aged nineteen years and ten months, he had begun training with the Pioneer Corps in Ilfracombe, Devon. He transferred to the Intelligence Corps on 15 March 1944, and finished the war with the rank of sergeant. Hans Max Wilmersdoeffer, who had been deported to Canada on the *Ettrick*, volunteered for the Pioneer Corps and was brought back to Britain to join it. He transferred to a regular unit, was commissioned, and late in the war, as a Lieutenant in the Special Air Service, parachuted into Enemy Occupied Italy on

Operation *Blimey*. He changed his name, and went on to have a distinguished career in civilian life in England after the war. Erik Nathan Kahnheimer joined the Pioneer Corps from the Isle of Man where he was interned. He moved on to the Royal Armoured Corps, and then he also joined the Special Air Service, now known as Eric "Lofty" Kennedy. He parachuted into Northern Italy with Operation *Galia* in December 1944. Those three were amongst over 3,600 "enemy aliens" who joined up and fought for Britain, starting in the Pioneer Corps, and moving on to other regiments. So much for the wild theories that they were dangerous Fifth Columnists. As we have already seen, German/Austrian and Italian refugees worked for the BBC, and many put their expertise into a wide variety of fields to the benefit of the Allies.

The position of the Italian internees was different to the Germans and Austrians. Although there were refugees amongst them, most had been living and working in Britain for many years, and had done well there. Some joined the Pioneer Corps but the majority, when released, returned to their businesses and homes in Britain. Most still loved their hometowns and villages in Italy, and before the war had returned there for holidays when they could, but Britain had become their home. When eventually they retired, some might return to their villages and towns in Italy and enjoy a comfortable life there, or they might choose to stay in Britain. The vast majority were friends of Britain, and not supporters of Mussolini.

After September 1939, when the war with Germany had started, those who believed that Mussolini would in due course bring Italy into the war on Germany's side had a genuine choice – to remain in Britain with their families or to return with their families to Italy. Initially, the fear was that the Germans would bomb the cities and towns. After the war had actually begun, and Britain began interning its enemy aliens [the Germans and Austrians], the message for Italians was clear – if Mussolini brought Italy into the war alongside Germany, Italian citizens in Britain would also be interned. Those of Italian descent who had been born in Britain were British citizens, and some long-term Italian residents had applied for and obtained naturalisation, but the substantial majority of Italians were still Italian nationals, and would become enemy aliens. The anomaly was that whilst Italian parents might be interned as enemy aliens, their British-born sons would be conscripted into the British Armed Forces.

The unsurprising result of the combined threat of bombing and internment was that many male Italians in Britain sent their wives and young families back to Italy once war against Germany had broken out, and sometimes the menfolk went as well, if there was somebody whom they could leave behind to look after the business. The family of Luigi Beschizza was an example. His parents returned to Bratto, Italy, whilst he himself insisted on staying in London. There was, of course, already a body of Italians who had returned from Britain to Italy before the war - those who had made sufficient money in Britain, and had retired and built a nice home in the village of their ancestors. Often these spoke good English. A third category, once Mussolini had declared war, was those who were caught in Italy by Mussolini's decision – those who had intended to return to Britain after a visit to Italy caused by business, family matters, education or simply a holiday, but who now found themselves unable to return because of the war. These were people who, even if they had succeeded in returning to Britain, would have been liable to be interned. What Winston Churchill and his Cabinet never realised was that these Italians would eventually become a very valuable British Fifth Column in Italy.

There was little that these accidental Fifth Columnists could do to help Britain in the early years of the war, whilst Mussolini remained firmly in control of Italy. However, once the Allies invaded Sicily in July 1943, all that changed. On 25 July, Mussolini was finally deposed as Italian Dictator. He was imprisoned, and on 8 September 1943, an armistice was announced, by which Italy withdrew from the war. At that time, there were between 80,000 and 85,000 Allied prisoners of war held in prisoner of war camps in Italy, the vast majority captured during the North African campaign.
Unfortunately, the lapse of time between Mussolini's fall and the signing of the armistice had given Germany plenty of time to prepare for what seemed to them to be inevitable – Italy's withdrawal from the war – and they made preparations to remain in Italy and fight on. Nonetheless, following Armistice Day, about 25,000 of the Allied

prisoners held by the Italians were freed or managed to escape from their prison camps. They went on the run in Italy, hoping to escape to freedom. Within days of the armistice, the Germans freed Mussolini from his mountain prison, and put him back on the throne of a new Italian Fascist Republic.

Using Mussolini as their puppet, the Germans fought to resist all Allied advances up Italy. Behind the German front line, a civil war was fought between the Fascists and the anti-Fascists. Many anti-Fascists joined the resistance – the *partigiani* – and, using sabotage and guerrilla warfare, they tried to shake off the German hold on their country. The thousands of Allied ex-prisoners wandered the country trying to find a way home, as Allied forces fought their way up Italy from the south. Potentially, the ex-prisoners were of great value to the Allies. Although they would no doubt be "rusty" after their time in captivity, they were all trained servicemen, with a wide variety of important military skills. Pilots and aircrew in particular were of value. A significant number of those who eventually escaped into Allied territory went on to fight with distinction in the invasion of Normandy, or elsewhere – at least two [Captain Bob Walker Brown and Lieutenant Jim Riccomini] returning by parachute into occupied Italy with the Special Air Service. Almost every escaped prisoner was helped on his way to freedom by Italians – an "Accidental Fifth Column." The "Accidental Fifth Column" became of great value to Allied fugitives after the armistice had been declared. There were many of them, and some had undoubtedly returned to Italy because of Britain's internment policy. The Foreign Office, the best informed of British government departments, had worried during the internment and deportation drive of June and July 1940 that the aggressive and mismanaged policy would turn friendly British Italians against their adopted country. Happily, if undeservedly, they were proved wrong. Despite all that had happened during May, June and July 1940, most British Italians retained a strong affection for their adopted country.

The sinking of the *Arandora Star* robbed the village of Bratto of five of its sons. From the Beschizza family, Anselmo, aged 62, who had married a Necchi-Ghiri, and Raffaele, aged 29 were both lost. There were three other members of the Beschizza family on board: Luigi,

Pietro and Sisto. From the Cattini family, Pietro, aged 58, and Giacobbe Pietro, aged only 22, were both lost. Another Brattese, Pietro Orsi, aged 52, also died, as did Domenico Chiodi, aged 27, from the neighbouring village of Braia. When the news eventually reached Bratto, the small and close community was shaken and shocked. In a village so inter-related, it is unlikely that there was a single person who was not affected by the tragedy. Their loss could only be blamed on the British state, who had imprisoned them and sent them to sea. Of course, the *Arandora Star* had been sunk by a German torpedo fired from a German U-Boat, but those who had died had been prisoners of the British who had committed no crime other than that of being Italians by birth and nationality, and they were exposed to great danger on their voyage to Canada. The *Arandora Star* was unescorted and an obvious target in an ocean where it was well-known that U-boats stalked. In Bratto, it must also be remembered that a number of the villagers spoke English as a result of the time that they had spent working in Britain, and would have been able to covertly listen to the BBC news on the radio. There was also the BBC's Radio Londra Italian language service. In addition, many had family members still in Britain. One villager, Matteo Pasquale Cocchi, who had previously lived in England for 42 years, claimed to have 43 nephews there.

The author is particularly grateful to Steve Schia, who was born in Bratto on 18 November 1936, for the details that he has been able to give of the families living in Bratto at that time. The village of Bratto had a population of about 400 people. They were nearly all *"contadini"* – peasant farmers - and they lived off potatoes, chestnuts and occasionally meat when it was available. There were six mills near the village for grinding the chestnuts into flour. Steve Schia's recollection is that at least a dozen citizens from Bratto were imprisoned in England on the Isle of Man. When Mussolini was deposed on 25 July 1943, there was a great feast of celebration in Bratto, and a service in the church of San Giorgio. Giovanni Schia, Steve's father, had been called up into the Italian army, and posted to Greece. He became one of many who refused to serve under the Germans once they took over Italy in September 1943, and decided to join the partisans [the resistance]. He later trained and served under British command.

The Italian Armistice was announced on 8 September 1943, and within days, fugitive Allied ex-prisoners of war began to arrive over the mountains, finding their way to Bratto en route for the west coast of northern Italy, where it was rumoured that an Allied landing was soon due to take place. On the other side of the Appenines from Bratto, prisoner of war camps at Veano and Fontanellato opened their gates and let all their prisoners out. The Germans and Fascists then began to hunt the escaped prisoners down – Germany retained control of most of Italy at that stage. The escaping prisoners were on foot, and most were still dressed in their military uniforms. They carried only emergency rations with them, taken from Red Cross parcels before they left camp, and they rarely carried any money. They needed everything – food, lodging, civilian clothing and guides to take them by safe paths on towards the front line or the coast. Coming to Bratto, it is highly unlikely that the fugitives knew anything of what had happened to the *Arandora Star* or the suffering that tragedy had caused to the villagers of Bratto. Nor would they have known that some Brattese were still held prisoner thousands of miles away from their families in Australia, having done absolutely nothing to justify their imprisonment. Amongst other nationalities, British and Australian fugitives came to Bratto, seeking help. The Brattese learned that they were British and Australian, and but still gave them nothing but help and comfort.

Amongst the first fugitives to arrive and seek refuge in the village were Lance Corporal D Russell of New South Wales, Australia and Roy Harris of Perth, Western Australia. They met and were looked after by Pietro Beschizza, namesake of a deportee on the *Arandora Star*. They probably did not fully appreciate the risk that Pietro Beschizza was taking by helping them. If re-captured, they would simply return to a life as prisoners of war, protected by the Geneva Convention, whilst any villagers of Bratto who had helped them were liable to be executed, and their houses burned to the ground. Pietro Beschizza not only sheltered the two Australians, he and his family also looked after four New Zealanders: Lance Corporal L. Roderick and Privates J. Devlin, L.E.Smith and M.B.McGregor. Finally, he took in a South African, R.P.Driver, making seven fugitives in all. When these seven moved on after two days on 16 September 1943, Lance Corporal Roderick wrote a note of thanks that all seven of them signed. They thanked not only Pietro Beschizza but all of the people of Bratto, saying: "Mr P.Beschizza and the people of the village, Bratto, acclaimed us, fed and gave us directions to enable us to evade the Germans, and assisted us in every way possible." Roderick, Devlin, Smith, Mcgregor, Harris and Driver also stayed with Clorinda Corsini in Bratto, and the four New Zealanders stayed with Clorinda Beschizza, a cousin of Pietro's. The South African, R. P. Driver moved on down towards Lucca, and was looked after for three months by a man called "Wally" Giannecchini. Another of the Beschizza family, Giorgio Beschizza, who had been born in London and spoke fluent English, was recruited by Major Gordon Lett, the author's father, to act as an interpreter in Lett's International Battalion of Partisans, based in the Rossano valley, Zeri.

Elvira Cattini, nee Venturini, was married with three small children, Bruno, Pasquale and Romana. Her husband Luigi had a restaurant business in London, and the family normally lived in New Cross. They had returned to Bratto for a holiday, and Elvira's youngest child, Romana, was born in Bratto in March 1940. After the birth, Luigi returned to London to work, and Elvira and the children remained for a while with their family in Bratto. Then war broke out, and Elvira was trapped in Italy, continuing to live in Bratto with her children. Her husband was arrested in London and interned. Although happily he was not sent off on any of the deportation ships, he remained a prisoner in England for years, eventually returning to Bratto in 1947. Elvira Cattini had not seen her husband, and her children had not seen their father, for more than three years by the time of the Armistice of September 1943. Nonetheless, when the escaped prisoners of war began to come over the mountains, Elvira Cattini, nee Venturini, helped and sheltered them.

Amabile Cattini was married to Mariuccia, and had a daughter called Rosina, born in 1936. Despite the enormous danger to himself and his family, Amabile looked after five British fugitives: Major P.A.Clayton, DSO, Major J.C.Blackmore, Squadron Leader N.P.Samuels, DFC, Able Seaman A.C. Capp and Trooper S.L.Moreton, Royal Hussars. On 20 September 1943, Major Clayton wrote: "Cattini Amabile has been of great assistance to the above officers and men in avoiding falling into German hands, by giving us food and shelter, and guiding us personally through a difficult part." Some time after Major Clayton's party went on their way, Amabile was betrayed to the Fascist authorities, and was arrested. Amabile was not executed, but was sent to a German concentration camp, almost certainly with the intention that he should be "exterminated by work." Somehow, Amabile managed to survive the war, and Steve Schia remembers him eventually returning to Bratto "very skinny indeed." Happily, Amabile was able to pick up the pieces of his life, to rejoin his wife Mariuccia, and to have further children.

Other members of the Cattini family also helped. Lieutenant Colonel V.J.L.Napier, Major C.P.G de Winton and Sapper Jones were looked after by two cousins, both named Luigi Cattini. Both had owned restaurants in London for many years, but had retired back to Bratto. Napier described them both as extremely hospitable. Napier left a note for the Allied authorities with one of the cousins, Luigi Cattini fu Andrea, of Bratto-Cerri, when he and his companions moved on after two nights on 23 September. It reads: "L.Cattini of Bratto, Pontremoli, has kindly given us food and shelter for two days, at risk both to himself and his household. Nothing could be more generous than the attention which we have received. They have bought special food available to us, offered a whole month of bread coupons and have pressed us to stay as long as we like. I should be most grateful if you would assist him if it lies in your power and repay a debt which I am unable".

Matteo Pasquale Cocchi, as previously mentioned, had lived in England for forty-two years before the war, and spoke perfect English. He was a man of about 60. Despite his age, he gave help to a total of ten escaped prisoners of war, including at least four British and two South Africans. He would shelter them in his barn overnight, and then guide them over the mountains on the next stage of their journey the following day. It was very risky, and on 4 October 1943, whilst guiding two South Africans, Cocchi was caught by German troops, and was imprisoned. After six months in custody, he managed to bribe his way to freedom in March 1944. After the war, he was compensated by the Allies for his time in prison – but not for the bribe which he had paid to secure his freedom.

Alberto Necchi-Giri was another who provided: "valuable assistance to many Allied Prisoners of War who escaped from Prisoner of War camps." Alberto was married with two young children, Marietta and Armando. He himself had never been to England, but according to Steve Schia [who was the same age as Armando], all Alberto's relatives were in London. Anselmo Beschizza, who died on the *Arandora Star* at the age of 62, had married a Necchi-Giri. However, perhaps the most unfortunate of the Bratto Necchi-Giris was Israele Necchi-Giri. He was arrested, and probably only because of his name and the fact that he had darker skin than many, he was believed to be Jewish [which he was not] and was exterminated in the gas chamber of a concentration camp. Between the Armistice of September 1943 and eventual liberation in the Spring of 1945, the German army sent squads of its soldiers to Bratto on five occasions. They had to march up each time, since there were no roads or paths fit for motor vehicles. Steve Schia recalls that the Germans behaved themselves, but that they took food, which was in short supply.

Guglielmo "Wally" Giannechini was another important Fifth Columnist. In September 1943, he was living in his home village of Vinchiana, near Lucca in Tuscany. The comune of Lucca had lost 31 souls on the *Arandora Star*. Giannechini had returned to Italy from Motherwell, Scotland, in early 1940, he said because of ill-health, but the British friends whom he was to make were sure that he had done so to avoid internment. Giannecchini was a successful café and billiard hall owner who had worked in Motherwell for eighteen years. He had rightly concluded that if Italy entered the war against Britain, those such as himself who were Italian citizens working in the United Kingdom would be interned. Giannecchini spoke fluent English, and had become known in Motherwell by the nickname "Wally" – the local pronunciation of the Anglicisation of his Christian name. He was Guiglelmo [William], Willy for short, pronounced Wally. Wally's sister, Mrs Paolina Fazi, still lived in Vinchiana.

For over three years, Wally lived a quiet life in Vinchiana, and "kept his head down". He no doubt enjoyed the delights of the weather and the dramatic local countryside around Vinchiana, which stands astride the Serchio river, and of being with his family, rather than in an internment camp on the Isle of Man, or travelling on a deportation ship such as the *Arandora Star* to Australia or Canada. He was strongly anti-Fascist, but kept his views to himself. He was an ideal Fifth Columnist – a "sleeper" until the day came when he could help the Allies.

Once the Armistice was signed in September 1943, escaped Allied prisoners of war soon began to move through the area around Vinchiana, and it was then that Wally began his work – providing them with shelter, food and clothing, and helping them to move on down towards the Allied front line which they hoped to cross in order to escape. Initially, he paid for them himself, using his own money, and then he borrowed money from friends without telling them the real purpose for the loans. The first ex-prisoners that he encountered [on 16 September] were South Africans, and he took them to the house of a friend, Alfredo Lazzarini, for shelter. They stayed with Lazzarini for two weeks, whilst their sore feet recovered. Before they left to head for the front line, they agreed on 26 September to go with Wally to find other escapers in the local mountains, since they could assure other escapers of Wally's good intentions. The expedition resulted in Wally being put in touch with more than a dozen fugitives. His sister, Paolina, was in charge of the distribution of money, food, clothes, medicines, and lodgings.

Before long, Wally had about ninety escapers in his care. He knew, as everybody did because it was well publicised, that the penalty for helping Allied escapers was death. That did not deter him. At the beginning of December, Wally was tipped off that there was going to be a German/Fascist *rastrellamento* [a raking through] to search for the ex-prisoners, using German soldiers and Fascist militia. Wally managed to move the ex-prisoners to safe lodgings before it took place. No-one was caught.

Wally was determined to mark Christmas for the fugitives with special Christmas parcels. Scraping together what he could, Wally put together Christmas parcels containing such things as trousers, suits, pullovers, cigarettes, toothpaste, biscuits, some wine, razorblades, and other luxuries, and distributed them to the escapers shortly before Christmas. The ex-prisoners in his care would often write messages to him about a variety of things, including their concerns that their hosts might be going without food in order to feed them, which was sometimes the case. Wally looked after them all until finally the Allied advance overran the area in late 1944.

Along with a number of other Italians, Wally was recommended and approved for a British medal for his unfailing courage, initiative and resolve. It was the British Empire Medal. His citation, drafted by British officers who knew what he had done, reads: "Signor Guglielmo Giannecchini started to help escaped prisoners of war in the Lucca area immediately after the Italian Armistice and worked tirelessly, with a complete disregard for personal danger, until December 1944. A most loyal and trusted member of an Escape Organisation, he arranged shelter, food and clothing for at least sixty escapers, caring for many of those men in his own home, and doing everything in his power to ensure their safety and well-being. Signor Giannecchini also carried food, medical aids and other necessities to a large number of Allied service personnel who were in hiding in the mountains. He gave warning when searches were likely to be made by the Germans, distributed money and gave valuable information as to the best escape routes. In addition, Signor Giannecchini frequently acted as guide, convoying escapers over long distances and completing all his missions successfully. All those with whom he came in touch, escapers and other helpers, speak of Signor Giannechini's unfailing courage, initiative and resolve. Signor Giannecchini has rendered outstanding service to the Allied cause, it is entirely due to his superb efforts that many escapers were able to regain their freedom."

Sadly, for reasons set out in the following chapter, Wally never got his medal.

Lazzaro Cura was a successful cafe owner in London, one of a number of members of the Cura family working in that city when war broke out in 1939. He came from the village of Gotra, Albareto, near Borgo Val di Taro in the province of Parma, and had built a fine house there which still stands. He lived with his wife and family in a flat above his café at 340, Edgeware Road, London. His eldest son, Vittorio [or Victor] was born in 1936. Lazzaro's wife fell ill not long before war broke out, and returned to Italy to recover – the fresh air around Gotra was a lot healthier than London in those days. In due course, Lazzaro Cura travelled to Italy to visit his wife, leaving the café temporarily in the hands of an Italian friend. He intended his visit to last only a month, but was then caught in Italy by Mussolini's declaration of war. He and his family were stuck in Gotra for the duration of the war.

Initially, Lazzaro Cura did what so many pro-British Italians did, he led a quiet life and did nothing to draw Fascist attention to himself or his family. Then in July 1943, came the fall of Mussolini after 21 years in power. On 3 September 1943, the Italian Armistice was signed. It was announced to the world on 8 September. The Germans had no intention of leaving Italy, and the Allies began to fight their way up the country, forcing the Germans and Mussolini's rejuvenated Fascists slowly back onto the Gustav Line, which ran through Monte Cassino.

This was the time for the "Accidental Fifth Column" to act, and to do whatever they could to loosen the German/Fascist grip on Italy. Lazzaro Cura, café owner from the Edgware Road, did just that. He linked up with Major Gordon Lett, an escaped prisoner of war and partisan resistance leader from the other side of the nearest mountain range. His job for Lett was one of the most dangerous – he became the custodian of Lett's radio transmitter, hiding it under the eaves of his house in Gotra. Gotra was a significant distance from Lett's partisan base in the valley of Rossano, which increased security. By use of the radio, Lett was able to communicate with Allied Special Force [he had been appointed as a Special Operations Executive partisan liaison officer], and to arrange supply drops of munitions, food and other equipment for his partisans. The whereabouts of his radio was a total secret, shared only by Lazzaro Cura and his immediate family. Lett did not tell any of his partisans where it was, and went secretly to Lazzaro Cura's house to send his messages. Cura knew that if he got caught, he would be tortured for whatever information he held and then shot. He knew also that in all probability his fine house would be ransacked and then burned to the ground, and his young family left homeless. At one point, a garrison of German troops occupied his house, but Lazzaro Cura remained steadfast in his support for Lett, and the Germans moved on, having murdered a young partisan whom they had captured and who had tried to escape, but not having discovered the radio. At the end of the war, Lazzaro Cura returned to London and continued his career as a café owner. His son Vittorio [or Victor] followed in his footsteps, until his own retirement.

Another who returned to his home town in Italy was Frank [Francesco] Berni. The exact date of Berni's return to his home town of Bardi is not known, but the explanation that he gave after the war was that he had been on a motoring holiday in Italy in 1939, and with war breaking out, he had been unable to return to his home in England. It seems therefore that he must have returned to Bardi before Mussolini declared war on 10 June 1940. During the war, he still owned two restaurants in Britain, and two sons of his, both British born, served in the British army. He had two sisters still living in England. Berni was a successful businessman, who had also lived in Dublin and run at least one cafe there. His home town of Bardi had a tradition of sending its men to work in Wales, and there were a large number of citizens from the town of Bardi working there in June 1940. With two British-born sons serving in the British army, Berni might have been expected to stay in Britain. However, the fact that he had British sons would not have protected him from internment there and possible deportation. It may be that he, like Wally Giannecchini, chose to return to his Italian home, because he did not wish to be interned in England.

Having returned, Berni became *podesta* [mayor] of his home town of Bardi, and held that post at the time of the Armistice in September 1943. Since the office of *podesta* was a Fascist appointment, it is to be presumed that the Fascist authorities did not know that Berni had two sons fighting for their enemies. In normal circumstances, he might have seemed an obvious candidate for the role of a Fifth Columnist supporting Britain in the war, but Bardi was a town which, on 2 July 1940, was the worst hit of all the Italian communes by the *Arandora Star* tragedy. Forty-eight of the victims of the *Arandora Star* came from the small but beautiful town of Bardi. One of them, Attilio Berni, aged 42, was undoubtedly a relative of Frank Berni's. Attilio had been working in Weston-super-Mare in

Somerset, England. Many of the Bardi victims would have been known to Frank Berni personally. The sinking and loss of life had had a massive impact on the town, and is still commemorated there every year. As with Bratto, but to a greater extent, it must have been difficult for many of the Bardini to forgive the British. However, their mayor, Frank Berni, led by example, and his help to the many Allied fugitives who passed through the Bardi area was outstanding.

Following the Armistice, Berni became a main organiser of help for escaped prisoners of war. He sheltered many of them, or found them safe lodging, obtained false identity documents for them, and gave them money to a total of about 144,000 lire, as well as food and cigarettes. After the war he refused any repayment of his costs. As *podesta* of Bardi, Berni had a difficult "double role" to play, seeming to be a good Fascist whilst working hard for the Allied fugitives. Parallel to the help that Berni was giving to Allied escapers, there was a resistance war going on between the anti-Fascist partisans and the Germans and Fascists. The partisans enjoyed great success in the Bardi area in 1944, and for a while were able to emerge from their covert partisan bases, and take control of the town of Bardi itself.

Berni, however, realised that the partisans could only retain control of the town for a short period. They were not strong enough to resist any determined attempt by the far superior German forces to recapture the town. He therefore did not declare his true colours, but stood down as *podesta* for as long as the partisans were in charge of the town, and inconspicuously provided all possible facilities to the acting mayor who took over. Berni was proved to be right when the partisans withdrew in the face of a German attack on the town. A punitive German occupation of Bardi followed, and when the Germans withdrew, Berni was able to return as *podesta*, and carry on his good work. Frank Berni helped escapers of every rank, including valuable aircrew, and of several different nationalities – but mainly British and South African.

Lieutenant Colonel Gordon de Bruyne, who was one of those Berni helped, wrote: "…Signor Berni has the confidence and respect of all parties. To my personal knowledge he has been of the greatest help to us all. He has been most generous in providing clothing and he has provided funds for innumerable prisoners of war. As Mayor of Bardi, he has supplied us with rations and personally supervised their delivery to us. His aid is always willingly forthcoming, and no prisoner of war has appealed to him in vain..."

After the liberation of Bardi by the Allies, Berni's valuable work was recognised, and he was recommended and approved for the award of Member of the British Empire. However, he like Giannecchini never received the award that he so richly deserved.

Emilio and Rosa Sartori had lived and worked in Cupar, Fifeshire, Scotland for nearly twenty years before the Second World War, running first a fish and chip shop in Cupar, and then a second shop in Comrie. Their son Pier Angelo Sartori was born in Cupar on 3 March 1927, and a little later a sister Maria arrived on 12 July 1929. Rosa's maiden name was Cura [no direct relation to Lazzaro Cura]. Both her family and Emilio Sartori's came from in and around the village of Buzzo, and from nearby Albareto, Parma. Rosa's father Giovanni [John] Cura had been the first of their immediate family to come to Britain. He had come initially to Dundee, and then moved to Cupar, where his daughter and Emilio Sartori joined him in 1920. All were driven to Scotland by poverty – at Buzzo there were too many large families squeezed into small houses, with no work available except in their few fields.

The boy Pier Angelo was schooled at Castlehill Primary School in Cupar until the age of eleven. Then his parents enrolled him in the Istituto Salesiano "San Benedetto", a Catholic school run by the clergy in Parma, Italy, since his mother Rosa wanted him to become a priest. Young Pier Angelo went off to school in Parma in 1938.

Neither Emilio nor Rosa Sartori had obtained British naturalisation, and following Mussolini's declaration of war on 10 June 1940, they were both interned, as was Rosa's father Giovanni. Thankfully, neither Emilio nor Giovanni were sent to Warth Mills or onto the *Arandora Star*. They were despatched with many other Italian detainees to the Isle of Man. Rosa was sent to Cultybraggan Camp near Comrie in Perthshire, and Maria went with her, since she was still only a child. As the panic of an expected invasion of Britain subsided, the Sartoris were allowed to obtain work, and eventually worked together at a hotel in Birmingham.

Pier Angelo Sartori, now 13, remained at school in Italy, trapped there by the war. In the confusion of June and July 1940, he may not have known what had happened to his parents and sister in Britain, but no doubt he would have learned in due course that they had been imprisoned by the British. He was only thirteen, and the news must have distressed him. However, he had family locally who were able to look after him when he was not at school. It seems that young Pier Angelo remained settled in his school, and kept on with his studies. However, after the Armistice of September 1943, it was the Germans who were running Italy, not Mussolini. Pier Angelo was Scottish born, and by May 1944 was aged seventeen. At some time before he eventually returned to Scotland, he gained the nickname "Jock", although whether that was at school or afterwards is not clear. In May 1944, "Jock" Sartori was advised by the Principal of the Silesian College to leave because the Germans were beginning to pay attention to the students there. Whether the Principal was worried about him because of his "Scottish" family and background, or because he was in effect close to military age, or both, is not recorded. Jock Sartori did not need to be warned twice. He left at once, and went to live with his maternal grandfather in the village of Buzzo.

It was not long before he joined the anti-Fascist resistance, the partisans. He wanted to fight against the Germans and Fascists. At first he joined a unit led by an ex-*maresciallo* of the carabinieri, battle name Richetto, who used him mainly as a courier, since he knew the mountains around his grandfather's home very well. Before long, he was recruited into a neighbouring unit, the British Special Operations Executive [SOE]'s Mission Blundell Violet, commanded by the escaped prisoner of war Major Gordon Lett, in the nearby valley of Rossano. Jock Sartori proved to be a brave and effective partisan and SOE agent. For Lett he acted mainly as a courier and an interpreter. Lett's International Battalion of partisans contained fighters of various nationalities, some of them British or English speaking. In late December 1944, Lett was reinforced by Operation *Galia* - a troop of 2 Special Air Service led by Captain

Bob Walker Brown, who were dropped in by parachute. Jock Sartori's language skills became invaluable as the SAS went into action with the International Battalion. In March 1945, Lett was ordered to ex-filtrate down through the front line to join the Allied forces awaiting an attack on the German Gothic Line. Jock Sartori received similar orders. He had his 18th birthday either in the valley of Rossano just before the perilous journey through the Gothic Line, or during that journey. Having crossed the lines he was formally attached to No.1 Special Force, a unit of SOE, and advanced with Lett and a partisan unit to take possession of the vital port of La Spezia as the Germans retreated in April. He was discharged from service by SOE on 15 May 1945, the war in Italy having been won. Jock Sartori is a fine example of a young man who, despite the way the British Government had treated his parents and his sister, was prepared to risk his life fighting for them, under Lett's command with SOE.

The work of the Accidental Fifth Column had been outstanding. However, the British Government failed to honour the recommendations for medals for the courageous Italians of its Accidental Fifth Column - a sad fact which lacked any justification of an imminent invasion, and was a decision made by a different British Government to Churchill's – the post-war Labour Government of Clement Attlee. At least 149 medals were initially approved for Italian Fifth Columnists who had shown exceptional courage, and the citations still exist. They included a George Medal, a DSO, OBEs, British Empire Medals, MBEs and many King's Medals for Courage – a medal that had been invented to reward the courage of non-British foreign nationals. As previously stated, Giannecchini and Berni were two of those medal winners. The author has dealt with the question of these medals elsewhere, but a brief synopsis of the situation is appropriate here.

The recommendations and citations for the award of medals to Britain's Fifth Column in Italy came through a body called the Allied Screening Commission [ASC], set up in 1944 following the fall of Rome. It was staffed by experienced British Officers from the Italian field, and all of the recommendations and awards were carefully vetted by senior British Officers. However, despite the fact that Field Marshal Alexander, the Allied Commander in Chief in Italy, was firmly in favour of the awards, on 31 May 1944 it is recorded that: "There is a complete ban on the giving of British awards and decorations to Italians." Until September 1943, Italy had been at war with Great Britain and her allies. Because of this, it was felt that it was too early in May 1944 to award any medals to Italians, irrespective of how outstanding their conduct in support of the Allied cause had been. The Americans were to award many medals to Italians, but not the British.

Field Marshal Alexander remained in favour of awards to Italians, and appreciated what the helpers had done. He made the following statement in support of the Accidental Fifth Column in 1945: "Before leaving Italy, I would like to pay tribute to all those civilians who at one time or another voluntarily rendered, at considerable personal risk, very valuable assistance to Allied fugitive ex-prisoners of war and airmen, who were escaping from the enemy in Occupied Territory. The gallant efforts of these countless helpers resulted in the safe and early return of thousands of our men to their homeland and families, and in many cases soon afterwards to further service with the armed forces. I know I am speaking on their behalf when I say they would all wish, if it were practicable, to thank their helpers personally, and endeavour in some way to repay the debts which they have incurred. It is however my intention that due recognition be awarded and all material debts be repaid to every individual civilian who rendered assistance of whatever nature to Allied escapers. I am glad to say that this immense task is already in hand. It will of course take many months to finish, but I give my assurance that everything will be done to see that no-one is forgotten."

On 17 May 1946, Sir Noel Charles, the British Ambassador, said in a speech in Rome: "I am well aware of the gallant efforts made by some 80,000 Italian civilians throughout Italy who, during the dark days of the Nazi-Fascist occupation, displayed boundless generosity and kindness to our men over a long and trying period; it must be remembered that, in doing so, not only did they refuse the financial rewards for the denunciation of Allied prisoners of war which the Germans offered and which would have been a fortune to them, but they also showed magnificent abnegation and courage in sharing their few clothes and scanty food, and, above all, risking their lives and the lives of their families and friends for disregarding the increasingly severe German injunctions against harbouring or helping Allied prisoners. A number of them indeed were shot by the Germans…We remember today with great sorrow those who no longer are with us, and who lost their lives in this noble cause."

Thus it is absolutely clear that both the military commanders and the British diplomats in Italy were well aware of the courage shown, and sacrifices made, by the Italian civilians of Britain's Accidental Fifth Column. Yet the position of the British Government never changed.

The Accidental Fifth Column contained both men and women. One of the most heroic of the women was Giuglelmina Petrelli, an eighteen year old who threw herself into the path of a bullet intended for a British escaped prisoner of war, in a moment of pure courage and self-sacrifice. She took the bullet for him, and he escaped. Even in her case, as with the others, all attempts to lift the ban on medals were of no avail. One of the last attempts which is still documented is a letter from Lord Selbourne [who previously had spoken in the 10 July 1940 debate in the House of Commons when he was Viscount Wolmer], who had been the Minister in charge of SOE. Written to Ernest Bevin, and dated 29 January 1948, it says: "I confess to considerable dismay at learning that it has been decided that no awards can be given to Italians for services in the late war, for fear of offending the relatives of our troops who were killed by the Italians…Thank heaven the British disposition is to forget and forgive, and I cannot visualise my numerous relatives, who have lost sons in the Italian campaign, taking other than the common sense view of the dilemma, which is that we should reward those who have helped us, and forgive those who fought against us, recognising that they only did so under orders of superior authority. I think it was the Duke of Wellington who said that when we made peace we ought to bury the hatchet altogether. I therefore deplore the decision, and I cannot help asking whether Field Marshal Lord Alexander was consulted…I very much hope that the decision does not include the King's Medal for Courage and the King's Medal for Service. These medals were struck particularly for foreigners who helped us…" Bevin replied that although he regretted the decision, it was final.

EPILOGUE

No formal apology has ever been given by the British Government for the multiple failings in the selection of internees for deportation on the *Arandora Star*, or for the fact that 452 of its survivors were shipped to Australia a mere seven days after they had been rescued from the Atlantic Ocean. Nor has any formal apology been given for the dreadful treatment of the deportees on the *Dunera*. In the individual case of Gaetano Antonio Pacitto, who was illegally interned and deported, and died on the *Arandora Star,* the new Home Secretary, Herbert Morrison, told the House of Commons on 8 October 1940 that: "the Government deeply regret this tragic error and are prepared to pay proper compensation", but that is all. Those who received compensation for their losses on the *Dunera,* received them as an ex-gratia payment without any concession of liability. Whilst there was an acceptance that the internment and deportation procedures were riddled with "mistakes", the excuse that was regularly given was the pressure of the existing national crisis i.e. the expected invasion by the Germans.

It is clear from the memorandum of 2 July 1940 that Churchill himself, with Chamberlain as his supporter, was the driving force behind the policy of "collar the lot", and from the memorandum of 22 June 1940 that the Government knew that the selection had not been done properly. The author suggests that the politicians arguing in the House of Commons on 10 July 1940 who described it as a panic were accurate – it was a panic move that completely ignored the basic human rights and the well-being of the deportees. The Italian Consul to Liverpool, Signor Rotini, was saying the same thing in his letter of 15 June 1940.

Following the evacuation from Dunkirk, the United Kingdom undoubtedly had its back to the wall, and was facing the imminent and totally unexpected prospect of a Nazi invasion. The United Kingdom Government was under enormous pressure, and the country was fighting for its life. The author has previously argued that human rights are often the first casualty when a national leader or politician considers how to deal with a pressing national problem. Not all national leaders pause to consider whether a proposed response to a current problem breaches human rights, or whether it can be justified as being a proportionate response to the crisis that threatens. The author has attempted to describe the British Government's decision to intern and deport accurately, and to set out the reasons behind it. Was it a panic decision? Would the action taken have been proportionate to the problem of Fifth Columnists and the threat of invasion had it been carried out properly? What caused the almost total failure of the selection process for both internment and deportation? The fatal intervention of Gunther Prien's *U-47* on 2 July 1940 simply confirmed what was already known, namely that the North Atlantic was a very dangerous ocean to cross in the summer of 1940.

On 15 July 1940, after the *Arandora Star* had been sunk, and the *Dunera* had sailed for Australia, the Foreign Secretary, Lord Halifax, wrote to the Home Secretary, Sir John Anderson, with copies to Neville Chamberlain, Anthony Eden and Lord Swinton. He began by saying: "I have been carefully into the matter [of the *Arandora Star*], and I find it difficult to write with complete restraint about what I cannot but think has been a very bad business…" The reader may conclude that Lord Halifax was absolutely right.

LISTS OF THOSE WHO DIED ON THE *ARANDORA STAR*

The author copies in the pages that follow a mixture of lists prepared by others in the years since the tragedy, and is indebted to them for their labours. He is particularly grateful for the work done by the author of the Colonsay History website and by Maria Serena Balestracci. There are many lists and part lists held in the National Archives, but none of them can be accepted as entirely reliable due to the circumstances in which they were compiled.

The United Kingdom was in a state of all out war, and an invasion was expected at any minute. The records that were kept of all personnel, both captors and captured, were not of high quality, and foreign names were confusing. There can be little doubt now that all the names on the lists in this book died on the Arandora Star, but it is certainly not beyond the bounds of possibility that there were others, whose presence on the ship was not recorded, and who died when she went down.

If the author, like many before him, has unknowingly included mistakes in the lists, then please forgive him

CREW

Rank	Name and Surname	Age	Place of Birth
Chief Steward	Percival Frederick Abbott	52	Southampton
Assistant Steward	Abraham Abrahams	25	Liverpool
Assistant Cook	Henry Lawrence Bache	59	Liverpool
Greaser	George Lowrie Bell	57	North Shields
Assistant Steward	Herbert Leslie Bleasdale	32	Birkenhead
Boatswain's Mate	Joseph Brindley	37	London
Writer	Denis Brook	20	London
Assistant Pantryman	William Ellis Castell	19	Liverpool
Purser	Harold Clegg	42	London
Steward	Robert Charles Cousins	59	London
Fireman	B. Darracotte	52	Liverpool
Pantry Boy	Henry Davies	18	Liverpool
Assistant Steward	Frederick John Edgecombe	34	Plymoouth
Assistant Steward	Thomas Ellis	49	Liverpool
Assistant Steward	J. Farquhar	20	Lerwick
Steward's Boy	J. Firth	18	Birmingham
Chief Officer	Hubert Henry Grace	51	Sheffield
Scullion	Jack Almo Halson	19	Portsmouth
Assistant Baker	William Thomas Halson	28	Portsmouth
Donkeyman	George Hamilton	57	South Shields
First Radio Officer	Charles Harris	46	Peterborough
Assistant Pantryman	William James Haslam	20	Liverpool
Assistant Steward	Wilfred Ernest Hayles	20	Isle of Wight
Assistant Steward	Frank Emil William Hobden	27	Worthing
Assistant Steward	Francis Edward Holohan	51	Kilkenny
Assistant Purser	George Pinkerton Hughes	26	Belfast
Writer	Alfred Charles Hutton	34	London
Assistant Steward	Christian Lauritz Jacobsen	46	Denmark
Able Seaman	John Morris Jones	49	Liverpool
Fireman	Richard Kehoe	52	Wexford
Assistant Steward	David Kelleher	59	Limerick
Sailor	Leonard Ernest King	18	Southampton
Second Radio Officer	Douglas Bernard Kirkham	28	Stourbridge
Able Seaman	John Joseph Kyte	59	Liverpool
Quartermaster	James Thomas Laurenson	21	Lerwick
Fourth Officer	Ralph Liddle	27	Essex
Assistant Steward	Ronald MacDonald	35	Fort William
Assistant Steward	Patrick Henry Pearse McNally	22	Belfast
Greaser	James McNamee	57	South Shields
Watchman	William Charles Moitie	60	Jersey
Master	Edgar Wallace Moulton	54	Liverpool
Fourth Engineer Officer	Alistair Richard Mowat	31	New Zealand
Fourth Engineer Officer	John Griffiths Mulcahy	28	Brisbane
Scullion	Gerald George Mulvey	25	Dublin
Fireman	Edward Murphy	53	New Zealand
Scullion	Karl Pontus	22	South Shields
Assistant Pantryman	John Patrick Quinn	39	Worcestershire
Second Officer	Stanley Ranson	40	Liverpool
Plumber	Thomas Ferguson Robson	22	Liverpool
Pantryman	Reginald Mathew Sharpe	36	Southampton
Greaser	Rocco Sinacola	23	London
Cook	Gilbert Lawton Smith	55	Liverpool
Fireman	Walter Varley Standing	49	Toronto
Assistant Pantryman	Charles Gordon Steward	22	London
Assistant Baker	George Allan Watson	55	Hull
Senior Ass Eng Officer	Robert John Wiggins	24	Monmouthshire
Chief Butcher	John Henry Williams	56	Liverpool
Steward	Albert Edward Young	39	London

MILITARY GUARD

NUMBER	RANK	NAME	REGIMENT
558173	Trooper	Arthur Richard Abbotts	Royal Armoured Corps, Staffordshire Yeomanry
556505	Gunner	Albert William Allison	Royal Artillery, 102 [Northumberland Hussars]
4035427	Private	Geoffrey James Barnett	4th Bn. Welch Regiment
2984552	Private	Thomas Barr	5th Bn. Argyll and Sutherland Highlanders
S/159411	Corporal	Leslie Sidney Barrett	Royal Army Service Corps
5620565	Private	Clifford Frederick Bartlett	4th Bn. Devonshire Regiment
326823	Gunner	William Edward Bates	Royal Artillery, 77 [Duke of Lancaster's Own Yeomanry]
5990254	Private	Herbert John Beckley	2nd Bn. Hertfordshire Regiment
326536	Trooper	Ronald Joseph Bee	Royal Armoured Corps, Nottinghamshire Yeomanry
5624085	Private	Alfred Henry Beer	5th Bn. Devonshire Regiment
5614593	Private	John Morton Bedlam	1st Bn. Devonshire Regiment
4935	Major	Christopher Aleck Bethell	Royal Tank Regiment, Royal Armoured Corps
5990106	Private	Alfred Joseph Birtchnell	2nd Bn. Hertfordshire Regiment
4126390	Private	Kenneth Philips Blackmore	7th Bn. Devonshire Regiment
557029	Trooper	James Blundred	Royal Armoured Corps, Staffordshire Yeomanry
3961176	Private	Henry George Brocklebank	2.5th Bn. Welch Regiment
7178754	C.S.M.	David Browne	9th Bn. Royal Warwickhire Regiment
2977971	Private	Robert Burrell	5th Bn. Argyll and Sutherland Highlanders
314715	Trooper	George William Buss	Royal Scots Greys [2nd Dragoons]
555851	Gunner	Thomas William Canterford	Royal Artillery
406216	Trooper	Frank Sidney Carter	Royal Armoured Corps, Royal Dragoons
98219	Lt [QM]	Thomas Cartman	General List
5726589	Private	William Frederick George Chick	4th Bn. Dorsetshire Regiment
5619912	Private	Peter Clarke	4th Bn. Devonshire Regiment
409839	Trooper	William Colquhoun	Lovat Scouts
318740	Trooper	John Connelly	Lovat Scouts
325094	Gunner	Alexander Cuthbert	Royal Artillery
S/149732	Private	Stanley Alfred John Darnell	Royal Army Service Corps
4033447	Private	Clive Darrall	4th Bn. Welch Regt
3966070	Private	Charles David	2.5th Bn. Welch Regiment
554079	Gunner	Leslie Dawson	Royal Artillery, 102 [Northumberland Hussars]
3964603	Private	Donald Ernest Vore Domican	5th Bn. Welch Regiment
4911816	Corporal	Charles Henry Edgington	Royal Armoured Corps, 1st Bn, Royal Dragoons
5619428	Private	Jack Alva Edmonds	4th Bn. Devonshire Regiment
5619731	Private	Richard Wilfred Ellis	7th Bn. Devonshire Regiment
3958788	Private	Alfred Robert Evans	4th Bn. Welch Regiment
3955542	Sergeant	Morgan Evans	2nd Bn. Hertfordshire Regiment
556746	Trooper	Albert Freeman	Royal Armoured Corps, Nottinghamshire Yeomanry
4126237	Private	Sidney Fredrick Arthur German	7th Bn. Devonshire Regiment
5623870	Private	Victor Basil Gibbons	7th Bn. Devonshire Regiment
562337	Private	John Frederick Glanfield	Devonshire Regiment
2981151	Corporal	William Glen	5th Bn. Argyll and Sutherland Highlanders
49339	Captain	Richard Henry Goddard	2nd Bn. Middlesex Regiment
5727272	Private	Robert Charles Godfree	4th Bn. Dorsetshire Regiment
318520	Gunner	Wallace Goodwin	Royal Artillery, 153 [Leicestershire Yeomanry]
323716	Trooper	Robert Grant	Lovat Scouts
406037	Trooper	James Grieve	Lovat Scouts
3963640	Private	Benjamin Griffiths	4th Bn. Welch Regiment
5623366	Private	Albert Richard John Hannaford	Devonshire Regiment
403988	Trooper	Frank Clifford Harley	Royal Armoured Corps, 1st Royal Dragoons
324110	Trooper	James William Hayles	Yorkshire Dragoons Yeomanry [Queen's Own]
3966133	Private	Harry Albert Holmes	2.5th Bn. Welch Regiment
5989833	Corporal	Harry Holt	2nd Bn. Hertfordshire Regiment
5624350	Private	Albert Ernest Hudson	4th Bn. Devonshire Regiment

5990188	Private	Robert Edward Humphreys	2nd Bn. Hertfordshire Regiment
5951293	Private	John Rylatt Jackson	2nd Bn. Hertfordshire Regiment
3963326	Private	William Samuel John	4th Bn. Welch Regiment
318248	Gunner	John Johnston	Royal Artillery
3963311	Private	Oliver Jones	4th Bn. Welch Regiment
3966164	Private	William John Jones	2 5th Bn. Welch Regiment
5723819	Sapper	Frederick Charles Kellaway	Royal Engineers
322429	Trooper	Norman James King	Warwickshire Yeomanry
5619142	Private	Edward George Lane	7th Bn. Devonshire Regiment
5989119	Private	Osmund Thomas Langley	2nd Bn. Hertfordshire Regiment
7562775	Gunner	Edward Macon	Royal Artillery
322158	Gunner	James McKenna	Royal Artillery, 155 [Lanarkshire Yeomanry]
112773	Lieut.	Edward Sydney William Miles	7th Bn. King's Royal Rifle Corps
5623901	Private	Owen Mitchell	7th Bn. Devonshire Regiment
317969	Gunner	Thomas Dunn Moore	Royal Artillery, 155 [Lanarkshire Yeomanry]
558176	Trooper	Thomas Mullis	Royal Armoured Corps, Staffs Yeomanry
326063	Trooper	Frank Geoffrey Munton	Yorkshire Hussars Yeomanry
325618	Gunner	John Frederick Murphy	Royal Artillery, 77 [Duke of Lancaster's Own Yeomanry]
4688185	Trooper	George Haller Newcombe	Royal Armoured Corps, Queen's own Yorkshire Dragoons
5989692	Private	James Thomas Oakley	2nd Bn. Hertfordshire Regiment
5612172	Private	Francis Percy Palmer	7th Bn. Devonshire Regiment
5718142	CQMS	Harry Gordon Payne	Somerset Light Infantry
3962740	Private	Maldwyn Phillips	2 5th Bn. Welch Regt
362437	Gunner	Francis Charles Price	Royal Artillery, 75 [Shropshire Yeomanry]
3952211	Private	David Thomas Rees	4th Bn. Welch Regiment
5990162	Private	Harold Alfred Robins	2nd Bn. Hertfordshire Regiment
2817123	Trooper	William Urquhart Ross	Lovat Scouts
5621426	Private	Cecil Arthur St. John-Clifford	7th Bn. Devonshire Regiment
5614987	Private	Percival George Sampson	7th Bn. Devonshire Regiment
5619117	Corporal	Roy James Skerrett	7th Bn. Devonshire Regiment
406316	Trooper	William Smith	Royal Armoured Corps, 1st Royal Dragoons
326332	Gunner	Alfred Nigel Whitley Sykes	Royal Artillery, 75 [Shropshire Yeomanry]
3248098	Rifleman	Peter Lluellyn Gordon Tarchetti	9th Bn. Cameronians [Scottish Rifles]
5990119	Private	Henry Ronald Taylor	2nd Bn. Hertfordshire Regiment
5726643	Private	Ronald Walter Terrell	4th Bn. Dorsetshire Regiment
318656	Trooper	Herschell Thompson	Yorkshire Dragoons Yeomanry [Queen's Own]
5990284	Private	Frederick William Wells	2nd Bn. Hertfordshire Regiment
325208	Trooper	Alexander Wilson	Lovat Scouts
3247652	Rifleman	John Wilson	9th Bn. Cameronians [Scottish Rifles]
5621415	Corporal	Douglas James Wyatt	7th Bn. Devonshire Regiment
CH/20011	Marine	Ernest Edward Warren	Royal Marines, H.M.S. President 111

GERMAN/AUSTRIAN PRISONERS

Surname and Christian name	D.o.b	Rank/Profession/Occupation	Nat.	Birthplace	Last place of abode
Rolf Baruch	05.05.22	Clerk	G	Hamburg	London
Heinrich Beck	26.01.98	Consulting Engineer	A	Zborowitz	Newcastle upon Tyne
Ludwig Beck	13.11.95	Master Tailor	A	Vienna	Northampton
Herman Bergemann	24.09.10	Music Hall Artist	G	Altona	Tenby, Wales
Fritz Bieber	10.02.07	Dress Designer	G	Berlin	Leeds
Wilhelm Biermann	01.04.06	Driller - SS *Leander*	G	Saltwarden	Oldenburg
Karl Birk	11.05.13	Naval Artificer - SS *Wagogo*	G	Freiendiez Unterlahn	Not Known
Bernhard Blankenhorn	23.06.09	Export Manager	G	Mulhouse	Ipswich
Bertold Bloch	05.07.00	Commission Agent	G	Randegg	Freetown
Samuel Blumens	13.01.93	Stocking Manufacturer	A	Neumarket, Poland	London
Alfons Blumenthal	21.04.07	Singer	G	Wiesbaden	London
Franz Breuer	17.11.85	Ship's Cook - SS *Adolf Woermann*	G	Neuss	Hamburg
Walter Buhtz	07.07.09	3rd Engineer - SS *Pomona*	G	Hermsdorf	Hermsdorf
Otto Burfeind	09.01.85	Captain - SS *Adolf Woermann*	G	Altona Blankensee	Hamburg
Friedrich Dabel	27.08.11	Physician	G	Stralsund	Lanlivery, Cornwall
Erich Dangl	18.02.10	Clerk	A	Waidhofen	Cambridge
Heinz Dellit	28.07.13	Technical Demonstrator	G	Jena	London
Steffen Dienes	04.04.23	Student	G	Dresden	London
Rudolf Dietze	02.09.11	3rd Officer - SS *Mecklenburg*	G	Hamburg	Hamburg
Karl Dippold	08.11.18	Ship's Baker - SS *Biscaya*	G	Hamburg	Hamburg
Hans Dobrin	25.08.93	Advertising Expert	G	Berlin	London
Emil Drews	06.04.97	2nd Engineer - SS *Leander*	G	Berlin	Danzig
Richard Erbert	31.07.84	Company Director	G	Stolzeman	West Byfleet
Hugo Erdmann	20.09.03	Steward - SS *Adolf Woermann*	G	Hamburg	Hamburg
Josef Eschborn	11.07.04	Clerk	G	Freiburg	Farnworth
Erwin Feinler	01.10.08	Sports Teacher	G	Berlin	Berlin
Adolf Feiltz	15.10.09	Engine Cleaner - SS *Adolf Woermann*	G	Lindow	Hamburg
Alexis Finkelstein	25.01.77	Retired Chemist	G	Leipzig	Cheltenham
Hugo Fleischer	26.02.13	Textile Representative	G	Cologne	Huddersfield
Julius Frank	10.04.91	Merchant	G	Zeilitzheim	London
Anton Fromeyer	04.05.07	Decorator	G	Thorn	Johannesburg
Hermann Gasteiner	14.01.80	Hairdresser	A	St. Veit	Hamburg
Rudolf Gellert	08.08.22	Mason	G	Gievertz, Silesia	London
Werner Gieske	08.10.12	Topographer	G	Berlin	Cirencester
Alexander Glaser	10.07.09	Insurance Agent	G	Vienna	London
Rubin Glucksmann	19.05.89	Company Director	A	Czernowitz	London
Heinz Gottfeld	08.02.07	Aeroplane Mechanic	G	Bad Polzin	Recife, Columbia
Hans Graboski	08.08.10	Motor Mechanic	G	Berlin	Cardiff
Otto Grebe	05.09.14	Housepainter	G	Klotzen	Essen
Walter Gremme	03.02.02	1st Officer - SS *Borkum*	G	Bochum	Hamburg
Walter Groskopf	18.03.90	Electrician	G	Lubben	Buenos Aires
Karl Guhl	04.05.89	Photographic Merchant	G	Spandau	Hove
Eduard Gumplowicz	15.05.23	Student	A	Vienna	Poole
Rudolf Hartmann	20.09.13	Circus Artiste	G	Stuttgart	Ascot
Gustav Haupt	15.09.10	Trader	G	Seidenschwauz	Wersenthal
Ferdinand Hebelka	21.05.97	Works Manager	A	Vienna	Newcastle upon Tyne
Walter Heinsohn	25.10.99	Quartermaster - SS *Adolf Woermann*	G	Hamburg	Hamburg
Simon Hermann	24.06.92	Watchmaker	S	Varschen	Leeds
Alfred Heyland	23.07.85	Teacher	G	Dusseldorf	London
Frank Hildesheim	20.03.76	Civil Engineer	B	Glasgow	Marlborough
Max Hirschfeld	13.03.89	Merchant	G	Berlin	London
Solomon Hochmann-Littmann	22.02.07	Electrical Fittings Trader	A	Kaluss	London
Karl Hoene	09.12.14	Radio Mechanic	G	Berlin	London
Friedrich Holdengraber	23.01.03	Ladies Outfitter	A	Vienna	London
Heinrich Holmes	27.09.22	None	A	Vienna	London
Mor Jam	30.06.93	Architect	A	Budafok, Hungary	London
Hero Jobus	05.02.97	Steward	G	Hanover	Hanover
Herbert Kastner	19.07.13	Seaman	G	Dohna	Dohna
Frantisek Kirst	22.06.07	Signwriter	G	Berlin	London
Valentin Klotzkowsky	23.09.96	Fitter	G	Nikolaiken	Hamburg
Rolf Korner	21.08.08	Dress Designer	G	Munchen Gladbach	London

Werner Krain	20.10.13	Printers Representative	G	Berlin	London
Richard Kuback	23.03.05	Diamond Mounter	A	Vienna	London
Conrad Lamberty	07.04.66	Chemist	G	Aachen	London
Heinrich Langheck	20.06.97	Engineer	G	Esslingen	London
Wilhelm Lauscher	04.03.92	Agent	G	Aachen	Leeds
Emil Lessmeister	21.03.84	Pensioner	G	Hutschenbausen	Nuremberg
Johann Letzke	21.01.77	Dyer's Foreman	G	Krefeld	Macclesfield
Rudolf Leutelt	11.06.07	Author	G	Innsbruck	Starnberg Munchen
Wilhelm Linke	07.05.07	Accountant	G	Hamburg	Calabar, Nigeria
Frido Lissauer	12.09.91	Stationer	G	Hamburg	London
Richard Loeb	20.03.02	Window Dresser	G	Munich	Liverpool
Friedrich Luetke	16.03.12	Company Director	G	Barmen	Leicester
Gustav Luppe	06.01.03	Planter	G	Kiel	Munchen
Richard Mai	22.06.10	Hosiery Foreman	G	Oberlungwitz	Mansfield
Richard Mai	29.01.86	Works Manager	G	Oberlungwitz	Mansfield
Fritz Marcus	19.02.89	None - formerly a Lawyer	G	Munster	London
Karl Meier	25.05.87	Locksmith	G	Konigstein	Birkenhead
Reinhart Melchior	24.03.21	Engineering Student	G	Charlottenburg	Loughborough
Ernst Meyer	23.02.79	Petroleum Chemist	S	Silesia	London
Willy Meyer	20.09.98	Army Contractor	G	Richmond, Surrey	London
Gustav Michaelis	09.09.84	Baker	G	Bruhesdorf	London
Hans Moeller	21.08.12	Student	G	Bremen	London
Curt Moll	10.06.76	Commercial Adviser	G	Breslau	London
Ernst Moser	27.10.89	Paper Manufacturer	G	Aachen	Wilmslow
Karl Moser	27.05.10	Cigar Factory Foreman	G	Denzlingen	Denzlingen
Walter Moszkowski	28.05.77	Journalist	G	Breslau	London
Karl Mueller	07.01.96	Ship's Engineer	G	Geestemunde	Bremen
Leopold Nagoschiner	11.01.03	Window Dresser	S	Berlin	London
Franz Brandus-Nathan	07.06.94	Company Director	G	Magdeburg	Cardiff
Fritz Neufeld	14.03.07	Insurance Manager	A	Vienna	London
Wilhelm Neumann	22.03.11	Tailor	G	Berlin	London
Alfred Neumann	05.01.82	Merchant	G	Vienna	London
Karel Olbrisch	24.11.02	Gardener	G	Essen	Horsham
Emanuel Oppers	25.06.90	Naval Architect	G	Hanover	Surbiton
Gottfried Paffen	29.11.82	Merchant	G	Aachen	London
Albert Pape	21.12.11	Photography Lecturer	G	Essen	London
Aegidius Pelzer	02.04.12	Assistant Engineer - SS Karfifanger	G	Koln	Berlin
Karl Peters	01.03.91	Electrical Fitter	G	Braunschweig	London
Karl Petersen	18.09.98	Merchant	G	Steinfeld	Reykjavale, Iceland
Karl Plath	17.08.74	Chef	G	Recklinghausen	London
Richard Plischke	26.07.89	Dr. of Chemistry	C	Liberec	London
Fritz Raab	00.11.95	Painter	A	Vienna	London
Rudolf Reichardt	24.03.15	Mechanic	G	Pleissa	Cardiff
Harry Reichenberger	31.07.96	Film Company Representative	A	Vienna	London
Emil Repenning	23.02.80	Engineer - SS Don Isidra	G	Kiel	Kiel
Karl Ritterfeld	21.08.17	Storekeeper	G	Bremen	Bremen
Hugo Rossman	03.05.21	Engine Boy	G	Graz	Graz
Walter Rostin	12.04.99	Civil Servant	G	Charlottenburg	London
Rudolph Schenk	08.04.12	School Teacher	A	Vienna	Bodrean nr. Truro
Hans Schiffer	16.06.93	Student of Law	G	Berlin	London
Heinz Schild	14.10.18	Student	G	Berlin	London
Ludwig Schild	27.02.91	Company Director	G	Magdeburg	London
Fritz Schlamowicz	27.09.08	Shoe Salesman	A	Vienna	London
Justus Schoenthal	27.02.88	Doctor of Law	G	Numberg	Whitehaven
Heinrich Schreiber	14.12.85	Export Merchant	G	Crombach	Manchester
Hans Schuldt	10.05.01	Captain- SS Uhenfels	G	Kiel	Mecklingberg
Bruno Schulze	27.03.85	Farmer	G	Leipzig	Leipzig
Hans Schutt	08.03.13	Commercial Traveller	G	Bergedorf	Hampton Hill
Oscar Schwengder	21.09.79	Cotton Buyer	G	Berlin	Stockport
Paul Selka	18.05.19	Student	A	Vienna	London
Rudolf Sengebusch	21.07.13	Merchant	G	Hamburg	Lagos, Nigeria
Hans Siems	22.09.79	Company Director	G	Lubeck	London
Friedrich Sittner	29.05.15	Assistant Manager	G	Berlin	Loughborough
Robert Spitzer	14.06.00	Silk Merchant	A	Vienna	London
Hans Steinbruckner	02.06.12	Engineer	G	Jena	London
Ewald Stern	22.07.00	None	G	Czernowicz	London
Heinrich Stoeppel	28.08.79	Chef	A	Danzig	London

Name	Date	Occupation	Nat.	Place	Residence
Nikolaus Strommer	04.12.04	Artist	G	Miskolecx	London
Walter Thurecht	07.04.02	Hotel Proprietor	G	Krefeld	Bournemouth
Rudolf Toth	22.10.11	Asbestos Joiner	A	Guntramsdorf	Sidcup
Walter Troetzer	05.08.19	Clerk	G	Duisburg	Surbiton
Hans Ultsch	09.12.02	Commercial Traveller	G	Leipzig	Munich
Max Waldowsky	30.04.92	Agent	G	Munster	Kineton
Harald Von Waldstaedt	18.02.99	Musician - SS *Adolf Woermann*	G	Heidelberg	Wesermunde
Christian Walter	30.12.84	Butcher	G	Bretzfeld	Stockport
Lorenz Weber	19.04.11	Private Secretary	G	Munich	London
Paul Weidlich	05.06.76	Engineer	G	Brunndobra	Macclesfield
Wilhelm Weil	27.10.14	None	G	Frankenthal	London
Julius Weiss	07.11.65	Industrial Agent	G	Stuttgart	London
Karl Wiese	29.10.72	Income Tax Collector	G	Unknown	Hamburg
Kurt Wilmowsky	16.05.16	Student	G	Essen-Hugel	Naumburg-Saaleland
Eberhard Wirth	15.12.06	Seaman	G	Munich	Tittmoning
Artur Wist	20.03.13	3rd Officer - SS *Poseidon*	G	Hamburg	Hamburg
Herman Wohlleten	16.11.05	Merchant	G	Bremen	Accra, Gold Coast
Karl Zimmermann	26.12.12	3rd Officer - SS *Pomona*	G	Konigssteele	Oberhausen

Key to Nationalities
G German
A Austrian
C Czechoslovakian
B British
S Stateless

ITALIAN PRISONERS

Name	Date of Birth	Place of Birth	Last Place of Residence
1. Abrardo, Eraldo Giuseppe	15.04.1892	Fubine	London
2. Abruzzese, Giocondino	26.08.1875	Filignano	Glasgow
3. Adami, Paolo	29.05.1909	Trieste	London
4. Affaticati, Riccardo	02.08.1893	Caorso	London
5. Aglieri, Mario	21.05.1887	Milano	London
6. Agostini, Oliviero	29.04.1904	Barga	Glasgow
7. Albertella, Giovanni	13.01.1893	Cannero	Lancaster
8. Albertelli, Carlo	30.05.1899	Morfasso	Pontypridd
9. Alberti, Humbert	28.10.1881	Barga	Manchester
10. Albertini, Constante	08.04.1885	Milano	London
11. Allera, Lorenzo	17.09.1900	Ivrea	London
12. Alliata, Publio	19.08.1884	Roma	London
13. Amodeo, Tullio Edouard	29.07.1882	Roma	London
14. Andreassi, Giuseppe	19.03.1880	San Demetrio	London
15. Angella, Emilio	02.07.1896	Pontremoli	Bolton
16. Angiolini, Domenico Giuseppe	15.03.1900	Genova	Glasgow
17. Aniballi, Giuseppe	06.09.1896	Amatrice	London
18. Antoniazzi, Bartolomeo	20.01.1908	Bardi	Newtown
19. Anzani, Decio	10.07.1882	Forlì	London
20. Arnoldi, Ercole	03.09.1910	Taleggio	London
21. Avella, Alfonso	04.07.1889	Tirreni	Glasgow
22. Avignone, Giovanni	02.05.1887	Port St Martin	London
23. Avignone Rossa, Italo	12.10.1907	Bollengo	London
24. Avondoglio, Fortunato	03.07.1888	Chiaversano	London
25. Azario, Efisio Remo Vitale	18.06.1885	Mosso, Santa Maria	London
26. Babini,Lorenzo	16.11.1885	Lugo	London
27. Baccanello, Marco	03.04.1898	Venezia	Harpenden
28. Bagatta, Angelo	26.03.1883	S.Columbano al Lambro	London
29. Baldieri, Armando	26.06.1912	Roma	London
30. Ballerini, Roberto	02.05.1895	Galluzzo	London
31. Banino, Luigi	21.08.1904	Cerione	London
32. Barone, Francesco	13.09.1889	San Paolo	London
33. Baroni, Alessandro	11.08.1880	Milano	London
34. Basilico, Cesare	15.06.1885	Cavonno Milanese	London
35. Basini, Bartolomeo	12.10.1908	Bardi	Tre Herbert
36. Battistini, Umberto	23.05.1899	Stazzema	Ayr
37. Bava, Claudio	20.03.1887	Montechiaro D'Asti	Gateshead
38. Belli, Antonio	08.11.1885	Bardi	Maeslag
39. Bellini, Pietro	08.07.1878	Morfasso	London
40. Belmonte, Gaetano	16.09.1876	Cassino	Edinburgh
41. Belotti, Leone	17.02.1904	Bergamo	West Wickham
42. Beltrami, Alessandro	20.12.1874	Egypt	Glasgow
43. Beltrami, Leandro	11.08.1890	Massemino	Middlesbrough
44. Benigna. Pietro	01.11.1904	Chiuduno	Leicester
45. Benini, Giuseppe	14.03.1881	Bologna	London
46. Berigliano, Antonio	17.01.1899	Dorzano	London
47. Berni, Attilio	10.05.1899	Bardi	Weston Sp Mare
48. Berra, Claudio Giacomo	16.07.1890	S.Quirico	London
49. Bersani, Carlo	07.06.1889	Sarmato	London
50. Bertin, Antonio	11.10.1901	Sequals	London
51. Bertoia, Luigi	04.06.1921	Montereale	Middlesbrough
52. Bertolini, Vincenzo Silvic	14.06.1876	Barga	Glasgow

53.	Bertoncini, Pietro	24.11.1887	Camporgiano	London
54.	Bertucci, Siro Celestino	01.02.1885	Vercelli	London
55.	Beschizza, Anselmo	29.04.1878	Bratto	London
56.	Beschizza, Raffaele	12.11.1910	Pontremoli	London
57.	Biagi, Luigi	16.04.1898	Gallicano	Ayr
58.	Biagioni, Ferdinando	06.07.1895	Barga	Glasgow
59.	Biagioni, Francesco	06.03.1897	Castelnuovo G.	Rothesay
60.	Biagioni, Umberto	23.04.1878	Castelnuovo G.	Glasgow
61.	Biagiotti, Carlo	04.06.1877	Pistoia	Glasgow
62.	Biagiotti, Nello	25.02.1893	Pistoia	Glasgow
63.	Bich, Clement Daniele	21.12.1887	Valtournenche	Thames Ditton
64.	Bigi, Mansueto	08.08.1885	Gualteri	Highcliffe on Sea
65.	Bivogna, Giuseppe	10.11.1900	Acqui	London
66.	Bissolotti, Carlo	24.11.1900	Soresina	London
67.	Boccassini, Altilio	10.10.1890	Barletta	London
68.	Bombelli, Mario	18.09.1885	Roma	Cardiff
69.	Bonaldi, Andrea Luigi	18.06.1898	Songavazzo	London
70.	Bonati, Alfonso	02.07.1893	Riccò Del Golfo	Glasgow
71.	Bonetti, Giovanni	23.02.1881	Lograto	Southampton
72.	Bongiovanni, Pietro	20.04.1891	Savona	London
71.	Bono, Luigi	24.01.1890	Arona	London
74.	Borgo, Carlo	03.04.1897	Casatisma	London
75.	Borrelli, Federico	12.12.1887	Schiava	London
76.	Borsumato, Alessandro	02.11.1896	Cassino	Middlesbrough
77.	Boccasso, Magno	02.06.1881	Montechiaro D'Asti	London
78.	Bragoli, Pietro	23.05.1880	Morfasso	London
79.	Bragoni, Ilario	14.01.1897	Villafranca	London
80.	Bravo, Francesco	30.03.1892	Bollengo	London
81.	Breglia, Salvatore Gaetano	13.07.1895	Napoli	Cambridge
82.	Broggi, Vittorio	08.07.1902	Gavirate	London
83.	Brugnoni, Mario Maximilian	25.08.1904	Paris	London
84.	Bucchioni, Lorenzo	23.03.1899	Pontremoli	London
85.	Caldera, Carlo	21.01.1896	Alice Castello	London
86.	Calderan, Emilio	06.09.1900	Torino	London
87.	Callegari, Luigi	27.03.1899	Torino	London
88.	Camillo, Giuseppe	04.10.1882	S.Cosmo	Glasgow
89.	Camozzi, Cesare	02.11.1891	Iseo	Manchester
90.	Capella, Giuseppe	13.04.1885	Borgotaro	London
91.	Capitelli, Carlo	28.04.1899	Borgotaro	London
92.	Capitelli, Eduardo	18.07.1882	Albareto	London
93.	Cardani, Carlo	28.04.1886	Sesto Calende	London
94.	Cardarelli, Quirino	17.05.1889	Roma	London
95.	Cardellino, Giovanni	18.12.1886	San Damiano	London
96.	Cardosi, Nello	17.02.1902	Brunswick	London
97.	Cardosi, Valesco	24.12.1910	Carnporgiano	London
98.	Carini, Francesco	15.07.1893	Bardi	Pontypridd
99.	Carini, Giuseppe	21.05.1898	Bardi	Ebbw Vale
100.	Carpanini, Giovanni	05.01.1919	Bardi	Britton Ferry
101.	Carpanini, Giuseppe	17.07.1892	Bardi	Cwmcarn
102.	Casali, Giuseppe	03.08.1909	Morfasso	London
101.	Castelli, Antonio	18.10.1894	Bettola	Aberdare
104.	Castellotti, Giovanni	15.06.1899	Pontremoli	London
105,	Cattini, Giacobbe Pietro	01.06.1918	Bratto	London
106.	Cattini, Pietro	02.11.1881	Bratto	London
107.	Cattolico, Mario Federico	16.04.1891	Napoli	Stanmore

108. Cavaciutti, Pietro	06.06.1893	Morfasso	London
109. Cavadini, Achille	26.03.1891	Como	London
110. Cavalli, Giovanni	04.02.1889	Bardi	Neath
111. Cavalli, Nicolas	06.05.1892	Felizzano	London
112. Ceresa, Antonio	20.06.1889	Bollengo	London
113. Ceresa, Eduardo	29.05.1890	Bollengo	Chorlton Medlock
114. Ceresa, Stefano	22.05.1900	Bollengo	London
115. Chiappa, Emilio Domenico	16.09.1900	Bedonia	Bridgend
116. Chiappelli, Oraldo	14.05.1920	Pistoia	Glasgow
117. Chiarcossi, Giovanni	09.01.1875	Gradisca di Sedegliano	London
118. Chietti, Emilio Ottavio	03.09.1886	Monte Folonico	London
119. Chiodi, Domenico	29.10.1912	Braia	London
120. Ciampa, Salvatore	07.02.1884	Messina	London
121. Ciarli, Vittorio	31.07.1897	Quagneto	Edinburgh
122. Ciotti, Pasquale	09.11.1890	Coseiago	London
123. Cimorelli, Giovanni	23.06.1875	Montaquila	Edinburgh
124. Cini, Armando	09.06.1886	Cairo	London
125. Colella, Vincenzo	25.04.1895	Viticuso	London
126. Coniola, Celeste	06.04.1883	Pontari Genova	Bradford
127. Conti, Abramo	04.09.1894	Venezia	London
128. Conti, Guido	26.12.1908	Bardi	Newport
129. Conti, Giuseppe	19.03.1898	Bardi	Treharris
130. Copolla, Philip	07.01.1895	Picinisco	Edinburgh
131. Coppola, Paolo	05.09.1878	Picinisco	Edinburgh
132. Corrieri, Leonello Giuseppe	16.10.1888	?	Wallasey
133. Cortesio, Giuseppe	13.01.1899	Savigliano	London
134. Cosomini, Giovanni	03.15.1880	Barga	Bellshill
135. Costa, Diamante	28.10.1882	Parma	London
136. Cristofoli, Domenico	14.04.1905	Sequals	Birmingham
137. Cristofoli, Ettore	12.09.1896	Sequals	London
130. Cristofoli, Renato	10.02.1908	Autun	London
139. Crolla, Alfonso	24.05.1888	Picinisco	Edinburgh
140. Crolla, Donato	07.09.1880	Paris	Edinburgh
141. D'Ambrosio, Francesco	02.12.1879	Picinisco	Swansea
142. D'Ambrosio, Silvestro	30.12.1872	Picinisco	Hamilton
143. D'Annunzio, Antonio	22.09.1905	Villa Latina	Glasgow
144. D'Inverno, Francesco	17.04.1901	Villa Latina	Ayr
145. Da Prato, Silvio	27.02.1878	Barga	Glasgow
146. Dalli, Pietro	10.10.1893	Barga	Ayr
147. Danieli, Daniele	23.03.1878	Monte di Malo	?
148. De Angeli, Mario	14.02.1906	Milano	London
149. De Gasperis, Carlo	01.09.1906	Tivoli	London
150. De Marco, Lorenzo	05.02.1885	Picinisco	Edinburgh
151. De Marco, Pasquale	10.04.1898	Caserta	Glasgow
152. De Rosa, Carlo	11.02.1882	Napoli	London
153. Del Grosso, Giuseppe	20.04.1889	Borgotaro	Hamilton
154. Delicato, Carmine	17.02.1900	Atina	Edinburgh
155. Delzi, Carlo	02.10.1913	Livorno	London
156. Di Ciacca, Aristide	06.10.1920	Picinisco	Glasgow
157. Di Ciacca, Cesidio	20.10.1891	Picinisco	Cockenzie
158. Di Cocco, Domenico	04.06.1876	Velliterro	Manchester
159. Di Luca, Pietro	29.09.1873	Rochetta al Volturno	Glasgow
160. Di Marco, Mariano	24.11.1897	Cassino	Hamilton
161. Di Marco, Michele	08.05.1890	Picinisco	Swansea
162. Di Vito, Giuseppe	25.11.1874	Casalattico	Crossgates

163. Dottori, Argilio	20.01.1882	Roma	Southampton
164. Ermini, Armando	28.08.1890	Chitta	London
165. Falco, Celestino	01.08.1891	Cuneo	London
166. Fantini, Guglielmo	03.08.1889	Napoli	Southampton
167. Farnocchi, Francesco	09.06.1906	Stazzema	Glasgow
168. Fellini, Ettore	25.09.1888	Savignoia	London
169. Felloni, Giulio	25.03.1905	Parma	Aberdeen
170. Fcraboli, Ettore Innocente	25.02.1885	Pessina	London
171. Ferdenzi, Carlo	12.06.1897	Vernasca	London
172. Ferdenzi, Giacomo	16.03.1858	New York	London
173. Ferdenzi, Giovanni	15.06.1879	Vernasca	London
174. Ferdenzi, Giovanni	20.05.1884	Vernasca	London
175. Ferrari, Francesco	19.08.1899	Zignago	Port Glasgow
176. Ferrari, Guido	01.09.1893	Valdena	Kirkcaldy
177 Ferrari, Luigi	19.10.1907	Bettola	Aberdare
178. Ferrero, Bernardo	14.09.1890	Montechiaro D'Asti	London
179. Ferri, Fiorentino	22.01.1886	Filignano	Bellshill
180. Ferri, Giovanni	12.07.1884	Vernasca	Hull
181. Filippi, Mario	15.03.1910	Castelnuovo G.	Ayr
182. Filippi, Simone	26.10.1878	Pieve	Ayr
183. Finazzi, Annibale	19.01.1903	Trescore	London
184. Fiorini, Clement	20.01.1888	Sora	Manchester
185. Fisanotti, Oreste	09.08.1897	Mathi	London
186. Foglia, Claudio Silvo	02.01.1891	Amatrice	London
187. Fontana, Giovanni	18.07.1892	Frassinoro	Carlisle
188. Forte, Giuseppe	03.01.1893	London	Belfast
189. Forte, Onorio	02.05.1880	Arce	Chorlton Medlock
190. Fossaluzza, Matteo	25.11.1897	Cavasso	London
191. Fracassi, Gaetano	18.04.1876	Pescarolo	Manchester
192. Franchi, Giacomo	06.08.1896	Bardi	New Tredegar
193. Franciscono, Nicola	03.12.1884	Alice Castello	London
194. Frattcroli, Giacinto	06.09.1900	Picinisco	Ayr
195. Friggi, Egidio	29.11.1886	Motta Visconti	Southampton
196. Frizzi, Carlo	13.12.1873	Caserta	Manchester
197. Fulgoni, Giacomo	10.07.1894	Grezzo Di Bardi	Hirwaun
198. Fulgoni, Giovanni	04.07.1900	Grezzo Di Bardi	Ponty Gwarth
199. Fusco, Antonio	26.08.1909	Casalattico	Belfast
200. Fusco, Giovanni Antonio	03.09.1877	Cassino	Dundee
201. Gabbini, Alfeo	11.10.1897	Cannero	London
202. Gadeselli, Vincenzo	15.09.1885	Bardi	London
203. Gagliardi, Battista	28.02.1890	Milano	London
204. Gallo, Emilio	20.11.1896	Belmonte	Edinburgh
205. Gargaro, Francesco	25.05.1898	Picinisco	Ayr
206. Gazzi, Andrea	02.08.1900	Bardi	Gorsewinon
207. Gazzi, Francesco	12.01.1922	Bardi	Pont Newydd
208. Gazzi, Lino	03.06.1881	Bardi	Ferndale
209. Gentile, Candido	17.08.1894	Ventimiglia	London
210. Gerla, Giuseppe	10.04.1893	Abbairati	London
211. Ghiloni, Ncllo	25.12.1909	Barga	Glasgow
212. Giannandrea, Vincenzo	16.12.1910	Belmonte Castello	Elgin
213. Giannotti, Alfredo	23.10.1885	Camporgiano	London
214. Giannotti, Ettore	20.05.1910	Brescia	London
215. Giovanelli Luigi	24.04.1890	Bardi	London
216. Giraschi, Enrico	22.02.1896	Pellegrino	London
217. Gonella, Francesco	01.01.1885	Pontstaira	London

218. Gonzaga, Luigi	11.02.1924	Bedonia	London
219. Gorgone, Alfeo	02.09.1909	Venezia	London
220. Gras, Davide	03.02.1882	Bobbio Pelice	London
221. Greco, Domenico	13.04.1885	Santo Padre	Middlesbrough
222. Greco, Tullio	26.10.1897	Arpino	Middlesbrough
223. Grego, Anthony	00.00.1891	Sora	Greet
224. Guarnori, Antonio	17.02.1884	Novara	London
225. Guerri, Lino	11.11.1914	Via Risasoli?	London
226. Gussoni, Ercole	12.02.1902	Roma	London
227. Gutkind, Curt Sigmar	29.09.1896	Manheim	London
228. Iannetta, Ferdinando	25.10.1889	Vilicuso	Edinburgh
229. Iannetta, Orazio	23.08.1901	Belmonte Castello	Methil
230. Iannetta, Vincenzo	25.10.1902	Belmonte Castello	Methil
231. Iardella, Pietro	05.07.1885	Pontremoli	London
232. Incerti, Rinaldo	17.04.1884	Villa?	London
233. Jordaney, Giuseppe	06.05.1888	Courmayeur	London
234. Landucci, Ernani	29.09.1894	Firenze	Chorlton Medlock
235. Lanzi, Ugo	01.04.1905	Milano	London
236. Lepora, Reino	29.07.1897	Alice Castello	London
237. Longinotti, Giovanni	17.05.1892	S.Maria Del Taro	Heywood
238. Lucantoni, Amedeo	16.02.1897	Roma	Middlesbrough
239. Lucchesi, Pietro	26.01.1894	Castiglioni	Prestwick
240. Luise, Raffaele	15.09.1905	Torre Del Greco	London
241. Lusardi, Tommaso Angelo	29.05.1909	Blaengaru	London
242. Lusardi, Vittorio	23.07.1892	Bedonia	Llanharan
243. Maccariello, Elpidio	16.05.1890	Casapulla	London
244. Maddalena, Marco Carlo	16.12.1909	Fanna	London
245. Maggi, Cesare	22.02.1887	Torino	London
246. Maiuri, Guido	30.04.1877	Napoli	London
247. Mancini, Antonio	03.08.1885	Atina	Ayr
248. Mancini, Domenico	22.04.1881	Sessa	Chorlton Medlock
249. Mancini, Umberto	02.07.1891	Picinisco	London
250. Mancini, Vittorio	19.04.1899	Picinisco	London
251. Manini, Cesare	25.11.1903	Palazzolo sul Senio	London
252. Marchesi, Charles Domenico	17.07.1872	Codogno	London
253. Marchetto, Ugo	18.04.1897	Venezia	London
254. Marello, Eugenio	30.03.1893	Alfieri	London
255. Marenghi, Giovanni	23.04.1897	Bardi	Pontypridd
256. Marenghi, Luigi	21.07.1893	Piacenza	London
257. Mariani, Amleto	24.05.1887	Torino	London
258. Mariani,Pietro	03.10.1921	Bardi	London
259. Marini, Luigi	06.01.1912	Cuccaro	London
260. Mariotti, Fulgenzio	23.09.1885	Costacciaro	London
261. Marre, Carlo	03.08.1880	Borzonasca	Manchester
262. Marsella, Antonio	15.10.1899	Casalattico	Bonnybridge
263. Marsella, Filippo	07.04.1897	Casalattico	Wishaw
264. Marsella, Orlando	22.08.1914	Glasgow	Glasgow
265. Martis, Orazio	18.07.1883	Sassari	New Malden
266. Marzella, Antonio	06.04.1899	Filignano	Glasgow
267. Massari, A.	Unconfirmed		
268. Mattci, Francesco	13.10.1885	Sesso	London
269. Matteoda, Leopoldo	30.07.1881	Saluzzo	London
270. Melaragni, Michelangelo	18.03.1890	Cassino	Manchester
271. Menozzi, Gioacchino	24.08.1894	Bardi	London
272. Meriggi, Mario	17.08.1892	Portalbert	London

273. Merlo, Giuseppe	29.03.1914	San Gallo	Trealaw
274. Meschi, Oscar	16.07.1920	Fornoli	Glasgow
275. Meta, Pasqualino	05.02.1899	Cassino	Paisley
276. Miele, Natalino	25.12.1898	Cassino	Edinburgh
277. Miglio, Filippo Luigi	19.05,1883	Trinilo Cuneo	London
278. Milani, Luigi	04.05.1890	Oggiono	London
279. Minetti, Giacomo	11.07.1905	Bardi	Neath
280. Mittero, Antonio	15.07.1908	Chieri	Stalybridge
281. Montagna, Giulio	31.10.1888	Napoli	London
282. Monti, Giuseppe	23.01.1889	Lacco Ameno	Manchester
283. Morelli, Luigi	01.09.1892	Borgotaro	London
284. Moretti, Giovanni	01.03.1900	Pardivarma	Greenock
285. Moruzzi, Ernesto	12.08.1879	Bardi	Neath
286. Moruzzi, Peter	31.05.1887	Bardi	Neath
287. Moruzzi, Pietro	24.11.1917	Bardi	London
288. Moscardini, Santino	02.01.1879	Barga	Motherwell
289. Musetti, Lorenzo	25.02.1897	Buenos Aires	London
290. Musetti, Pietro	31.01.1890	Pontremoli	London
291. Muzio, Enrico	12.12.1892	Napoli	London
292. Nannini, Oreste	28.05.1891	Pievepelago	Edinburgh
293. Nardone, Antonio	20.10.1882	Cassino	Middlesbrough
294. Nichini, Giulio	04.05.1896	Orla Novarese	London
295. Notafalchi, Lorenzo	08.08.1885	Piacenza	London
296. Novelli, Vincenzo	08.07.1893	Fubine	London
297. Olivelli, A	Unconfirmed		
298. Operti, Egidio Ferrucio	26.08.1890	Torino	Southampton
299. Orsi, Giuseppe	22.06.1890	Albareto	London
300. Orsi, Pietro	01.05.1888	Pontremoli	London
301. Ottolini, Giovanni	21.07.1876	Lucca	Birmingham
302. Pacitti, Alfonso	03.08.1887	Cerasuolo	Glasgow
303. Pacitti, Carmine	03.06.1876	Filignano	Carfin
304. Pacitti, Gaetano	10.12.1890	Villa Latina	Edinburgh
305. Pacitto Gaetano Antonio	19.10.1875	England	Hull
306. Palleschi, Nicola	16.12.1884	Sesto Campano	Glasgow
307. Palumbo, Gioacchino	21.03.1897	Minori	London
308. Paolozzi, Alfonso Rodolfo	29.03.1901	Viticuso	Edinburgh
309. Papa, Pietro	02.10.1909	S. Biagio	Glasgow
310. Pardini, Agostino	09.09.1901	Capezzano	Greenock
311. Parmigiani, Giuseppe	17.11.1889	Tourolo	London
312. Pastecchi, Enrico	06.03.1896	Roma	London
313. Paulone, Arnadeo	24.03.1885	Scanno Aquila	Southampton
314. Pellegrini, Domenico	22.10.1894	Varsi	London
315. Pelosi, Paul	23.03.1882	Picinisco	Edinburgh
316. Pelucco, Francesco	12.04.1882	Quariento	London
317. Perella, Luigi	03.12.1893	Picinisco	Edinburgh
318. Peretti, Luigi	01.10.1880	Agrano	London
319. Pettiglio, Carlo	05.05.1878	Cassino	Edinburgh
320. Piancastelli, Annino	26.07.1894	Busighella	London
321. Picozzi, Carlo	04.10.1889	Milano	London
322. Pieri, Alfredo	08.11.1898	Lucca	Carlisle
323. Pieroni, Giuseppe	31.01.1889	Pieve	Ayr
324. Piloni, Battista	24.05.1897	Crema	London
325. Pinchera, Angelo Antonio	31.08.1898	Cassino	Glasgow
326. Pinchiaroli, Luigi	01.12.1894	Albareto	Pontypridd
327. Pino, Antonio Cesare	18.10.1889	Lonigi	London

328. Piovano, Giacomo	25.02.1892	Castelnuovo G.	London
329. Piscina, Giovanni	16.05.1884	Parma	London
330. Plescia, Andrea	16.01.1905	Palermo	London
331. Plescia, Baldassarc	01.01.1915	Palermo	London
332. Poli, Amedeo	10.03.1896	Barga	Glasgow
334. Pollini, Manlio	20.03.1883	Milano	Southampton
335. Pololi, Francesco	06.03.1881	Toliggio	London
336. Pompa, Ferdinando	16.09.1876	Picinisco	Swansea
337. Pontone, Domenico	13.08.1885	Cassino	Hartlepool
338. Pozzo, Giacinto	20.04.1906	Viverone	Whitton, Middx
339. Prati, Carlo	04.11.1877	Lugagnano	Hull
340. Previdi, Lodovico	12.06.1895	Gropparello	London
341. Prister, Camillo Flavio	28.06.1890	Gradisca	Ilminster
342. Puchoz, Marcello	26.08.1896	Courmayeur	London
343. Pusinelli, Pietro	03.04.1897	Naso	London
344. Quagliozzi, Angelo	30.08.1881	Cassino	Sheffield
345. Quaranta, Domenico	30.01.1883	Carbonara Napoli	London
346. Rabaiotti, Antonio	20.10.1885	Bardi	Newport
347. Rabaiotti, Bartolomeo	23.03.1881	Bardi	Pontypridd
348. Rabaiotti, Domenico	12.02.1912	Bardi	Ogmore Vale
349. Rabaiotti, Francesco	06.03.1894	Bardi	Swansea
350. Rabaiotti, Luigi	11.12.1910	Bardi	Swansea
351. Raffetti, Carlo	22.09.1901	Genova	London
352. Raggi, Luigi	15.08.1880	Bardi	London
353. Ranaldi, Antonio	16.01.1884	Arpino	Middlesbrough
354. Ravetto, Carlo	09.01.1897	Alice Castello	London
355. Ravina, Cristoforo	06.01.1882	Fulbrino	London
356. Ravina, Giuseppe	26.03.1884	Fubine	London
357. Razzuoli, Enrico	15.12.1909	Stazzema	Darvel
358. Rea, Camillo	06.10.1878	Arpino	Middlesbrough
359. Rea, Domenico	07.01.1900	Arpino	Middleshrough
360. Ricaldone, Alessandro Angelo	03.12.1892	Fubine	London
361. Ricci, Lazzaro	24.03.1891	Bardi	Treharris
362. Rinaldi, Giovanni	31.03.1883	Arlenes	Leith
363. Rivaldi, Patrocco	18.01.1879	Cremona	London
364. Roccantonio, Francesco	23.10.1875	Rocca D'Arce	Peebles
365. Rocchiccioli, Caesar	06.12.1909	Barga	Troon
366. Roffo, Ernesto	14.01.1896	Picinisco	London
367. Rosi, Guglielmo	25.12.1893	Pontremoli	London
368. Rosi, Luigi	16.12.1886	Grondola	London
369. Rossetto, Ferdinando	19.06.1888	Bollengo	London
370. Rossi, Emilio	08.09.1888	Viticuso	Edinburgh
371. Rossi, Eugenio	17.10.1893	Paris	Mountain Ash
372. Rossi, Flavio	15.06.1902	Bardi	Port Glasgow
373. Rossi, Giovanni	11.09.1923	Bardi	Cardiff
374. Rossi, Luigi	14.08.1908	Bardi	Swansea
375. Rossi, Mario	03.04.1889	Pisa	London
376. Rossi, Pietro	23.12.1875	Viticuso	Edinburgh
377. Rossi, Vitale	05.05.1898	Cavaglia	London
378. Rossotti, Carlo	09.03.1899	Chieri Torino	London
379. Rota, Carlo	20.03.1898	Giarole	London
380. Ruffoni, Giovanni Battista	05.05.1885	Chignolo Verbano	London
381. Ruocchio, Michele Andrew	06.07.1908	?	Larkhall
382. Russo, Carmine	24.07.1886	Cassino	London
383. Rustioni, Oreste	09.07.1913	Milano	London

384. Sagramati, Vilfrido	19.10.1910	Roma	London
385. Sala, Emilio	21.10.1912	Monza	Luton
386. Salsano, Luigi	14.06.1921	Tramonti	London
387. Sangalli, Gianetto	12.07.1882	Milano	London
388. Santarello, Ferruccio	17.12.1892	Venezia	London
389. Santi. S	Unconfirmed		
390. Santini, Quinto	29.07.1880	Pistoia	Paisley
391. Santuz, Antonio	27.01.1884	Fanna	Birmingham
392. Sartori, Luigi	14.04.1885	Morfasso	London
393. Scarabelli, Angelo Mario	19.04.1892	S.Maria Della Verra	London
394. Sidoli, Giovanni	17.08.1894	Bardi	Glyncorrwg
395. Sidoli, Luigi	29.12.1882	Bardi	London
396. Siliprandi, Olimpio	10.01.1883	Mantova	Pettswood
397. Silva, Luigi Antonio Mario	11.11.1893	Via Anano?	London
398. Silvestrini, Giovanni	24.04.1894	Verona	London
399. Simeone, Francesco	27.01.1891	S.Vittorio Lazio	London
400. Sola, Carlo Federico	28.06.1882	Torino	London
401. Solari, Federico	05.09.1914	Vernasca	London
402. Solari, Luigi	24.04.1888	Bardi	Neath
403. Sottocornola, Edmondo	02.04.1897	Gargallo	London
401. Sovrani, Giovanni Jean	13.07.1882	Saludecio	London
405. Spacagna, Giuseppe	09.03.1881	Cervaro	Eastleigh
406. Spagna, Antonio	10.10.1894	Bardi	Maesteg
407. Spelta, Giuseppe	07.03.1897	Milano	Scarborough
408. Speroni, Ermete	27.11.1898	Milano	Beckenham
419. Stellon, Giovanni Maria	14.09.1891	Fanna	Newport
410. Sterlini, Giuseppe	31.05.1900	Bardi	Wellington
411. Sterlini, Marco	17.10.1891	Bardi	Tenby
412. Storto, Giuseppe	18.11.1900	Monferrato	London
413. Stratta, Giacomo	07.03.1894	Bollengo	Croydon
414. Strinati, Giovanni	26.03.1880	Bardi	Cwmaman
415. Taffurelli, Giuseppe	29.03.1892	Bettola	Dowlais
416. Taglione, Benedetto	14.11.1883	Arpino	London
417. Tambini, Giovanni	13.03.1899	Bardi	Newport
418. Tapparo, Luigi	22.10.1898	Bollengo	Edinburgh
419. Tedesco, Raffaele	03.09.1889	Mocera	Edinburgh
420. Tempia, Giuseppe	04.07.1896	Bollengo	London
421. Todisco, Antonio	14.04.1893	Vallerotonda	Redcar
422. Togneri, Giuseppe	19.03.1889	Barga	Dunbar
421. Tortolano, Giuseppe	12.08.1880	Cassino	Middlesbrough
424. Tramontin, Riccardo	24.11.1890	Cavasso Nuovo	London
425. Traversa, Italo Vittorio	06.06.1918	Carisio	London
426. Trematore, Severino	24.05.1895	Torre Maggiore	London
427. Trombetta, Pietro	01.08.1892	Minori	Chertsey
428. Tuzi, Pasquale	01.04.1898	Picinisco	Edinburgh
429. Vairo, Cesare	26.07.1891	Milano	London
430. Valente, Adolf	15.06.1900	Cervaro	Edinburgh
431. Valli, Giovanni	20.09.1901	Novarro	London
432. Valmaggia, Elio	12.11.1896	Gemonio	London
433. Valvona, Enrico	05.09.1885	Villa Latina	London
434. Vercelli, Emilio Giacomo	01.08.1894	Mombercelli	London
435. Viccari, Antonio	28.02.1890	Pontremoli	London
436. Viccari, Giulio	31.05.1901	Pontremoli	London
437. Viccari, Pietro	27.09.1889	SS.Cosmo e Damiano	London
438. Virno, Giovanni Battista	07.10.1888	Cava Dei Tirreni	London

439. Zambellini, Luigi	04.12.1887	Como	London
440. Zanelli, Ettore	03.11.1893	?	Tonypandy
441. Zanetti, Antonio	09.07.1898	Varsi	Swansea
442. Zangiacomi, Italo	16.04.1879	Verona	London
443. Zani, Guido	30.11.1900	Pontremoli	London
444. Zanolli, Silvio	09.04.1880	Monteforte	London
445. Zavattoni, Ettore	19.08.1882	Villate	London
446. Zazzi, Luigi	03.01.1895	Borgotaro	London

Reference Material and Bibliography

The majority of the references are to files held at the National Archives, Kew, London. They are referred to simply by the file references beginning HO, FO, KV, T, LCO etc.

Recorded interviews held at the Imperial War Museum, London, are referred to as IWM.

Files from the US National Archives, College Park, Washington are referred to as USNA.

Chapter One: For a useful summary of internment in World War One, see Chapter 2 of "Collar the Lot" by Leni and Peter Gillman, Quartet Books, 1980; KV 4/364; IWM Oral History 4382; LCO 2/1377; Collar the Lot" op.cit. p.56.

Chapter Two: "Italian Fascism in Britain", Claudia Baldioli, UMI Disertation Publishing 2014; "Guida generale degli italiani a Londra", Edward Ercoli and Sons 1933; IWM Oral History 13149; FO 371/25192; "The Internment of Aliens", Francois Lafitte, Penguin Books, 1940; "Anderson's Prisoners" Victor Gollancz, 1940

Chapter Three: "Collar the Lot" op.cit; IWM Oral History 4300; KV 4/373; "The Man Who Took Trains" written under the pen name John Grane by Ulrich Boschwitz, Hamish Hamilton, 1939; re-published as "The Passenger" Puskkin Press, 2021; IWM Oral History 16506; KV 4/366; KV 4/370; Sport Australia Hall of Fame, and many obituaries of Franz Stampfl; HO 283; HO 382/261; HO 213/1721.

Chapter Four: "The Internment of Aliens" op.cit.p.38,166,170; "Anderson's Prisoners" op.cit. p.20; FO 371/25189; FO 371/25210; FO 371/25244; "Collar the Lot" op. cit. p.133.

Chapter Five: "The Internment of Aliens" op.cit. p.187; "The Finest Years" Max Hastings, 2009, p.14, 70-1; "Hitler's Hangmen", Brian Lett, Frontline Books, 2019; FO 371/25193; CAB 93/2; Daily Express 31/5/40; KV 4/366 ; KV 4/371 ; FO 371/25210 ; T161/1081.

Chapter Six : Daily Sketch 11 June 1940; HO 213/1721; Glasgow Herald 25/7/2012; The Warth Mills Project – BBC Witness [Joe Pieri]; FO 371/25193; IWM Oral History 11485; IWM Oral History 11190; www.britishnewspaperarchive.co.uk re Enrico Muzio;

https://archive.thestage.co.uk re Enrico Muzio; FO 371/25210; "The Internment of Aliens" op.cit. p.128; FO 371/25192; T 161/1081.

Chapter Seven: KV 2/677; KV 2/678; HO 45/24895; KV 2/841.

Chapter Eight: Hansard 10 July 1940; FO 916/2576; www.warthmillsproject.com; IWM Oral History 12911; "A political exile relived – Paolo Treves in Great Britian [1938-1945]" Francesca Fiorani 2020; T 161/1127.

Chapter Nine: FO 916/2581; FO 371/25210; www.bluestarline.org; BT 389/2/25; "Collar the Lot" op.cit. p.187, 189; "The Campaign in Norway" T.K Derry, Naval and Military Press, 1952; WO 106/1615; www.royalpioneercorps.co.uk/rpc/history_lancastria.htm: account of Stanley Scislowski; www.naval-history.net – this appears accurate, but its source is unknown; IWM Oral History 11484; IWM Oral History 11485; news.bbc.co.uk – Wales, 16 May 2009; IWM Oral History 11190; IWM Oral History 16506.

Chapter Ten: "Enemy Submarine" by Wolfgang Frank, William Kimber, 1954; Levie on the Law of War, International War Studies Vol.70PREM; "Gunther Prien and U-47", Dougie Martindale, Frontline Books, 2018; "U-47 in Scapa Flow", Angus Konstam, Osprey Publishing, 2015; ADM 116/5790; ADM 199/158; ADM 116/5790.

Chapter Eleven: "Gunther Prien and the U-47", op.cit; FO 916/2581; IWM Oral History 16506; IWM Oral History 13149; IWM Oral History 11190; IWM Oral History 11485; IWM Oral History 11484; news.bbc.co.uk – Wales 16/5/2009; FO 371/25210.

Chapter Twelve: PREM 3/49; IWM Oral History 16506; FO 916/2581.

Chapter Thirteen: T 161/1081; "Invasion 1940" St Ermin's Press 2000; "The Black Book", Sybil Oldfield, Profile Books, 2020; HO 214/4; The Annals of Fondazione Luigi Einaudi, Vol LIV, December 2020 p.215; HO 213/1721; FO 371/25192; colonsayhistory.info; "Arandora Star, From Oblivion to Memory" Balestracci, Monte Universita Parma Editore 2008.

Chapter Fourteen: FO 916/2581; Hansard 2 July, 9 July, 10 July 1940; HO 214/2; HO 214/12; Anderson's Prisoners, op.cit., p.36, p.59.

Chapter Fifteen: Report of the Directorate of Prisoners of War and Internees at Army Headquarters, Australia, 1939-51 – "The Melbourne

Report"; FO 371/25192; HO 215/213; HO 215/1 Embarkation list; "Collar the Lot" op.cit, p.215, p.243, p.316-7; IWM Oral History13149; HO 213/1959; BBC News 10/7/2010 – Cacciottolo; The Royal Pioneer Corps Association Magazine, April 2013; HO 215/257; "Into the Arms of Strangers" Warner Brothers film, 2000 – interview with Gorbulski; T 161/1127.

Chapter Sixteen: Hansard July 16, 6 and 15 August 1940; FO 916/2581; FO 371/25210.

Chapter Seventeen: FO 371/25210; T 161/1127; HO 213/1959; HO 215/213; The Royal Pioneer Association Magazine, April 2013.

Chapter Eighteen: "Gunther Prien and U-47" op.cit. p.143; ADM 358/1158; HO 214/71.

Chapter Nineteen: USNA ASC File 46,986; USNA ASC File 46,989; USNA ASC File 46,988; USNA ASC File 30,462; USNA ASC File 18,758; USNA ASC File 28,818; Sartori/Cura family archive; HO 9/1315/3; "Italy's Outstanding Courage", Brian Gordon Lett, Della Cresa Publishing 2018; FO 371/67771

Epilogue: Hansard 8 October 1940, Barrister Magazine October 2023, FO 371/25192

Illustrations: The author is very grateful to the Padgett/Pacitto family for granting permission to use the photographs on p.132/3, to the Sartori/Penman family on p.133, and to the Liverpool Maritime Museum for the photographs of the *Arandora Star*, Captain Moulton and his family.

Acknowledgements

History books do not get written without a lot of help from other people, and I express my very sincere thanks to the many who helped me with this book - in particular the descendants of those who suffered or died on the *Arandora Star*, or suffered on the *Dunera*. Also, the author has been able to listen to many of the voices of the survivors giving their accounts of what happened, thanks to the Imperial War Museum's Oral History archive. Steve Schia of Bratto has been a fund of knowledge, and there are many more, including, of course, Coraggio Brunoletto and his team at Della Cresa Publishing. I thank also those authors who have written about this tragedy before me, including Leni and Peter Gillman, Maria Serena Ballestracci, and the authors of the Colonsay History website.

INDEX

Printed in Great Britain
by Amazon

40993226R00158